MULTICULTURALISM AS A FOURTH FORCE

MULTICULTURALISM AS A FOURTH FORCE

edited by

Paul Pedersen

Department of Human Studies
School of Education
University of Alabama at Birmingham

USA	Publishing Office:	BRUNNER/MAZEL *A member of the Taylor & Francis Group* 325 Chestnut Street Philadelphia, PA 19106 Tel: (215) 625-8900 Fax: (215) 625-2940
	Distribution Center:	BRUNNER/MAZEL *A member of the Taylor & Francis Group* 47 Runway Road Levittown, PA 19057 Tel: (215) 269-0400 Fax: (215) 269-0363
UK		BRUNNER/MAZEL *A member of the Taylor & Francis Group* 1 Gunpowder Square London EC4A 3DE Tel: +44 171 583 0490 Fax: +44 171 583 0581

MULTICULTURALISM AS A FOURTH FORCE

1 2 3 4 5 6 7 8 9 0

Printed by Hamilton Printing Company, Castleton, NY, 1998.

Cover design by Michelle Fleitz.

A CIP catalog record for this book is available from the British Library.
⊗ The paper in this publication meets the requirements of the ANSI Standard Z39.48-1984 (Permanence of Paper).

Library of Congress Cataloging-in-Publication Data

Multiculturalism as a fourth force / edited by Paul Pedersen.
     p.   cm.
    Includes bibliographical references and index.
    ISBN 0-87630-929-5 (case : alk. paper). – ISBN 0-87630-930-9
(pbk. : alk. paper)
    1. Cross-cultural counseling.   2. Pluralism (Social sciences) –
– Psychological aspects.   I. Pedersen, Paul, 1936– .
BF637.C6M845   1999
155.9'2–dc21   98-42486
                                                 CIP

ISBN   0-87630-929-5 (case)
ISBN   0-87630-930-9 (paper)

This book is dedicated to Ms. Doris Chang Hsiao Feng
who *inspires* and *motivates*!

CONTENTS

PART II
PARTICULAR ISSUES: PRODUCTIVITY WITHIN THE
MULTICULTURAL PERSPECTIVE

6   Multiculturalism and Mental Health in a Changing South Africa

7   Multiculturalism and the Deaf Community: Examples Given From Deaf People Working in Bicultural Groups

CONTRIBUTORS

Gunnel Backenroth-Ohsako, Ph.D., is an Associate Professor, Senior University Lecturer in psychology, licensed psychologist, psychotherapist, and specialist in clinical psychology. Her major research focuses on counseling, rehabilitation, communication, and disability. She conducts a research program regarding social relations between hearing and deaf people in working life (i.e., bicultural working groups) financed by the Swedish Council for Work Life Research. Backenroth-Ohsako teaches learning psychology, developmental psychology, personality psychology, social psychology, differential psychology, research methodology, crisis intervention, counseling, culture, rehabilitation, and disability. She supervises psychology students at the undergraduate and graduate levels, as well as audiological assistants at the University College of Health Sciences, and students in vocational counseling at Teachers' College. Backenroth-Ohsako is in command of five languages, including SSL, the Swedish Sign Language.

Jessica Ball, M.P.H., Ph.D., is a Clinical-Developmental Psychologist in the Department of Psychology at the University of Victoria, Canada. She completed her doctoral studies in psychology and public health at the University of California, Berkeley. Subsequently, she spent a decade working in several countries in Southeast Asia developing participatory, community-based approaches to research, training, and service delivery in education and community mental health. She has also worked as a therapist and public health consultant in Asia. Dr. Ball's program of research has been aimed at understanding the ongoing reproduction and reconstitution of culture as seen in the development of personal identity and health behaviors. She has been working in Canada with rural aboriginal communities in the delivery of training programs that are predicated on an understanding of the ways in which culture is reflected in and recreated by a community's construction of childhood and provision of care for young children.

Stephen Bochner is a cross-cultural scientist-practitioner. Half his time is spent as a Visiting Professor in the School of Psychology at the

University of New South Wales in Sydney, Australia, where he teaches cross-cultural aspects of applied psychology to graduate students in the professional program. His research interests include culture contact, particularly as it occurs in culturally diverse work places. The rest of his time is devoted to action-oriented research in multicultural social and industrial settings. He has published extensively, and his books include *The Mediating Person* (Boston: Schenkman), *Culture Shock* (with Adrian Furnham; London: Methuen), and *The Psychology of the Dentist-Patient Relationship* (New York: Springer-Verlag). Extended sojourns abroad have included Visiting Fellowships at Oxford and Cambridge Universities in England, and the East-West Center at the University of Hawaii. For recreation, he and his wife spend most of their spare time on their yacht, cruising in Sydney Harbour and nearby waterways.

Guler Okman Fisek, Ph.D., is Professor of Psychology and director of the Center for Psychological Research and Services at Bogazici University. She received her B.A. from Connecticut College and her M.A. and Ph.D. from the University of Connecticut. After working in the United States for some time as a licensed clinical psychologist, she returned to Turkey where she has been teaching and practicing since 1977. Her current interests and publications focus on the development of selfhood, health and pathology in the family context, family coping with social and contextual change, and the effects of migration on family functioning.

Michael J. Karcher graduated from the Human Development and Psychology doctoral program at Harvard University. He currently is an intern at the University of Texas at San Antonio Health Sciences Center, and is completing a Ph.D. in counseling psychology at the University of Texas at Austin. He has published several papers on the use of Pair Therapy to promote intercultural competence among youth.

Cigdem Kagitcibasi is a Professor of Psychology at Koc University in Istanbul, Turkey. She received her B.A. at Wellesley College and her Ph.D. at the University of California, Berkeley. She is the Vice-President of the International Union of Psychological Science, Past President of the International Association for Cross-Cultural Psychology and the Turkish Psychological Association, and is a member of the Turkish Academy of Sciences. She holds several honors and awards, including the American Psychological Association 1993 Distinguished Contributions to the International Advancement of Psychology Award, the 1998 International Association of Applied Psychology Award for Distinguished Scientific Contribution to the International Advancement of Applied Psychology, the Wellesley Alumnae Achievement Award and Phi Beta Kappa. She was a Fulbright Scholar at Harvard, a Fellow at the Netherlands Institute for Advanced Study and at Bunting Institute, Radcliffe. Her publications include more than 100 journal articles/book chapters and 17 books, among which is *Family and Human Development Across Cultures* (Mahway, NJ: Lawrence Erlbaum Publications). She is involved in both theoretical and applied work with the family, and parenting and human development in cultural context.

Frederick Leong is an Associate Professor of Psychology at The Ohio State University. He obtained his Ph.D. from the University of Maryland with a double specialty in counseling and industrial/organizational psychology. Currently, he serves as a faculty member in both the Counseling and Industrial/Organizational Psychology Programs at The Ohio State University. He has authored or co-authored over 65 publications in various counseling and psychology journals and 16 book chapters. He was the co-editor of *Womanpower: Managing in Times of Demographic Turbulence* (with Uma Sekaran; 1992) from Sage Publications (Thousand Oaks, CA), and the APA Bibliography, entitled *Asians in the United States: Abstracts of the Psychological and Behavioral Literature, 1967–1991* (with James Whitfield; 1992). In 1995, he published an edited volume, *Career Development and Vocational Behavior of Racial and Ethnic Minorities* with Lawrence Erlbaum Associates (Mahway, NJ). His latest book, also from Sage Publications (co-edited with James Austin; 1996) is entitled *Psychology Research Handbook: A Guide for Graduate Students and Research Assistants*. He is also the Editor of a book series at Sage Publications on racial and ethnic minority psychology. Dr. Leong is a Fellow of the American Psychological Association (Divisions 2, 17, and 45). His major research interests are in vocational psychology (career development of ethnic minorities), cross-cultural psychology (particularly culture and mental health and cross-cultural psychotherapy), and organizational behavior.

Professor Magoroh Maruyama has been on faculty at the University of California Berkeley, Stanford University, University of Illinois Urbana, Uppsala Universitet in Sweden, Université de Montpellier in France, National University of Singapore, Aoyama Gakuin University in Tokyo, and currently teaches at Aomori Graduate School in Japan. His 170 publications include "The Second Cybernetics" (1963; in *American Scientist*), "Mindscapes and Science Theories" (1980; in *Current Anthropology*), and "Beyond Post-Modernism" (1997; in *Cybernetica*).

Azara L. Santiago-Rivera is an Assistant Professor in the Department of Counseling Psychology, and Latin American and Caribbean Studies Departments at SUNY-Albany. She obtained a B.A. in psychology and an M.A. in guidance and counseling from Interamerican University in Puerto Rico. She obtained a Ph.D. in counseling from Wayne State University in 1991. She has published on counseling the bilingual Spanish-speaking client, and Latino ethnic identity; individual differences in the appraisal of and reactions to stressful life events; and the study of the effects of environmental contamination on the psychological and physical well-being of individuals. She is currently a principal investigator on a major research project funded by the National Institute of Environmental Health Sciences involving the study of the effects of PCB exposure on a Mohawk community in Northeastern New York. Professor Santiago-Rivera is also on the editorial boards of the *Journal of Counseling and Development* (American Counseling Association), and the *Latino Review of Books* (Center for Latino, Latin American, and Caribbean Studies, University at Albany).

Wayne Schlapkohl is a doctoral student in human development and applied psychology at the University of Toronto. His thesis research is on the role of self-efficacy beliefs in college students' responsiveness to an intervention designed to alleviate academic underachievement.

Barry H. Schneider is Associate Professor of Psychology at the University of Ottawa and Associate Professor of Human Development and Applied Psychology at the University of Toronto. His research interests include the dynamics of children's friendships in different cultures; the social relations of children who display patterns of atypical development; and interventions to prevent and treat peer-relations problems.

Leslie Swartz is a clinical psychologist trained at the University of Cape Town, where he is currently Professor of Psychology based at the Child Guidance Clinic. His research has centered on two main areas: culture and mental health in the South African sociopolitical context; and the development of community clinical psychology in South Africa. His current research includes an intervention study of support for mothers and infants in an informal settlement, and he is completing a manuscript for Oxford University Press entitled *Culture and Mental Health: A Southern African View.*

FOREWORD

Humans see the world according to the information that they sample from the environment. Members of different cultures sample different types of information. For example, members of Western, individualist cultures, when explaining what people do, sample mostly internal processes such as beliefs, attitudes, personality, personal goals, aspirations, and values. Members of the cultures of the majority of the rest of the world sample mostly external processes, such as the views of the in-group, the norms and roles that have developed in the in-group, and the in-group's goals, aspirations, and values. This sampling is so pervasive that we are not even aware of it. As members of a culture we do this sampling automatically, the way Americans behave when entering a car and driving on the right side of the road without even thinking. Similarly, without thinking, we make assumptions about the way the world is, and what standard operating procedures we must use to get things done. For most of us it is *obvious* that there is one and only one way to look at the world.

This way of behaving serves us well as long as we interact with others who have been exposed to the same culture. But as the world is getting to be more multicultural, what is helpful in a culturally homogeneous environment becomes a trap that leads to misunderstandings, conflict, and even war. In a global society where we depend on the cooperation of others, such outcomes are unacceptable. This book explores what needs to be done to avoid these unacceptable outcomes.

The book treats multiculturalism broadly: Even the deaf are included as a different culture. It has an international cast of authors who discuss the many uses of culture in psychology. The aim is to make psychology more complete and more accurate. Thus, in addition to humanism, behaviorism, and psychodynamism, cultural psychology can become the fourth dimension of psychology.

The majority of the authors emphasize that the West is but a small part of humankind, yet most of the subject matter of psychology has been generated in the West, often in de-contextualized settings such as in experiments. While the information derived from such research methods is

very useful in cultures where most people pay little attention to the context of events, it becomes much less useful in cultures where the context
is used much more extensively. When the best predictor of behavior is an
attitude (internal process) our methods can be useful; but when the best
predictor is norms that change with each ingroup (external process), our
methods are much less effective.

When client and counselor share a cultural background, the context is
less important than it is when they come from different cultures. When
the distance between the two cultures is large they literally live in different
worlds, and they communicate past each other. In that case the counselor's
sampling of "helping responses" is inappropriate and unhelpful to the
client. For example, in individualist cultures people value "choice." The
counselor is likely to suggest more than one course of action to the client.
But in most vertical collectivist cultures people want to be told "this is
what you must do." When given many choices and asked to select among
them, instead of enjoying the freedom and self-determination that such
choices imply, they feel frustrated, confused, and even angry.

This book assesses the prospect that culture may become a fourth dimension in psychology. What changes in psychology and in the training of
practitioners will be necessary for the therapists to become effective when
working with clients from other cultures? The book explores the advantages and disadvantages of this happening and discusses whether it is likely
that it will happen. The authors differ in their assessments, and that leads
to healthy debate.

One of the authors examines the international scene. Is there a chance
that the fourth dimension can become significant in that setting? He discusses different ways in which the cultures of the world might change. For
example, one direction might be that each culture will emphasize its differences from other cultures and seek separation from other cultures, while
the opposite direction may be that a unified world culture will eventually
emerge. Both extremes are assessed as undesirable.

Within a country should we aim toward a melting pot or a mosaic? How
can we help people develop multiple cultural identities that allow them to
function effectively in many cultural environments? What are the barriers
toward that goal? What does it mean to become effective in many cultural
environments? Would a person become "internally more heterogeneous"
or "migrate to different cultural settings" or both?

One of the pessimisms concerning the possibility that psychology will
become a fourth dimension points out that we are all ethnocentric, and
the false consensus effect makes us assume that others see the world the
way we do. We tend to be attracted to people like us, to select them, and
if we do not get along with them we reduce our interactions with them.
For culture to become the fourth dimension in psychology the discipline

and profession will require much change. Change is always difficult, and when people are asked to change too much, they react to the pressures and often do the opposite of what we had hoped they would do. Furthermore, psychologists often think that it would be desirable if their findings were universal, and are just as subject as other humans to the "values-belief fallacy" that "what is desirable is true." In any case, the majority of psychologists ignore culture and many of us have a tendency to go along with the majority. In short, in this author's assessment, the prospect that culture will become the fourth dimension in psychology is very dim.

The book provides case studies and data from many cultures, such as Turkey, South Africa, Hungary, and Japan. It deals with intriguing topics, such as indigenous healing in South Africa and why the literature on such healing is so positive about it although the evidence about its effectiveness is non-existent. It explores the problems when client and therapist do not have a common "best" language, and the need for therapists to learn the languages of their clients. It presents interesting case studies and perspectives on conflict in different settings, such as in schools and in international contexts.

As we become more and more a global village, the discussions of this book will be of vital importance to the future of psychology.

Harry C. Triandis, Ph.D.
Professor Emeritus
Department of Psychology
University of Illinois
at Urbana-Champaign

PREFACE

Psychological publications have increasingly included *culture* as an important factor, due largely to the pressure of the civil rights movement, the feminist movement, and various special interest groups who have been undervalued and marginalized to the extent that they deviated from the mainstream of white, middle-class, urban, male measures of normal behavior. Although the rhetorical support for multiculturalism is evident, the actual changes toward a culture-centered psychology have been much slower. This book is directed toward the question of whether or not multiculturalism qualifies as a "Fourth Force" or dimension of psychology to supplement and, ideally, to strengthen the three earlier theoretical forces of humanism, behaviorism, and psychodynamism.

One advantage of the term "multicultural" is that it implies a wide range of multiple groups without grading, comparing, or ranking them as better or worse than one another, and without denying the very distinct and complementary or even contradictory perspectives that each group brings with it. This definition of culture is complicated and dynamic but not chaotic. Each of us belongs to many different cultures at different times, in different environments, and in different roles. Within-group differences are at least as important as between-group differences in the multicultural perspective. This book will attempt to identify both the unique perspectives of specific cultural groups and some of the more universal perspectives different groups share with one another in the broad definition of multiculturalism (Pedersen, 1991).

Before we were born, cultural patterns of thought and action were already prepared to guide our ideas, influence our decisions, and help us take control of our lives. We inherited these cultural patterns from our parents and teachers who taught us the "rules of the game." Only later (sometimes much later and sometimes never) did we learn that our culture was one of the many possible patterns of thinking and acting from which we could choose. By that time, most of us had already come to believe that "our" culture was the best of all possible worlds. Even if we recognized that traditional values were false or inadequate, when challenged by the stress of radical social change, it was not always possible to replace the worn-out habits with new alternatives.

Multiculturalism as a fourth force combines the alternatives of universalism and relativism by explaining behavior both in terms of those culturally learned perspectives that are unique to our particular background, and our search for common-ground universals that are shared across cultures. The "melting pot" metaphor made the mistake of overemphasizing the universal common-ground generalizations to the neglect of culturally unique perspectives. The phenomena of racism, sexism, ageism, and other exclusionary perspectives, overemphasize culturally unique perspectives while neglecting the common-ground universals and within-group differences that are shared across cultures. An inclusive multicultural fourth-force perspective recognizes both similarities and differences at the same time.

This book explores the possibility that we are moving toward a generic theory of multiculturalism that recognizes the psychological consequences of each cultural context, where each behavior has been learned and is displayed. The description of multiculturalism as a fourth force has grown out of work by many persons (Pedersen, 1990, 1991, 1994; Ponterotto & Casas, 1991; Sue & Sue, 1990). The label of "fourth force" emphasizes that multiculturalism is relevant throughout the field of psychology as a generic rather than an exotic perspective. Labels tend to oversimplify complicated relationships, and to that extent they are dangerous. The label of Multiculturalism as a Fourth Force, however, calls attention to the way in which a culture-centered perspective has changed the way we look at psychology across fields and theories.

The book is divided into two parts. The first part is focused on the issue of multiculturalism as a fourth force generally. The importance of culture-centered interventions in counseling as an increasingly recognized and consistently important perspective is reviewed in Chapter One. Accurate assessment, meaningful understanding, and appropriate intervention require that each behavior be understood in the cultural context where that behavior was learned and is displayed. The chapter by Maruyama explores the complicated epistemological issues of culture in the field of psychology. The multicultural perspective changes both the content and the process of psychological analysis. The chapter by Leong is critical of a fourth-force perspective as premature, given the extent of racism and cultural bias in the contemporary psychological literature. While a generic multicultural perspective may be aspirational, Leong posits that it may be too soon to apply that label.

The second part is focused on particular contexts where the multicultural perspective demonstrates its productivity. The chapter by Fisek and Kagitcibasi clearly demonstrates the importance of a culture-centered perspective, providing Turkish case examples as supporting data. The generic utility of multiculturalism across cultures is a powerful factor in the theory and practice of psychology. The chapter by Swartz applies a multicultural perspective to mental health issues in South Africa. Psychological literature not typically cited in Euro-American psychological publications demonstrates by its presence the importance of taking an international and multicultural perspective. Backenroth applies the multicultural perspective to the deaf population in a broad definition of culture. The chapter demonstrates the generic utility of reframing relationships into a multicultural perspective which allows for both similarities and differences as examples of quantum thinking. The chapter by Ball discusses the importance of multiculturalism in issues of identity, particularly focusing on Confucian heritage societies. While culture may be defined differently in each social context, the underlying principles of identity across cultures share a foundation of cultural process. The chapter by Barry Schneider likewise emphasizes the importance of culture in the Canadian setting with particular emphasis on counseling.

Whether or not multiculturalism emerges as a truly generic approach to psychology and whether or not it emerges as a fourth force with an articulated impact on psychology equivalent to behaviorism, psychodynamics, and humanism, culture does provide a valuable metaphor for understanding ourselves and others. It is no longer possible for psychologists to ignore their own culture or the cultures of their clients. Until the multicultural perspective is understood as making a psychological perspective more accurate, dear, and meaningful instead of more obscure, troublesome, and awkward, little change toward multiculturalism being a fourth force is likely to occur.

☐ References

Pedersen, P. (1990). The multicultural perspective as a fourth force in counseling. *Journal of Mental Health Counseling 12*(1), 93–95.

Pedersen, P. (1991). Multiculturalism as a generic approach to counseling. *Journal of Counseling and Development: Special Issue on Multiculturalism as a Fourth Force*, 70(1), 6–12.

Pedersen, P. (1994). *A handbook for developing multicultural awareness*. Alexandria, VA.: American Association for Counseling and Development.

Ponterotto, J. G., & Casas, J. M. (1991). *Handbook of racial/ethnic minority counseling research.* Springfield, IL.: Charles C. Thomas.

Sue, D. W., & Sue, D. (1990). *Counseling the culturally different: Theory and practice.* New York: John Wiley & Sons.

PART

I

THE GENERAL
ISSUES OF
MULTICULTURALISM
AS A FOURTH FORCE

CHAPTER 1

Paul Pedersen

Culture-centered Interventions as a Fourth Dimension of Psychology

A "fourth force" or dimension of psychology is emerging from a variety of contrasting perspectives in the social sciences. This fourth alternative is characterized by an inclusive nature that goes beyond the psychodynamic, behavioral, and humanistic perspectives and is best described by cultural metaphors. A broad definition of culture which includes all salient features of personal identity provides a psychological construct adaptable to contemporary theories of counseling and psychological intervention. The advantages of a culture-centered perspective as a fourth-force alternative are identified and discussed in this chapter.

Culture is emerging as one of the most important and perhaps one of the most misunderstood constructs of contemporary theories of psychology. Culture may be defined narrowly, limited to ethnicity or nationality; or broadly, to include any and all potentially salient ethnographic, demographic, status, or affiliation identities. There are hundreds of working definitions for the culture construct which contrast with and sometimes contradict one another (Berry, Poortinga, Segall, & Dasen, 1992; Pedersen, 1990; 1997). At the same time, the fundamental importance of cultural constructs in psychology are clearly documented.

If each behavior occurs in a cultural context then all theories of human behavior are fundamentally, but usually implicitly, cultural theories. Attempts to accurately assess, meaningfully understand, and appropriately change behaviors without regard for their cultural contexts are misguided, naive, and dangerous. A culture-centered perspective provides a "fourth dimension" to the psychological interpretation of human behavior which gives additional meaning to psychodynamic, humanistic, and behavioral interpretations much as the fourth dimension of time gives meaning to three dimensional space. The culture-centered perspective is not intended to displace or compete with the other psychological perspectives but rather to complement them by framing them in the cultural contexts where all psychological interpretation occurs.

Segall, Dasen, Berry, and Poortinga (1990) affirm that ecological forces are the prime movers and shapers of cultural forms which in turn shape behaviors: "... given these characteristics of culture, it becomes possible to define it simply as the totality of whatever all persons learn from all other persons" (p. 26). Cultural psychology presumes that every sociocultural environment depends on the way humans give each cultural context meaning and are in turn changed in response to that sociocultural environment. Cultural psychology studies the ways cultural traditions and social practices regulate, express, and transform people in patterned ways. "Cultural psychology is the study of the ways subject and object, self and other, psyche and culture, person and context, figure and ground, practitioner and practice live together, require each other, and dynamically, dialectically and jointly make each other up" (Shweder, 1990, p. 1).

A culture-centered perspective introduces a new paradigm for psychology. Smith, Harre, and Van Langenhove (1995) contrast the new with the old paradigms in psychology. The new paradigms emphasize: understanding and description more than measuring, counting, or predicting; meaning rather than causation or frequencies; interpretation rather than statistical analysis; language, discourse, and symbols rather than reduction of data to numbers; holistic rather than atomistic perspectives; particularities rather than universals; cultural context rather than context-free perspectives; and subjectivity as well as objectivity.

☐ The Development of a Fourth Dimension in Psychology

To the extent that culture in addition to ethnographic categories also refers to broadly defined social systems, variables of demographic, status and formal or informal affiliation, then a culture-centered dimension of all psychological theory emerges as a fourth dimension. According to the broad definition of culture, the underlying principle of a culture-centered perspective is to emphasize both the culture specific characteristics which differentiate and the culture-general characteristics which unite. The accommodation of both similarities and differences provides a complementary and comprehensive context for psychological understanding.

The notion of a fourth force is not new. Tart (1975) described the position of transpersonal psychology as a "fourth force" based on the spiritual revolution in modern society. The transpersonal psychologists suggested that their "fourth force" provided an alternative to scientific psychology. Transpersonal psychology was the first of many psychological perspectives to call attention to an emerging fourth alternative to the three prevailing psychological theories.

Mahoney and Patterson (1992) suggest that counseling and perhaps all psychology is at a "pivotal period" in which the rules are being changed in ways that we are only beginning to appreciate. The early history of psychology began with psychoanalytic theory as the first force of psychology emphasizing belief in the power of unconscious forces, biological impulses, and other internal processes of a client which determine behaviors. The second force began as a revolution toward positivism and objectivity as the explicit ideals of the scientific psychology of behaviorism. This changed the focus from the unconscious to behaviors which can be directly observed. Later, the third force of existentialism in Europe, and humanism in the U.S., with its positive view of human nature, emerged. This perspective, usually combined with phenomenological/experiential elements, saw clients as interactive and interdependent with environmental factors. Mahoney and Patterson (1992) claim that a fourth force cognitive revolution emerged in the late 1950s and 1960s as an interdisciplinary perspective in which human behavior is described as reciprocal and interactive rather than linear and unidirectional.

Other psychologists discuss the emergence of a fourth force without mentioning culture. Wrightsman (1992) describes how the perspectives of behaviorism, psychoanalysis, and humanism are supplemented by a "fourth alternative" based on George Kelly's personal construct theory. Wrightsman describes this new movement as more collectivistic, resembling non-Western indigenous psychologies. "We are living in a time when the conventional wisdom about human nature and the nature of society is under attack. Technology has run amok; many now question our ability to bring technology under manageable control. Bureaucracy—a social structure originally established to provide for person growth—now stifles human development and generates a philosophy that human nature is lazy, irresponsible and extrinsically motivated. The communal movement has challenged a pessimistic drift in our society. Through study of the movement's assumptions, aims, procedures and outcomes, we may gain an understanding of the future of philosophies or human nature" (Wrightsman, 1992, p. 293).

Culture provides a convenient construct to describe the complex and dynamic changes in psychological thinking which are redefining the rules of psychology. The new rules advocate tolerance of ambiguity rather than reductionism, multidimensional reality rather than unidimensionalism, the validity of subjective as well as objective evidence as proof and the validity of qualitative as well as quantitative methods for psychological research (Smith, Harre, & Van Langenhove, 1995).

Psychology in the near future promises to become a culture-inclusive science, that is, a science that routinely takes cultural variables into account (Berry, 1996). In contrast, psychology has routinely neglected and underestimated the power of cultural variables. Soon there will appear in connection with many psychological theories and methods a series of questions: "Under what circumstances and in which culturally circumscribed situations does a given psychological theory or methodology provide valid explanations for the origins and maintenance of behavior? What are the cultural boundary conditions potentially limiting the generalizability of psychological theories and methodologies? Which psychological phenomena are culturally robust in character, and which phenomena appear only under specified cultural conditions?" (Geilen, 1994, p. 38).

This multidimensional theory of cultural relationships accommodates both the perspective of cultural relativism and a universalistic perspective. The universal explanation of human behavior more frequently associated with the discipline of psychology is based on Nomothetic truth in the aggregate and lends itself to quantitative analysis across individual cases. The relativist perspective, more frequently associated with the field of anthropology, describes the ideographic truth of the particular instance but does not lend itself to generalizations across instances. The culture-centered perspective seeks to combine anthropological and psychological perspectives for a more balanced and comprehensive interpretation of human behavior than either discipline can provide separately.

There has been some controversy between those supporting cross-cultural psychology and those supporting cultural, transcultural, multicultural, or intercultural psychology, and other descriptions of the relationship between culture and psychology. These disagreements have been a distraction to the genetic application of culture to psychology.

Much has been made recently of the relatively small differences in approaches to the study of relationships between culture and behavior. I believe that the main goal of the field is to convince general psychology that culture is an important contributor to the development of human behavior, and to our understanding and study of it. I also believe that our combined efforts should be directed towards achieving this goal, rather than towards establishing claims of the correctness of one particular orientation over another (Berry, 1996, p. 96).

A multicultural counseling theory (Sue, Ivey, & Pedersen, 1996) is needed to provide a conceptual framework that recognizes the complex diversity of a plural society while at the same time suggesting bridges of shared concern which bind culturally different persons to one another. The ultimate outcome of a multicultural theory, as Segall et al. (1990) suggest is a contextual understanding. "There may well come a time when we will no longer speak of cross-cultural psychology as such. The basic premise of this field—that to understand human behavior we must study it in its sociocultural context—may become so widely accepted that all psychology will be inherently cultural" (p. 352).

The notion of culture is not new to psychology. Cross-cultural psychology has been an established area of psychology for nearly half a century. Cross-cultural psychology has more often been described as a method than as a theory. To the extent that "culture" refers exclusively to narrowly defined ethnographic categories such as nationality, race, or ethnicity, then cross-cultural psychology might indeed best be considered to be a method of analysis. The methods of cross-cultural psychology have usually applied to understanding the encounter of specific cultural groups with one another, while emphasizing the culture-specific categories of each group.

This trend toward cultural identification is not limited to the field of psychology. Huntington (1993) has described a "change in the rules" of national and international political engagement. In his opinion, a clash of deep seated ethnocultural differences will become more important than will nationalism for understanding the science of political conflict in the future. There is a pervasive awareness of cultural similarities and differences in the social sciences today which is changing the rules in ways that will require a rethinking of established theories of human behavior.

Two contrasting definitions of culture have emerged. One views culture as the values, beliefs, norms, rationalizations, symbols, ideologies, and other "mental products" which provide descriptive categories. The other views culture as the total way of life of a people including their interpersonal relations as well as their attitudes. The broad and more inclusive perspective of culture is emerging as the preferred perspective (Thompson, Ellis, & Wildavsky, 1990). Berry et al. (1992) point out the implications of a broad and inclusive perspective in an interdisciplinary study of behavior from multiple perspectives. "Thus in our frame of reference we need to avoid reducing culture to the level of psychological explanations, of psychological phenomena to biological explanations, biological to chemical, and so on. That is, we must recognize that there are, for example, cultural phenomena that exist and can be studied at their own level" (p. 6).

Definitions of cultural identity depend on a broad definition of culture. By defining culture broadly, to include demographic (e.g., age, gender, place of residence, etc.), status (e.g., social, educational, economic, etc.), and affiliation (e.g., formal and informal) variables as well as ethnographic variables of nationality and ethnicity, the construct of culture becomes generic to all counseling relationships in context. The narrow definition of culture has limited culture to what might more appropriately be called ethnographic relationships between groups with a shared sociocultural heritage and history. Ethnicity and nationality are important cultural variables but they are not unidimensional. The broad definition of culture includes the many within-group variables in a multidimensional description of cultural identity.

Attempts to describe cultural identity as unimodal or unidimensional rather than orthogonal (Berry, 1970, 1980; Oetting & Beauvais, 1991) have led to glossing over within-group differences and imposing a pseudo cultural identity on those with simultaneous membership in more than one culture at the same time. The five most used alternative models of identity are less complex. The dominant majority model simply imposes a dominant culture as an appropriate adjustment. The alienation model seeks to avoid stress from anomie by assisting persons in transition to make successful adjustments. The multidimensional model presumes transition on several dimensions at the same time, with different degrees of change on each dimension. The bicultural model presumes that one can adapt to one culture without losing contact with the earlier culture.

The orthogonal model, however, suggests that adapting simultaneously to more than one culture combines the preceding five alternative models in a higher level of comprehensive and inclusive complexity. This orthogonal perspective offers several important advantages. First, cultural groups may exist in association with one another without isolating themselves or competing with one another. Second, minority cultures need not be eliminated or absorbed in order to coexist. Third, a permanent multicultural society may be possible that is multifaceted and multidimensional without becoming a "melting pot." Fourth, conflicts of value and belief do not present insurmountable barriers but may be combined in a realistic pluralism. Fifth, cultural conflict may become a positive rather than a negative force from the perspective of shared common-ground expectations. Sixth, members of minority groups may be less inclined toward militancy when their survival is not threatened. Seventh, interaction between minority and majority cultures may be less destructive to all parties. Eighth, there are economic advantages of releasing resources previously consumed by cultural conflict. Ninth, there are already models of orthogonal relationships in healthy bicultural and multicultural families or social units.

Just as differentiation and integration are complementary processes, so are the emic (culture specific) and etic (culture general) perspectives necessarily interrelated. The terms emic and etic were borrowed from phonemic (language-specific) and phonetic (language-general) analysis in linguistics describing the rules of language. Even Pike (1966) in his original conceptualization of this dichotomy suggested that the two elements not be treated as a rigid dichotomy but as a way of presenting the same idea from two complementary viewpoints. All people experience loneliness (etic) but each specific group has learned to deal with loneliness in a particular and unique way (emic). Although research on the usefulness of emic and etic categories has been extensive, the notion of a culture-free (universal) etic has been just as elusive as attempts to capture a culture-pure (totally isolated) emic. Combining the specific and general viewpoints provides a broadly-defined culture-centered perspective. This more inclusive perspective is an essential starting point for psychological interventions that are accurate, meaningful, and appropriate. The exclusive narrowly-defined alternative is likely to result in cultural encapsulation.

The broad definition of culture is also represented in the literature about social constructivism. Hermans, Kempen, and Van Loon (1993) propose a dialogical as opposed to a monological view of self for psychology, which assumes that identity is formed out of the construction and reconstruction of encounters with others. We are connected with other groups and cultures through reciprocal influences. People are guided by what Hermans and colleagues call "root metaphors" to guide their perceptions and thinking. Metaphors become spotlights on each particular view of reality. Each spotlight is focused in a particular angle and, therefore, offers only one view. Metaphors, like perspectives, create views and at the same time restrict these views. The broadly-defined culture-centered perspective provides a dynamic metaphor for interpreting human behavior in the context of where that behavior was learned and is displayed.

There are some functional benefits in defining each complicated cultural context broadly rather than narrowly. First, the broad definition allows and forces counselors to be more accurate in matching a client's culturally learned expectation with the client's behavior learned in that cultural context. Second, a broad definition helps counselors become more aware of how their own culturally learned perspective predisposes them toward a particular decision outcome. Third, a broad perspective helps the counselor become more aware of the complexity in culturally defined identity patterns which may or may not include the obvious indicators of ethnicity and nationality. Fourth, the broad definition encourages counselors to track the ever changing salience of a client's different interchangeable cultural identities within a counseling context or the cultural contexts of their clients. The culture-centered perspective is proposed as a way of making the counselor's job easier instead of harder, and for increasing rather than decreasing the quality of a counselor's life, so that change toward acknowledging the importance of culture in psychology is more likely to happen.

There are at least twelve uniquely positive contributions of a broadly defined culture-centered perspective in psychology.

1. Since all behavior is learned and displayed in a cultural context, accurate assessment, meaningful understanding, and appropriate interventions are culturally contextual constructs.
2. The common ground of shared values or expectations can be expressed by contrasting culturally learned behaviors to express shared common ground values.
3. An articulate awareness of the thousands of culture teachers accumulated throughout our lifetime will help us comprehend the complexity of our multicultural identity.
4. A healthy socio-ecosystem requires a diversity of cultural perspectives just as a healthy bio-system requires a diverse gene pool by analogy.
5. A culture-centered perspective protects us from inappropriately imposing our own culturally encapsulated self-reference criteria in the evaluation of others.
6. Contact with culturally different groups provides an opportunity to rehearse adaptive functioning skills for our own multicultural future in the global village.
7. Understanding social justice and moral development in a multicultural context helps us differentiate fundamental non-negotiable beliefs from negotiable applications of those beliefs.
8. A culture-centered perspective reflects the complementarity of the quantum metaphor by emphasizing both similarities (of values) and differences (of behaviors) in each multicultural context.
9. All learning and change involves some degree of culture shock to the extent that it influences our basic beliefs.
10. A culture-centered perspective enhances our spiritual completeness by linking culturally-different spiritual representations of the same ultimate reality.
11. A culture-centered perspective builds pluralism as an alternative to authoritarianism or anarchy for social organizations.
12. A culture-centered perspective will strengthen contemporary theories of psychological intervention rather than weaken or displace them by interpreting them in the client's cultural context.

☐ The Dangers of Cultural Encapsulation

The monocultural perspective has served the purposes of a dominant culture by protecting the cultural assumptions of the dominant culture (Pedersen, 1994). The first assumption is that we all share the same single measure of normal behavior which is presumed to be universal across social, cultural, economic, and/or political backgrounds. The second assumption is that individuals, rather than the families or groups to which they belong, are the basic building blocks of a modern society, as reflected in the terminology (e.g., self-awareness, personality, identity) of psychological intervention. The third assumption is that psychological interventions are bounded by areas of specialization and special expertise rather than the more holistic perspective typical of a hurting client. The fourth assumption involves the rigid use of professional and abstract psychological classification without regard for the complex and dynamic cultural contexts to which those classifications are applied, especially in cultures that put a high emphasis on context. A fifth assumption is that independence is desirable and dependence is undesirable, devaluing the connectedness in collectivistic cultures. A sixth assumption is to prefer formal counseling to the client's natural support system as an appropriate intervention, even though 80 percent of the world's population relies on alternative therapies (Eisenberg et al., 1993). A seventh assumption is that everyone depends on linear thinking, where each cause has an effect and each effect is tied to a cause, disregarding the nonlinear alternatives to cognition. An eighth assumption is that psychological interventions change individuals to fit the system and not the system to fit the individual, sometimes even when the individual is right and the system is wrong. A ninth assumption is that historical background is not a high priority for understanding contemporary events even though many cultures believe that knowing the historical context defines civilized societies. A tenth assumption is that we already know all of our culturally learned assumptions and biases, causing us to unintentionally continue to socialize our clients and students into the dominant culture to which we belong.

There is a history of moral exclusion when individuals or groups are perceived as outside the rules that define fairness, and as nonentities, expendable or undeserving (Opotow, 1990). This exclusionary perspective has been described as a form of encapsulation (Wrenn, 1962; 1985). It assumes five basic identifying features. First, we define reality according to one set of cultural assumptions and stereotypes which become more important than the real world. Second, we become insensitive to cultural variations among individuals and assume that our view is the only real or legitimate one. Third, each of us develops unreasoned assumptions which we accept without proof and which we protect without regard to rationality. Fourth, a technique-oriented job definition further contributes toward and preserves the encapsulation. Fifth, when there is no evaluation of other viewpoints, then there is no responsibility to accommodate or interpret the behavior of others except from a self-referential perspective.

The politics of minority versus majority culture provides examples of cultural encapsulation in the cultural context of counseling. Ponterotto and Casas (1991) document the perception that "the majority of traditionally trained counselors operate from a culturally biased and encapsulated framework which results in the provision of culturally conflicting and even oppressive counseling treatments" (pp. 7–8). Counselor training programs are often presumed by minority clients to be proponents of the status quo, stimulating considerable criticism regarding counseling research about racial/ethnic minority groups (Sue & Sue, 1990).

The Task Force of the U.S. National Advisory Mental Health Council (1996) in their national plan for behavioral science research identified areas where social and cultural factors were evident in the research literature. While this report is focused on mental health and mental illness, the implications for other fields of psychological intervention are clear: (1) Anthropological and cross-cultural studies demonstrate that cultural beliefs about the nature of mental illness influence a community's view of its course and treatment; (2) diagnosis of mental illnesses differ across cultures and subcultures; (3) research has revealed differences in how individuals in different cultures experience and express symptoms of mental illness; (4) culturally based variations in diagnosis also occur because current diagnostic categories are derived largely from research among majority populations; and (5) the vast majority of providers come from the White majority culture, while most of their clients are members of ethnic minorities.

Culture provides the context through shared experiences that influence how basic psychological processes are expressed, provided, and consumed. Basic psychological theories describe the "false uniqueness effect," a tendency to underestimate the extent to which others also possess one's desirable traits; this effect applies much better to some Western cultures than to other non-Western cultures (Pedersen, 1997). The "fundamental attribution error" applies much more to cultures that are individualistic than to those that are collectivistic (Segall et al., 1990). The role of appropriate achievement motivation is also connected with the individualistic striving for success. How we experience emotions themselves will change and vary from one cultural context to another.

There are several reasons why the pressure is on to reduce cultural encapsulation, though a more culture-centered perspective has become globally popular in recent years (Sloan, 1990). First, there is a growing psychological concern for Third World development and global awareness resulting from increased access to international communication and transportation resources. These developments have not always been positive and have contributed to problems as well as solutions in newly industrialized societies. Second, there is an attempt to redefine international relationships in the search for a post-colonial and/or post-imperial future for the dominant cultures. Third, the social sciences have been internationalized at both the practical and theoretical levels to match geopolitical developments. The impetus for development as a goal of the social sciences has become prominent. Fourth, the interests of Third World countries and minority interest groups has become radicalized through national liberation movements. Plans for gradual political and economic transformation have lost credibility in many Third World countries. Fifth, there has been a paradigm shift in methodology that advocates practical applications over abstractions. The contemporary emphasis on indigenous psychologies and alternative therapies demonstrate this movement. Sixth, professionals from the activist generation of the 1960s have gained professional maturity. The enthusiasm for human rights monitoring and research, international cooperation and peace research, has grown out of their leadership. Seventh, there is more interdisciplinary cooperation and concern for practical relevance in social science research. Scientific and technological advances have been challenged to become more relevant to all populations. Eighth, new forms of cultural diversity have emerged with attention to immigrants, refugees, migrant workers, students, tourists, and migrants across cultures. The problems resulting from voluntary and, particularly, involuntary cultural contact requires new solutions. Finally, the educational exchange and collaboration of social scientists has contributed to a global perspective which is more proactive than reactive. Social scientists from around the world spend more time than ever before in direct contact and conversation.

Levine (1985) suggests that the social sciences have preferred less complicated perspectives because of the problems in managing ambiguity as an empirical phenomenon, difficult to measure in objective terms. "The toleration of ambiguity can be productive if it is taken not as a warrant for sloppy thinking but as an invitation to deal responsibly with ideas of great complexity" (p. 17). Cultural encapsulation is no longer acceptable in psychology. Increased attention to context has required increased ability to manage ambiguity, as Lonner and Adamopoulos (1997) point out. "In general, what we observe in our analysis, above all, is an invigorated attempt to reintroduce some form of contextualism in a psychology that has long ignored the importance of the environment, broadly defined, as a constitutive component of human behavior" (p. 77).

☐ Implications for Psychology in the Future

Multiculturalism as a fourth dimension psychological perspective provides the framework for an active response. Recognizing that accurate assessment, meaningful interpretation, and appropriate intervention require attention to the cultural environment in which behaviors are learned and displayed, the culture-centered perspective as a fourth force has profound consequences for psychology in the future. In defending the importance of "meaning" as a central concept of psychology, Bruner (1990) makes two arguments: "The first is that to understand man you must understand how his experiences and his acts are shaped by his intentional states, and the second is that the form of these intentional states is realized only through participation in the symbolic systems of the culture" (p. 33). Psychological research, for example, will be guided by new and different assumptions according to a culture-centered perspective.

Research directions for the future were identified by the National Advisory Mental Health Council (1996) to include the following: (1) Research is needed that explores how ethnicity influences social cognition and achievement motivation as well as how cultural differences affect the expression and labeling of emotion; (2) research is needed on such issues as the role of culture in the expression of psychiatric symptoms, the factors that place poor and minority persons at elevated risk for misdiagnosis; (3) research is needed on how and in what settings ethnic discrimination continues to be expressed and how it affects various groups; (4) increased research is needed on discrimination in school and work settings, successful strategies for dealing with disempowerment, and the mental health consequences of acculturation for migrants and immigrants; (5) basic research is needed to identify those processes that mediate the effect of SES (socioeconomic status) on mental health; (6) future research should emphasize the interdependence of work environments with family constellations; and (7) research should focus on those key aspects of communities that either threaten or protect mental health and well being.

Sue et al. (1996) have attempted to describe the future directions of multicultural counseling theory based on six propositions. First, each Western or non-Western theory represents a different worldview. Second, the totality and interrelationships of client/counselor experiences and contexts must be the focus of treatment. Third, a counselor or client's racial/cultural identity will influence how problems are defined and dictate or define appropriate counseling goals or processes. Fourth, the ultimate goal of a culture-centered approach is to expand the repertoire of helping responses available to counselors. Fifth, conventional roles of counseling are only some of the many alternative helping roles available from other cultural contexts. Sixth, multicultural counseling theory emphasizes the importance of expanding personal, family, group, and organizational consciousness in a contextual orientation to clients.

One promising movement in the social sciences which provides a contextual alternative to simplistic encapsulation is based on the concepts of chaos theory, nonlinear dynamics, and self-organizing systems (Barton, 1994). This new paradigm for understanding how systems interact has been described as chaos theory, and later, as complexity theory, with their shared emphasis on nonlinear dynamics, self organization, and nonlinear dynamical systems theory. When chaos theory was originally invented to describe weather forecasting (Gleick, 1987) it described chaotic systems as unpredictable locally, although when viewed globally they were essentially stable. Psychology has typically depended on unidimensional models of human behavior based on linear, positivistic, and empirical epistemologies as the exclusive avenue to proof or evidence. Nonlinear dynamics suggests that people are multidimensional, functioning at multiple interactive levels simultaneously. To the extent that psychological analysis is focused on only one level, it will result in incomplete data and misunderstanding. The culture-centered perspective provides the possibility of an orthogonal (Oetting & Beauvais, 1991) identity based on many different and dynamic cultural affiliations at the same time. Belonging to one group does not exclude the possibility of belonging to many other groups at the same time. Each individual is a complex adaptive system for which a salient identity is both complicated and dynamic in each cultural context.

Complexity theory in the hard (and, more recently, in the soft) sciences has evolved from chaos theory, redefining conventional categories of analysis. Advocates of the nonlinear dynamics in the social sciences see themselves as pioneers of a dramatic new perspective. "They believe that they are forging the first rigorous alternative to the kind of linear, reductionistic thinking that has dominated science since the time of Newton—and that has now gone about as far as it can go in addressing the problems of our modern world" (Waldrop, 1992, p. 13). Lifton (1993) describes these postmodern survivors as "shape-shifters" with multiple identities, in contrast with the "fundamentalist" self who avoids fragmentation by being consistent whatever the consequences. If discontinuous change is a permanent feature of the post-modern world this need not result in confusion or abandonment of conventional rules of thinking. Rosenau (1992) distinguishes between "skeptical post-modernists" who react against any quest for certainty and unitary truth and the "affirmative post-modernists" who react against modernism but reject a world without meaning and recognize the importance of plural identities, ambiguous truth, and multiplicity of truths even without having all the answers.

The social constructivist perspective is also a relevant perspective for the future, based on the premise that we do not have direct access to a singular, stable, and fully knowable external reality, but rather depend on culturally embedded, interpersonally connected, and necessarily limited notions of reality. This emphasis on personal reality and constructed meaning provides a subjective understanding of knowledge. Rather than define the self as self-contained, self-reliant, independent, standing out, egocentric, and selfish, Hermans et al. (1992) promote a dialogical view of self beyond rationalism and individualism, based on the stories, patterns, or dialogues by which we understand ourselves and reality. "The embodied nature of the self contrasts with conceptions of the self found in mainstream psychology, which are based on the assumptions of a disembodied or rationalistic mind" (p. 23). If the world is objective then our different perceptions are inaccurate, our beliefs and perceptions are not relevant, context is unimportant, and all experiences are judged by universally applied rational rules. Reality, according to the contextual and constructivist view, is not based on absolute truth, but rather, on an understanding of complex and dynamic relationships in a cultural context.

Life is the narrative of culturally learned stories about the self in each cultural context. Life is not abstract, but told through relationships in a developmental rather than linear or stage-based hierarchy (Steenbarger, 1991). Howard (1991) describes how life is a series of stories about our collective experiences in a lifetime. "A life becomes meaningful when one sees himself or herself as an actor within the context of a story—be it a cultural tale, a religious narrative, a family saga, a march of science, a political movement, and so forth. Early in life we are free to choose what life story we will inhabit—and later we find we are lived by that story" (p. 196).

If we believe that culture is the context in which all behavior is learned, then culture is complicated and dynamic. It is complicated because of the many different perspectives in each context. It is dynamic as the salience changes within each context. Our cultural identity grows out of what we have learned and are learning in each cultural context. Culture controls our lives across all theories. Values and worldviews have been constructed to better understand each cultural context and are a product of that context. Each cultural context is experienced differently according to time, place, person, and circumstance to be understood through the patterns, rules, and stories of that context. Individual behaviors change only when their cultural context has been changed. The culture-centered perspective assumes that all measures and theories are biased by the implicit/explicit perspectives of the context in which that measure or theory was developed, requiring skilled adaptation or reinterpretation in each other context.

☐ Conclusion

There is a confluence of observations that we are going through a paradigm shift in the social sciences, and particularly in psychology, resulting in a "fourth force" or dimension to supplement the prevailing theories of psychodynamics, behaviorism, and humanism. These changes are more than a continuation of historical patterns and present a significantly different set of rules or patterns for the future. The development of this fourth alternative is described and documented from a variety of different disciplines. The opportunities and advantages of this new fourth alternative are described and discussed in the context of accurate assessment, meaningful understanding, and appropriate interventions from a psychological viewpoint.

A key feature of this fourth force is the broad definition of culture to include demographic, status, and affiliation as well as ethnographic variables. Support for the broad definition of culture is identified and the functional utility of defining culture broadly is discussed as a culture-centered point of view. There are specific positive advantages of a culture-centered approach from a psychological perspective for managing social issues more constructively.

The dangers of cultural encapsulation resulting from a unimodal and monocultural viewpoint are identified and discussed from a variety of social perspectives. The global forces favoring a culture-centered perspective and diminishing encapsulation are identified and discussed.

Implications for the future identify how a broadly-defined culture-centered perspective provides a useful metaphor for managing complexity in an increasingly complicated society.

☐ References

Barton, S. (1994). Chaos, self-organization and psychology. *American Psychologist, 49*(1) 5–14.
Berry, J. W. (1970). Marginality, stress and ethnic identification in an acculturated Aboriginal community. *Journal of Cross-Cultural Psychology, 1*, 239–252.
Berry, J. W. (1980). Acculturation as varieties of adaptation. In A. Padilla (Ed.), *Acculturation: Theory, models, and findings* (pp. 9–25). Boulder, CO: Westview.
Berry, J. W. (1996). On the unity of the field: Variations and communalities in understanding human behavior in cultural context. *Interamerican Journal of Psychology, 30*(1), 85–139.
Berry, J. W., Poortinga, Y. H., Segall, M. H., & Dasen, P. J. (1992). *Cross-cultural psychology: Research and applications.* Cambridge, England: Cambridge University Press.
Eisenberg, D. M., Kessler, R. C., Foster, C., Norlock, F. E., Calkins, D. R., & Delbauco, T. L. (1993). Unconventional medicine in the United States: Prevalence, costs and patterns of use. *New England Journal of Medicine, 328*(4), 246–252.
Gielen, U. P. (1994). American mainstream psychology and its relationship to international and cross-cultural psychology. In A. L. Comunian and U. P. Gielen (Eds.), *Advancing psychology and its applications: International perspectives* (pp. 26–40). Milan, Italy: Franco Angeli.
Gleick, J. (1987). *Chaos: Making a new science.* New York: Viking-Penguin.
Hermans, H. J. M., Kempen, H. J. G., & Van Loon, R. J. P. (1993). The diological self: Beyond individualism and rationalism. *American Psychologist, 47*(1), 23–33.
Howard, G. S. (1991). Culture tales: A narrative approach to thinking, cross-cultural psychology and psychotherapy. *American Psychologist, 46*, 187–197.
Huntington, S. (1993). The clash of civilizations. *Foreign Affairs, 72*, 22–49.
Levine, D. N. (1985). *The flight from ambiguity.* Chicago: The University of Chicago Press.
Lifton, R. J. (1993). *The protean self.* New York: Basic Books.

Lonner, W. J., and Adamopoulos, J. (1997). Culture as antecedent to behavior. In J. W. Berry, Y. H. Poortinga, & J. Pandey (Eds.), *Handbook of cross-cultural psychology: Volume 1* (pp. 43–83). Needham Heights, MA: Allyn & Bacon.

Mahoney, M. J., & Patterson K. M. (1992). Changing theories of changes: Recent developments in counseling. In S. D. Brown, & R. W. Lent (Eds.), *Handbook of counseling and psychology: Second edition* (pp. 665–689). New York: John Wiley & Sons.

National Advisory Mental Health Council (1996). Basic behavioral science research for mental health: Sociocultural and environmental processes. *American Psychologist, 51*(7) 722–731.

Oetting, E. R., & Beauvais, F. (1991). Orthogonal cultural identification theory: The cultural identification of minority adolescents. *The International Journal of the Addictions, 25,* 655–685.

Opotow, W. (1990). Moral exclusion and injustice: An introduction. *Journal of Social Issues, 46*(1) 1–20.

Pedersen, P. (1990). The multicultural perspective as a fourth force in counseling. *Journal of Mental Health Counseling, 12*(1) 93–95.

Pedersen, P. (1994). *A handbook for developing multicultural awareness: Second edition.* Alexandria, VA: American Counseling Association.

Pedersen, P. (1997). *Culture-centered counseling interventions: Striving for accuracy.* Thousand Oaks, CA: Sage Publications.

Pike, R. (1966). *Language in relation to a united theory of the structure of human behavior.* The Hague: Mouton.

Ponterotto, J. G., & Casas, J. M. (1991). *Handbook of racial/ethnic minority counseling research.* Springfield, IL: Charles C. Thomas.

Rosenau, P. M. (1992). *Post-modernism and the social sciences.* Princeton, NJ: Princeton University Press.

Segall, M. H., Dasen, P. R., Berry J. W., & Poortinga, Y. H. (1990). *Human behavior in global perspective: An introduction to cross-cultural psychology.* New York: Pergamon.

Shweder, R. A. (1990). Cultural psychology—What is it? In J. W. Stigler, R. A. Shweder, and G. Herdt (Eds.), *Cultural psychology: Essays on comparative human development* (pp. 73–112). New York: Cambridge University Press.

Sloan, C. (1990). Psychology for the third world? *Journal of Social Issues, 46,* 1–20.

Smith, J. A., Harre, R., & Van Langenhove, L. (1995). *Rethinking psychology.* London: Sage Publications.

Steenbarger, B. N. (1991). All the world is not a stage: Emerging contextualist themes in counseling and development. *Journal of Counseling and Development, 70*(2), 288–296.

Sue, D. W., Ivey, A., & Pedersen, P. (1996). *A multicultural theory of counseling and psychotherapy.* Pacific Grove, CA: Brooks/Cole.

Sue, D. W., & Sue, D. (1990). *Counseling the culturally different. Theory & Practices.* New York: John Wiley & Sons.

Tart, C. (1975). *Transpersonal psychologies.* New York: Harper & Row.

Thompson, M., Ellis, R., & Wildavsky, A. (1990). *Cultural theory.* San Francisco: Westview.

Waldrop, M. M. (1992). *Complexity: The emerging science at the edge of order and chaos.* New York: A Touchstone Book.

Wrenn, C. G. (1962). The culturally encapsulated counselor. *Harvard Educational Review, 32,* 444–449.

Wrenn, C. G. (1985). Afterward: The culturally encapsulated counselor revisited. In P. Pedersen (Ed.), *Handbook of cross-cultural counseling and therapy* (pp. 323–329). Westport CT: Greenwood.

Wrightsman, L. S. (1992). *Assumptions about human nature: Implications for researchers and practitioners.* Newbury Park, CA: Sage Publications.

Stephen Bochner

Cultural Diversity Within and Between Societies: Implications for Multicultural Social Systems

In this chapter, the term "multiculturalism" refers to social arrangements characterized by cultural diversity. In practice, this means non-trivial interpersonal contact between individuals and groups who differ in their ethnicity. In multicultural societies, such contact occurs within a climate of tolerance and mutual respect. A distinction is drawn between the processes of multicultural contact, which include the behaviors, attitudes, perceptions and feelings of the participants; and the institutional structures which characterize and either support or hinder benign intercultural contact, which include legislation, government policy, and employment practices.

There is considerable evidence for the existence of multicultural processes and structures within particular culturally heterogeneous societies. However, before multiculturalism can become a global fourth force, similar processes and structures will have to evolve at the inter-society level to a greater extent than is presently the case. Such a global system of multiculturalism will be modelled on the within-society arrangements that characterize successful multicultural nation states. Moral arguments to persuade people to adopt an international multicultural mind-set are less likely to be effective than a cost-benefit analysis showing that the two other plausible alternate futures, separatism on the one hand, and one homogeneous global culture on the other, have highly undesirable consequences.

It is vital to anchor this discussion to a definition of multiculturalism that is both inclusive and exclusive. The topic is politically sensitive as well as conceptually fluid, and unless extreme care is taken to specify what is being talked about, there is a real danger of disappearing into a semantic black hole. Let me illustrate. In a recent article which appeared in the *American Psychologist*, a journal presumably read or at least scanned by most psychologists in the U.S.A., Fowers and Richardson (1996) defined multiculturalism as ".... a social-intellectual movement that promotes the value of diversity as a core principle and insists that all cultural groups be treated with respect and as equals" (p. 609). So far, so good. But in almost the same breath, they assert that " .... multiculturalism is, at its core, a moral movement that is intended to enhance the dignity, rights, and recognized worth of marginalized groups" (p. 609), and devote the rest of the article to defending that position.

So what is wrong with that approach? Apart from implanting the kiss of death on a quite useful working construct by calling it a moral movement, this is a prime instance of muddled thinking. The fallacy consists in jumping from describing a phenomenon in terms of its defining characteristics (in this instance, diversity), to the conclusion that diversity is a compelling moral good (p. 610). At least two major objections can be raised to this conclusion, in addition to its poor logic: (a) It is inconsistent with one of the other main characteristics of cultural diversity, the doctrine of the cultural relativity of values (Herskovits, 1948), according to which values are not absolute but specific to particular cultures. The mare's nest that this proposition raises in the present context, including the quite plausible contention that under some cultural and/or practical conditions diversity may not be a desirable outcome, suggests that it would be advisable to leave the issue of values out of any scientific discussion of multiculturalism; and (b) exhorting people to behave morally has a sad history of failure right across the board of social issues. For instance, the literature on modifying the environmental behavior of people in areas such as getting them to recycle, conserve energy, or use car pools has shown that appealing to their higher moral and altruistic motives is less effective than extrinsic factors such as legal compulsion, monetary reward, and in the case of recycling, convenience (e.g., curbside collection of waste and the provision of household receptacles). It also helps if such initiatives are supported by clearly stated objectives and widespread information about the availability of these facilities, their specific benefits to the community, and the sanctions imposed on non-compliance (e.g., Oskamp, Zelezny, Schultz, Hurin, & Burkhardt, 1996). In the context of the present discussion, individuals and groups are much more likely to adopt a multicultural mind-set if they can be convinced of the personal and commercial advantages of such a policy and the disadvantages of the alternatives, a sub-theme of this chapter. We shall return to this issue in a more explicit way in the concluding section, which will compare and contrast the consequences of three alternate global futures on the quality of life on this earth. Consequently, the key elements of the "coat hanger" or working model guiding the present discussion will eschew moral arguments. Rather, the discussion will concentrate on the theoretical and empirical findings as identified in the relevant literature, in particular: (a) the distinction between multicultural processes and multicultural structures; (b) cultural diversity as a defining characteristic of both multicultural processes and structures; and (c) culture contact as the variable at the personal and group level which determines multicultural outcomes.

Multicultural processes refer to the psychological reactions of individuals and groups caught up in culturally heterogeneous settings. Specifically, these include their behaviors, perceptions, feelings, beliefs and attitudes as a function of various antecedent conditions, as described by relevant empirical research. Multicultural structures refer to the socio-political attributes of particular societies, which can be used in an operational definition of multiculturalism, and include legislation, government policies, and societal norms consistent with such an orientation.

A defining attribute of both processes and structures is the extent to which they reflect and support cultural diversity, empirically described as the amount of culture contact occurring, and the nature of such contact, in particular whether it is benign or hostile. Two types of culture contact will be distinguished, that which occurs within culturally diverse societies among its culturally heterogeneous residents; and that which occurs between societies when members from one nation embark on a sojourn abroad for varying lengths of time and purposes, in locations varying in culture distance from the country of origin.

It will be argued that the construct of multiculturalism is appropriate in describing both the process and structures of within-society culture contact, and in that context, referring to multiculturalism as a generic force is a useful conceptual advance. Australia will be used as an example to support this proposition. However, it is much more difficult to find empirical instances of multiculturalism in between-society contacts in the strict sense that this term is being used in this chapter. This is really not surprising, because at the global level the key structures that support within-society multiculturalism are absent; and because the nature and extent of between-society contacts, relative to within-society relations, tend to be stressful, short term, and superficial. Examples and empirical evidence consistent with these assertions will be provided, leading to the conclusion that at the global level, for multiculturalism to become a generic force, some of these problems will have to be resolved first.

Finally, this topic is not just of academic interest, but has non-trivial practical consequences. It is therefore advisable to link the discussion to events in the so-called real world, such as productivity, job and life satisfaction, inter-group relations, and national cohesion. And although it is outside the scope of this chapter, ultimately the question cannot be avoided as to whether some of the practical consequences of multiculturalism could be adverse, and if so, what sorts of interventions or techniques can be developed to reduce such undesirable effects.

☐ A Bottom-Up Definition of Multiculturalism

Let us begin by distinguishing between two sets of multicultural characteristics which differ in kind. The first cluster consists of the processes that define multiculturalism as they are studied by psychologists, and include the behaviors, attitudes, perceptions, feelings, and emotions that are the consequences or correlates of the as-yet-to-be-defined state. The second cluster consists of the institutional structures that characterize multicultural living, for example, a country's immigration policy, school curicula, employment laws, anti-discrimination legislation, a climate favoring or opposing cultural diversity, and all the other regulatory and normative social arrangements that affect the lives of its citizens. These features tend to be studied by sociologists, political scientists, and historians, although psychologists ignore these contextual aspects of behavior at their peril.

☐ Multicultural Processes

Let us first deal with the process which, for the past 20 or so years, I have been studying under the label of "culture contact," referring to critical incidents (Flanagan, 1954) where people from different cultural, ethnic, or linguistic backgrounds come into social contact with each other. These interactions will vary according to their purpose, their duration, and their degree of intimacy, and will have a variety of different but mostly predictable effects and outcomes, some positive and some negative (for a review of this literature see Bochner, 1982, 1994; Furnham & Bochner, 1986). The contacts can be classified into two broad categories: whether they occur among the members of a culturally diverse society or nation; or whether the contact takes place when a person from one society visits another country, for example to work, study, exploit, convert, assist, or recreate. Thus the within-society versus between-society distinction is based on the geographic location of the interactions. One reason why we are drawing on this distinction in the present context is because there are some important differences between the two categories of contact, which in turn have implications for a discussion of multiculturalism.

Between-society Contacts

In the literature, culture travellers who fit the between-society contact category have been labelled as "sojourners," (e.g., Ady, 1995; Klineberg & Hull, 1979) to emphasize that their stay is temporary and that at least implicitly there is the intention to return to the culture of origin. The persons with whom the visitors come into contact during their sojourn have been referred to as "host nationals" (e.g., Schild, 1962), a term which emphasizes the imbalance in power, rights, territorial assumptions, and role expectations distinguishing temporary sojourners from members of the permanent receiving majority. Examples of sojourners include business people (Torbiorn, 1994), overseas students (Klineberg, 1981), tourists (Pearce, 1982), Peace Corps Volunteers (Guthrie, 1975, 1981), and technical experts (Seidel, 1981).

Within-society Contacts

Let us now turn to the second category of culture contact, that which occurs within culturally heterogeneous societies. When lay as well as professional commentators use the term multiculturalism, it is almost certain that they are describing this form of contact. For instance, in the article referred to at the outset of this chapter, the authors (Fowers & Richardson, 1996) refer almost exclusively to racial and minority issues in the United States, and most of the references they cite likewise deal with intra-society cross-cultural interactions. In general, these analyses are based on judgments about the amount of actual or perceived cultural diversity which characterizes a particular society, and the extent to which the observer regards such heterogeneity as desirable.

Although it is unlikely that any contemporary nation is totally monocultural, some societies are clearly more culturally diverse than others. For instance, Japan and Korea are often used as examples of relatively monocultural societies (Kashima & Callan, 1994), and contrasted with more culturally diverse, and hence more multicultural societies such as Australia, the U.S.A., or Canada (Berry, Kalin, & Taylor, 1977; Bochner, 1986; Bochner & Hesketh, 1994; Hesketh & Bochner, 1994; Triandis, Kurowski, & Gelfand, 1994).

☐ Multicultural Structures

The term multiculturalism has also been used to refer to the policies and institutional practices that provide the context within which the process of

2

culture contact occurs. These societal structures, whether deliberately put in place, or having evolved over time, can either welcome, support, and celebrate cultural diversity; or they can ignore, undermine, and hinder it (in terms familiar to cross-cultural psychologists, they can promote assimilation, segregation, the marginalization of minorities, or integration) (Berry, 1994; Bochner, 1986). Furthermore, monocultural societies can, if they wish or are forced, transform themselves into culturally diverse countries (for instance, through conquest or immigration).

It is, in principle, possible to empirically establish where a nation stands on these matters by looking at its immigration policies and practices. For instance, the Australian Government Statistician (McLennan, 1996) publishes annual levels of migrant intake as a proportion of the existing population, the origins of the new settlers, and their categories (e.g., whether they are business migrants, refugees, or come in under the family reunion program). Such information can provide a reasonably objective picture of whether the official immigration policies of particular nations are non-discriminatory or whether they favor some categories of new settlers, or indeed seek to exclude immigrants altogether. Berry et al. (1977) reviewed a whole raft of demographic, documentary, and attitudinal data to provide an empirical assessment of multiculturalism in Canada.

Integration

The definition of multiculturalism being developed in the present chapter pertains to societies that explicitly promote integration as their goal, although there is some debate as to what that means in practice. Broadly speaking, integration refers to the expectation that ethnic immigrant groups will retain and take pride in the core aspects of their culture of origin, while at the same time embracing a unifying, umbrella national identity that reflects the culture of the receiving society (Throssell, 1981). Such arrangements are fairly common in other walks of life. For instance, most Americans would regard themselves as residents of a particular state such as California or New York, but have no difficulty in also thinking of themselves as U.S. citizens.

At the ethnic level, the term bicultural has been used to describe such a resolution, which in Australia means Italian-Australians, or Greek-Australians, or Anglo-Australians. Bochner (1981) has referred to such individuals as "mediating persons" who, by virtue of their membership in two ethnic reference groups, can act as links or bridges between them. The term was also used by Eide (1970) in connection with overseas students. Such individuals are an embodiment of the multicultural construct. They are also extremely useful in a practical sense. For instance, Australia's growing commerce and trade with the countries in South-East Asia has been greatly facilitated by Australian citizens whose ethnic origins are from the region, and who, by virtue of their education and upbringing in both cultures and language groups, are uniquely placed to foster joint ventures between Australian and Asian companies.

☐ Melting Pot or Mosaic?

The other issue is whether the pattern of integration follows a melting pot or a mosaic paradigm (de Lacey & Poole, 1979), because each can lead to a different outcome. As Bochner (1986) has argued, under a melting pot model, all ethnic groups, including the receiving dominant host population, would have to cede some of their ethnic identity because, by definition, a melting pot is a new mixture that replaces existing characteristics. In practice, even in societies that explicitly promote integration under the melting pot model, the various ingredients do not retain or exert equal influence over the outcome. Usually, the original, host components tend to dominate because of the numerical advantage of hosts relative to new settlers, and because despite good intentions and policy, assimilation pressures exist that new comers, particularly second-generation ones, may not be able to resist. In describing this process in Australia, Bochner (1986) has suggested that to the extent that a melting pot model can be sustained, the mixture will have a predominantly eucalypt flavor.

The mosaic model of multiculturalism provides a much closer approximation of the process of integration. As the term implies, all the elements (ethnic groups) retain the core aspects of their original identity, but in combination create a new super-ordinate form where the whole is greater than the sum of its parts.

There are both theoretical and practical difficulties with the mosaic model. As mentioned earlier, assimilationist pressures are impossible to eradicate. As well, cultures vary with respect to how "loose" or "tight" (Pelto, 1968) they are, or in the present context, how much of a grip they maintain on their members in the face of pressures to assimilate to a dominant majority ethic. There is also the problem that the values, beliefs, and practices of some groups in the so-called mosaic may be diametrically opposed to the norms of other members, a situation that is incompatible with the notion of a cohesive society. Still, we live in an imperfect world, and the existence of an approximation of either model would provide some evidence in support of the existence of multiculturalism as a generic force in such societies.

Australia is a good example of a successfully emerging multicultural nation. From being a basically monocultural Anglo-Celt society for the first 150 years of its existence, in the 50 years since the end of the Second World War, Australia has been transformed into a country which now embraces 140 different ethnic groups. One in three of its 20 million citizens were born overseas or are the offspring of persons born overseas in non-English-speaking countries (McLennan, 1996). Until relatively recently, Australia had an explicit White Australia policy. The relevant act was repealed in 1966, but many of its practices lingered on until the election of a Labor Government in 1972 (Department of Labour and Immigration, 1975; Grassby, 1973). Since then, Australia has progressively enacted non-discriminatory immigration legislation, resulting in a substantial presence of ethnic Chinese, Vietnamese, and other non-European communities. And although there is some opposition from a few special-interest groups to these developments, Australia can be described as a multicultural nation by whatever criteria are used to support that claim.

However, this plurality in the population does create specific problems in some workplaces where there is substantial cultural diversity, particularly with respect to interpersonal and communication difficulties between workers from different cultures, between workers and their supervisors, and between workers and their customers (Bochner & Hesketh, 1994). Still, these problems are relatively minor, and can be tackled through work-based training programs, which many companies are now introducing. For instance, in collaboration with a Human Factors psychologist, we have conducted research on the effectiveness of safety hazard warning signs in heavy industry. These work sites are inherently dangerous, and employ many workers from non-English-speaking backgrounds, a combination which increases the risk of accidents (Adams, Bochner, & Bilik, 1998).

Between-society Contact

Let us now return to the other category of culture contact, that which occurs not within but between societies. The focus is on culture travellers in foreign lands, who in the course of their sojourns come into contact with host members of the country they are visiting. This kind of contact is certainly on the increase, partly due to the greater ease and lower cost of travel, but mainly due to the globalization of commerce, industry, education, and leisure (Erez, 1994). Civil wars, famines, and natural disasters also contribute to this mass movement of people. However, refugees and migrants should be excluded from this category because they are not sojourners as that term is being used here, in that they have no intention of returning to their country of origin.

The number of foreign students, multinational employees, international agency workers (including peace-keeping military personnel), tourists, and other types of sojourners has vastly increased in the last 30 years, and in absolute terms refers to millions of people annually on the move. Again, Australia is a good example of this type of culture contact. It is host to large numbers of foreign students attending universities, and it is a mass destination for tourists, many of them from Japan, Korea, and other non-European countries. For instance, in 1994, 721,000 Japanese tourists visited Australia (McLennan, 1996). In addition, Australians are inveterate overseas travellers and sojourners, whether for business, study, or pleasure. But it is not all plain sailing. To illustrate some of the problems these contacts generate, Bochner and Coulon (1997) have conducted a major diagnostic study of host-visitor communication difficulties between the Australian hospitality industry and the masses of Japanese tourists who visit Australia each year. On the basis of these findings, we developed a Japanese culture assimilator for the training of Australian hotel and airline staff, using the principles and methods pioneered by Triandis and his colleagues in the seventies (Fiedler, Mitchell, & Triandis, 1971).

☐ Between-society Multiculturalism

The crucial issue is whether between-society culture contact can be regarded as an instance of multiculturalism. In particular, is there any utility in extending the term to this category of contact, or would this merely muddy the conceptual waters. One way to answer that question is to examine whether the characteristics and criteria which have been used to identify within-society multiculturalism are present in between-society contact. This question will now be pursued, again looking separately at both process and structural characteristics.

Between-society Multicultural Processes and Structures

There is little doubt that the process of culture contact is very much in evidence at the between-society level. A great many sojourners from a variety of different ethnic backgrounds enter into significant interpersonal relationships with a great number and variety of host nationals (Bochner, McLeod, & Lin, 1977; Boxer, 1969; Smith & Bond, 1993; Torbiorn, 1994). However, the integrating contextual structures that are absolutely vital to support the processes are much more likely to be absent than present in this type of contact. Undoubtedly, some sojourners and some host nationals regard themselves as members of an interdependent world order, and often provide a systematic bridging function linking different cultural groups. Bochner (1981) used the term "mediating person" to describe such individuals. Eide (1970) called them "links between cultures." Useem & Useem (1967), and Useem, Useem, & Donoghue (1963) called them "Third Culture members," by which they meant that such persons will identify strongly with some super-ordinate, supranational group that transcends or at least runs parallel with their particular national allegiances.

Empirically, such people are usually long-standing employees of international agencies such as the United Nations or the World Health Organization (WHO), or have moved through the various branch offices of their global companies; are at home (and may have had homes) in several countries; probably have dual nationality; may have married out of their cultural group or were the offsprings of mixed marriages; and most importantly, have institutional support for their global cultural identity, and social support in the form of other individuals who are similarly situated and provide a salient reference group.

However, the overwhelming majority of sojourners do not operate in a mediating framework. They regard themselves and are regarded by their hosts as temporary visitors, no matter how welcome they may feel in their host country (Schild, 1962). And sometimes sojourners are not clasped warmly to the bosoms of the locals (Tajfel & Dawson, 1965). In London during the height of the season, t-shirts with the slogan "I am not a tourist" can be glimpsed on the backs of passers-by. There is no doubt that for both sojourners and their host-national counterparts, the in-group/out-group distinction is highly salient, as countless studies have demonstrated (Smith & Bond, 1993). In practical terms, therefore, sojourners are unlikely to integrate into their host culture's social systems, even those who do not remain mere observers but actively participate in the host country's affairs. If visitors do integrate, it is likely that they will cease to be sojourners and will become immigrant settlers, and their culture contacts will then shift from the between- to the within-society category.

☐ Barriers to the Establishment of Global Multiculturalism

There is no doubt that it would be highly desirable for the world to move towards an integrated multicultural social system, along the lines that some of our more successful multicultural nation states have achieved. But at present, there is little chance of this happening. There are four main reasons for this pessimistic view, all implied by the theoretical model of multiculturalism as an outcome of benign culture contact.

Short-term, Superficial Contacts

First, although a great many people do undertake sojourns abroad, the majority of these are short-term visitors whose exposure to a second culture is fairly superficial. Even international students, in theory the group most likely to develop social networks with their hosts, tend in the main to remain isolated from their local peers, as studies conducted by the author and his colleagues in Australia, Britain, and the United States have conclusively shown (Bochner, Buker, & McLeod, 1976; Bochner, Hutnik, & Furnham, 1985; Bochner et al., 1977; Bochner & Orr, 1979). Indeed, most of humankind has not experienced significant interpersonal contact with members of other cultures, either as sojourners or as hosts. Those who have, and they include all of the contributors to this book, are in a minority. Which leads to the second reason for being pessimistic.

Lack of Institutional Supports

Unlike the structures present in the political systems of some nation states, there are very few supra-national institutions to support and explicitly affirm multiculturalism at the international level. Organizations such as the United Nations are preoccupied with reducing conflict between individual cultures and nations, rather then devoting their energies to creating a multicultural world. Organizations such as the Food and Agriculture Organization (FAO) and WHO spend their time and resources on providing emergency aid and the basic requirements of existence when disaster strikes.

Global sport, including the Olympic movement, is supposed to foster an international perspective and a sense of universalism. In fact, some of the worse excesses of chauvinism, jingoism, parochialism, and intergroup friction and hostility are spawned by international sporting tournaments. And the same can be said for the supposedly unifying force of a belief in God, with more people being killed in the name of religion than for any other ideological reason.

Organizations such as the World Bank and UNESCO are closer to the mark—their brief being the health of the global economy or raising the global level of educational attainment—but their contribution to the emergence of a multicultural world is only indirect, as their focus still is on individual national economies or educational systems (e.g., Gagliardi, 1995). Multinational business does have a global perspective, but because of its emphasis on profits and its responsibilities to its shareholders, not all of its effects are desirable, particularly when their presence tends to erode or swamp indigenous cultures. In terms of the culture contact model described earlier, a major effect of multinational commerce is assimilation to "head office" values, or coca-colonization as it has been called (Lambert, 1966).

Global Assimilation Pressures

Third, some of the most prominent commercial institutions that are globally ubiquitous are McDonald's hamburgers, Holiday Inn, Coca-Cola, and now the Internet. Their effect, in their respective domains, is to eliminate diversity, and to impose world-wide uniformity. A Big Mac and Coke taste, look, and cost the same irrespective of whether this assault on the consumer's digestive system occurs in Beijing, Sydney, Vienna, or Paris. Likewise, every Holiday Inn contains virtually the same furnishings, facilities, and ambience (or lack thereof). International business is mainly in the business of assimilation, although in theory some of its structures could be harnessed towards the aims of multiculturalism.

The serious point here is to draw attention to a fundamental distinction between MULTIculturalism and MONOculturalism. Opponents of cultural diversity often point to the high degree of strife that exists in some culturally heterogeneous nations, such as the former Yugoslavia, Israel, and countries in Africa. Their solution is to eradicate the diversity, by methods such as assimilating minority groups into the dominant majority, ethnic cleansing, separate enclaves, and in extreme instances genocide. These, of course are pseudo-solutions. The only real solution is to achieve some form of integration, and to create a social system in which cultural diversity is tolerated, better still accepted, better still encouraged and celebrated. Indeed, we have here a weak, medium, and strong definition of multiculturalism.

About the only global institution which is compatible with the integration criterion is international education. However, even it has been accused of creating what Alatas (1972, 1975) called the "captive mind" syndrome, by which he meant that students from traditional societies who attend universities abroad are often influenced into adopting Western thoughts, precepts and practices which might not be appropriate to their professional and personal conduct in their own societies. On returning from their sojourn, such students, who may have been on government scholarships, have difficulty in readjusting to their home culture, and show cultural insensitivity in their approach to solving the problems their societies face. Becoming dissatisfied with their lot, they may join the brain drain (Adams, 1968; Rao, 1979) and emigrate, thus constituting an economic loss for their already impoverished countries.

Cross-cultural Contact Is Stressful

The fourth reason why world multiculturalism is unlikely to be attained in the foreseeable future, is that as extensive research has shown, between-society culture contact is stressful. Oberg (1960) called this reaction of sojourners to their new setting "culture shock," a term which features in the title of one of the editor's recent books (Pedersen, 1995), as well as in one of our books (Furnham & Bochner, 1986). The latter publication explored the theoretical basis for culture shock, the empirical evidence establishing the conditions under which it occurs, and the methods and procedures which can be employed to reduce culture shock.

Salient features of this author's model include the similarity-attraction hypothesis (Byrne, 1969), the idea that individuals are more likely to seek out, enjoy, understand, and interact harmoniously with people with whom they share salient features such as interests, personal characteristics, and values; the culture distance hypothesis (Babiker, Cox, & Miller, 1980; Dunbar, 1992; Furnham & Bochner, 1982; Torbiorn, 1994), stating that the larger the cultural distance between participants, the greater the communication difficulties that they will encounter; the process of social categorization (Abrams & Hogg, 1990), which in the present context refers to the tendency for individuals to classify other persons as belonging either to their own group (the in-group), or to some other (the out-group); the process of stereotyping (Katz & Braly, 1933; Lippman, 1922), which attributes to individuals the traits that allegedly characterize the group to which the target person belongs, or has been categorized into by the perceiver; primary socialization (Deaux, 1976), describes a process through which we acquire core values early in life which we then regard as absolutely true. These values are highly resistant to change, and may not be shared by, or may even be contradicted by people who experienced different primary socializing influences; and the pervasive in-group bias (Tajfel, 1970, 1981), which is a complex function encompassing all of these processes in combination, that leads to ethnic prejudice, inter-group friction, hostility, and, in extreme cases, to physical violence and war.

☐ Conclusion

Taking everything that has been said into account leads to the inescapable conclusion that multiculturalism at the between-society global level is not a feasible idea at this stage in the world's development. If global multiculturalism is to come about, it will do so indirectly, through the strengthening and the proliferation of individual multicultural nation states, because theoretically, an increase in within-society cultural diversity should facilitate benign between-society contact. For instance, as was mentioned earlier, many of the growing number of ethnic Chinese-Australians are now engaged in promoting trade between Australia and the South-East Asian region, that is, they serve as mediating persons between these two cultural systems. Replicate that mediating model worldwide with a variety of ethnic groups and for a variety of contact purposes, and the conditions may be present for the arrival of the Fourth Force as in the Editor's vision. The means to achieve that outcome will be largely political, but applied psychology will also have a role to play in describing, facilitating, and supporting this process of global multiculturalism. Some of these procedures are described in some detail elsewhere in this book, and include culture training techniques, developing cultural sensitivity, and intercultural communication skills.

Future Worlds

With respect to the "Fourth Force" construct, three possible futures for the world can be envisaged. All three already exist in a rudimentary form at present. All three share the condition that the nation state as we know it today will either disappear or become a much less important influence in managing human affairs.

A Single Global Culture

It is quite likely that one bland, dominant global culture will emerge, driven by Western commercial values and interests, and underpined by the Internet and by the Hollywood-based entertainment industry, itself controlled by a monopoly or duopoly of multinational media corporations. Within this system there will exist a few boutique subcultures, but their role, function, and influence will be restricted to a niche audience. The Fourth Force will have become the First Force, and humankind will be in deep trouble, if the analogy from biology about the crucial role of diversity (Bochner, 1979; Mayr, 1976) can be transferred into sociology.

It is true that some of the internecine conflicts that bedevil a diverse world may be reduced, but there is also the likelihood that other problems will emerge. These will probably include the suppression of innovation, the emergence of an underclass that is intellectually, physically, or temperamentally unable to participate in the dominant practices, and a population that may literally bore itself to death.

Separatism

The second future, also easily glimpsed in many parts of the world today, is for nation states to disintegrate into warring tribal factions. Separatism is a growth industry, practiced virtually everywhere and not just in the former Yugoslavia. Great Britain threatens to divide up into England, Scotland, and Wales. The Irish have already done it, as has the Soviet Union and the Czech Republic. The Indian sub-continent achieved it when gaining independence from the British, and Malaya did soon after. There is talk of it in Indonesia, most parts of Africa, Sri Lanka, and China, not to mention Canada. Hot heads in Queensland want to secede from Australia. The list is endless, and if only some of these countries break up into less than the sum of their parts, cultural diversity will be a major defining characteristic of the global order. However, I doubt if it will satisfy one of the key criteria of multiculturalism—mutual respect and understanding. The Fourth Force will have become the Chaos Force, with endless, lethal, inter-ethnic squabbles making life miserable for most of the world's inhabitants.

Integration

The third future is also in existence but, compared to the other two, is in a precarious condition. It is, of course, multiculturalism as we have described it in this chapter, as a genuine Fourth Force. Perhaps one strategy that could be effective in persuading people to give it a go, to use an Australian expression, is to draw attention to the alternative futures that will overwhelm humankind if multiculturalism falls by the wayside. Appealing to people's moral instincts is unlikely to get us very far, although it probably can't do too much harm. But a cool, rational cost-benefit analysis backed up by hard data is a good way to start, and the present chapter has provided some suggestions as to how one might go about doing it.

☐ References

Abrams, D., & Hogg, M. A. (Eds.). (1990). *Social identity theory: Constructive and critical advances*. London: Harvester Wheatsheaf.

Adams, A., Bochner, S., & Bilik, L. (1998). The effectiveness of warning signs in hazardous work places: Cognitive and social determinants. *Applied Ergonomics 29*, 247–254.

Adams, W. (Ed.). (1968). *The brain drain*. New York: Macmillan.

Ady, J. C. (1995). Toward a differential demand model of sojourner adjustment. In R. L. Wiseman (Ed.), *Intercultural communication theory* (pp. 92–114). London: Sage Publications.

Alatas, S. H. (1972). The captive mind in development studies: Some neglected problems and the need for an autonomous social science tradition in Asia. *International Social Science Journal, 24*, 9–25.

Alatas, S. H. (1975). The captive mind and creative development. *International Social Science Journal, 27,* 691–700.

Babiker, I. E., Cox, J. L., & Miller, P. (1980). The measurement of cultural distance and its relationship to medical consultations, symptomatology, and examination performance of overseas students at Edinburgh University. *Social Psychiatry, 15,* 109–116.

Berry, J. W. (1994). Acculturative stress. In W. J. Lonner and R. Malpass (Eds.), *Psychology and culture* (pp. 211–215). Needham Heights, MA: Allyn and Bacon.

Berry, J. W., Kalin, R., & Taylor, D. M. (1977). *Multiculturalism and ethnic attitudes in Canada.* Ottawa, Canada: Supply & Services Canada.

Bochner, S. (1979). Cultural diversity: Implications for modernization and international education. In K. Kumar (Ed.), *Bonds without bondage: Explorations in transcultural interactions* (pp. 231–256). Honolulu, HI: The University Press of Hawaii.

Bochner, S. (1981). The social psychology of cultural mediation. In S. Bochner (Ed.), *The mediating person: Bridges between cultures* (pp. 6–36). Boston: Schenkman.

Bochner, S. (1982). The social psychology of cross-cultural relations. In S. Bochner (Ed.), *Cultures in contact: Studies in cross-cultural interaction* (pp. 5–44). Oxford: Pergamon.

Bochner, S. (1986). Coping with unfamiliar cultures: Adjustment or culture learning? *Australian Journal of Psychology, 38,* 347–358.

Bochner, S. (1994). Culture shock. In W. J. Lonner & R. Malpass (Eds.), *Psychology and culture* (pp. 245–251). Needham Heights, MA: Allyn and Bacon.

Bochner, S., Buker, E. A., & McLeod, B. M. (1976). Communication patterns in an international student dormitory: A modification of the "small world" method. *Journal of Applied Social Psychology, 6,* 275–290.

Bochner, S., & Coulon, L. (1997). A culture assimilator to train Australian hospitality industry workers serving Japanese tourists. *The Journal of Tourism Studies, 8,* 8–17.

Bochner, S., & Hesketh, B. (1994). Power distance, individualism/collectivism, and job-related attitudes in a culturally diverse work group. *Journal of Cross-Cultural Psychology, 25,* 233–257.

Bochner, S., Hutnik, N., & Furnham, A. (1985). The friendship patterns of overseas and host students in an Oxford student residence. *Journal of Social Psychology, 125,* 689–694.

Bochner, S., McLeod, B. M., & Lin, A. (1977). Friendship patterns of overseas students: A functional model. *International Journal of Psychology, 12,* 277–294.

Bochner, S., & Orr, F. E. (1979). Race and academic status as determinants of friendship formation: A field study. *International Journal of Psychology, 14,* 37–46.

Boxer, A. H. (1969). *Experts in Asia: An inquiry into Australian technical assistance.* Canberra, Australia: Australian National University Press.

Byrne, D. (1969). Attitudes and attraction. In L. Berkowitz (Ed.), *Advances in experimental social psychology, Volume 4.* New York: Academic Press.

Deaux, K. (1976). *The behavior of women and men.* Monterey, CA: Brooks/Cole.

de Lacey, P. R., & Poole, M. E. (1979). *Mosaic or melting pot: Cultural evolution in Australia.* Sydney, Australia: Harcourt Brace Jovanovich.

Department of Labour and Immigration, Committee on Community Relations. (1975). *Final report.* Canberra, Australia: Australian Government Publishing Service.

Dunbar, E. (1992). Adjustment and satisfaction of expatriate U.S. personnel. *International Journal of Intercultural Relations, 16,* 1–16.

Eide, I., (Ed). (1970). *Students as links between cultures.* Paris: UNESCO.

Erez, M. (1994). Toward a model of cross-cultural industrial and organizational psychology. In H. C. Triandis, M. D. Dunnette, and L. M. Hough (Eds.), *Handbook of industrial and organizational psychology, Volume 4* (2nd ed.) (pp. 599–607). Palo Alto, CA: Consulting Psychologists Press.

Fiedler, F. E., Mitchell, T., & Triandis, H. C. (1971). The culture assimilator: An approach to cross-cultural training. *Journal of Applied Psychology, 55,* 95–102.

Flanagan, J. C. (1954). The critical incident technique. *Psychological Bulletin, 51,* 327–358.

Fowers, B. J., & Richardson, F. C. (1996). Why is multiculturalism good? *American Psychologist, 51,* 609–621.

Furnham, A., & Bochner, S. (1982). Social difficulty in a foreign culture: An empirical analysis of culture shock. In S. Bochner (Ed.), *Cultures in contact: Studies in cross-cultural relations* (pp. 161–168). Oxford: Pergamon.

Furnham, A., & Bochner, S. (1986). *Culture shock: Psychological reactions to unfamiliar environments.* London: Methuen.

Gagliardi, R. (Ed.). (1995). *Teacher training and multiculturalism: National studies.* Paris: UNESCO International Bureau of Education.

Grassby, A. J. (1973). *A multi-cultural society for the future.* Canberra, Australia: Australian Government Publishing Service.

Guthrie, G. M. (1975). A behavioral analysis of culture learning. In R. W. Brislin, S. Bochner, and W. J. Lonner (Eds.), *Cross-cultural perspectives on learning* (pp. 95–115). New York: Sage Publications.

Guthrie, G. M. (1981). What you need is continuity. In S. Bochner (Ed.), *The mediating person: Bridges between cultures* (pp. 96–112). Boston: Schenkman.

Herskovits, M. J. (1948). *Man and his works.* New York: Knopf.

Hesketh, B., & Bochner, S. (1994). Technological change in a multicultural context: Implications for training and career planning. In H. C. Triandis, M. D. Dunnette, and L. M. Hough (Eds.), *Handbook of industrial and organizational psychology, Volume 4* (2nd ed.) (pp. 191–240). Palo Alto, CA: Consulting Psychologists Press.

Kashima, Y., & Callan, V. J. (1994). The Japanese work group. In H. C. Triandis, M. D. Dunnette, and L. M. Hough (Eds.), *Handbook of industrial and organizational psychology, Volume 4* (2nd ed.) (pp. 609–646). Palo Alto, CA: Consulting Psychologists Press.

Katz, D., & Braly, K. (1933). Racial stereotypes of one hundred college students. *Journal of Abnormal and Social Psychology, 28,* 280–290.

Klineberg, O. (1981). The role of international university exchanges. In S. Bochner (Ed.), *The mediating person: Bridges between cultures* (pp. 113–135). Boston: Schenkman.

Klineberg, O., & Hull, W. F. (1979). *At a foreign university: An international study of adaptation and coping.* New York: Praeger.

Lambert, R. D. (1966). Some minor pathologies in the American presence in India. *Annals of the American Academy of Political and Social Science, 368,* 157–170.

Lippman, W. (1922). *Public opinion.* New York: Harcourt & Brace.

Mayr, E. (1976). *Evolution and the diversity of life: Selected essays.* Cambridge, MA: Harvard University Press.

McLennan, W. (1996). *Year book Australia. Number 78.* Canberra, Australia: Australian Bureau of Statistics.

Oberg, K. (1960). Cultural shock: Adjustment to new cultural environments. *Practical Anthropology, 7,* 177–182.

Oskamp, S., Zelezny, L., Schultz, P. W., Hurin, S., & Burkhardt, R. (1996). Commingled versus separated curbside recycling: Does it matter? *Environment and Behavior, 28,* 73–91.

Pearce, P. L. (1982). *The social psychology of tourist behavior.* Oxford: Pergamon.

Pedersen, P. (1995). *The five stages of culture shock: Critical incidents around the world.* Westport, CT: Greenwood Press.

Pelto, P. J. (1968). The difference between "tight" and "loose" societies. *Transaction, 5,* 37–40.

Rao, G. L. (1979). *Brain drain and foreign students.* St. Lucia, Australia: University of Queensland Press.

Schild, E. O. (1962). The foreign student, as stranger, learning the norms of the host culture. *Journal of Social Issues, 18,* 41–54.

Seidel, G. (1981). Cross-cultural training procedures: Their theoretical framework and evaluation. In S. Bochner (Ed.), *The mediating person: Bridges between cultures* (pp. 184–213). Boston: Schenkman.

Smith, P. B., & Bond, M. H. (1993). *Social psychology across cultures: Analysis and perspectives.* Hemel Hempstead, England: Harvester Wheatsheaf.

Tajfel, H. (1970). Experiments in intergroup discrimination. *Scientific American, 223,* 92–102.

Tajfel, H. (1981). *Human groups and social categories.* Cambridge: Cambridge University Press.

Tajfel, H., & Dawson, J. L. (Eds.). (1965). *Disappointed guests.* London: Oxford University Press.

Throssell, R. P. (1981). Toward a multicultural society: The role of government departments and officials in developing cross-cultural relations in Australia. In S. Bochner (Ed.), *The mediating person: Bridges between cultures* (pp. 246–272). Boston: Schenkman.

Torbiorn, I. (1994). Operative and strategic use of expatriates in new organizations and market structures. *International Studies of Management and Organizations, 24,* 5–17.

Triandis, H. C., Kurowski, L. L., & Gelfand, M. J. (1994). Workplace diversity. In H. C. Triandis, M. D. Dunnette, & L. M. Hough (Eds.), *Handbook of industrial and organizational psychology. Volume 4* (2nd ed.) (pp. 769–827). Palo Alto, CA: Consulting Psychologists Press.

Useem, J., & Useem, R. H. (1967). The interfaces of a binational third culture: A study of the American community in India. *Journal of Social Issues, 23,* 130–143.

Useem, J., Useem, R. H., & Donoghue J. (1963). Men in the middle of the third culture: The roles of American and non-Western people in cross-cultural administration. *Human Organization, 22,* 169–179.

CHAPTER 3

Magoroh Maruyama

Self-heterogenization and Cultural Milieu Selection: Two New Directions in Counseling

Until now two of the main aims of counseling have been the establishment of ego identity and adaptation to social milieu. These goals may appear to be two opposites but are actually two sides of the same coin: homogenism. Ego identity strived for self-homogenization, while adaptation assumed social homogeneity to be normal and desirable. Ironically, ethnic movements which advocated cultural heterogeneity fell into the trap of in-group homogeneity. In contrast, two emerging individual and social processes can replace the two old aims and can provide new models for counseling. They are: individual self-heterogenization; and cross-cultural migration.

In the past, adaptation to social milieu and formation of ego identity were two of the most frequent aims of counseling. "Maladjusted" individuals had to become well-adjusted or well-adapted. Confused, drifting, aimless, or weak egos had to be strengthened. These two aims had an implicit assumption of homogenism in common. On the one hand, behind the aim of social adaptation, social homogeneity was assumed to be good and desirable. On the other hand, ego identity was sought to make the individual coherent, consistent, and resistant to swaying influences.

With the rise of ethnic minority movements in the 1960s, social heterogeneity became recognized and legitimized, but at the same time, these movements were conducive to in-group homogenization and in-group conformity.

Since then, in more recent years, new types of individual and social processes have emerged, and are proving to be healthier than the old principles of sociocultural adaptation and homogeneous ego identity. Two new processes which we will discuss in this chapter are: self-heterogenization without geographic displacement; and cross-cultural migration to select a sociocultural milieu compatible with one's own logical and epistemological structure.

Multiculturalism can be conceptualized in the new way as well as in the old way. In the old way as advocated in the 1960s, there are many cultures within one society. For example in the United States of America (herein, U.S.A.), there was first the Black Power movement, then Brown Power (Hispanics), Red Power (Native Americans) and Yellow Power (Asian Americans). At that time the older trend for assimilation to the "White" society was reversed, and ethnic groups asserted themselves. Individuals of the various ethnic groups then were eager for in-group homogenization, proud to be black, brown, red, or yellow. Also at that time, counselors were eager to recognize cultural differences, but in so doing, they fell into stereotyping each ethnic group.

Individual and social processes have changed since then. Elements of foreign cultures such as music, food, and dress became accessible and available to anyone anywhere, and people, especially young people, began to create individually unique patterns of combinations of elements from many cultures, even though some are inevitably more followers and imitators than creators.

Migration has usually been explained in terms of economics. Such explanations still hold true to some extent. However, there have always been other causes of migration. Political and religious oppression as a cause of migration was well-known. Relatively unrecognized is selection of cultural milieu to match the individual's logical and epistemological type. This has existed in a small scale, but the trend is for its increase.

The individual is no longer limited to be just Irish or Norwegian. She or he can self-heterogenize inside Ireland or Norway. She or he can also emigrate. Such strategies can be incorporated in counseling.

This chapter consists of four parts: (1) Multiculturalism as a source of self-heterogenization and cross-cultural migration; (2) heterogeneity of individual epistemological types that cut across cultural boundaries; (3) cases of selection of cultural milieu; and (4) new directions of counseling, and educational and vocational equal opportunity for all logical and epistemological types.

☐ Multiculturalism as a Source of Self-heterogenization and Cross-cultural Migration

Isolationistic Multiculturalism and Interactive Interwoven Multiculturalism

The second half of the 20th century has been characterized by political, social, and cultural movements toward localized, regionalistic, and isolationistic heterogeneity. After the end of the Second World War we saw a surge of many new independent nations freed from colonial subjugation. In the 1960s we saw two types of movements in the U.S.A.: ethnic minority groups asserting their own cultures and civil rights, in the form of Black Power, Brown Power, Red Power, and Yellow Power; hippies turning inward individually or forming secluded groups with slogans such as "Drop out!," "Turn on!," and "Grow your own potatoes!" The first was an assertion, revival, and consolidation of suppressed ethnic cultures. The second was a withdrawal. Actually a similar withdrawal had occurred in Germany after the Second World War in the form of ohne-mich-ism (without-me-ism), in which freedom was interpreted as freedom *from* social and political involvement. By the 1970s, the minority group movements expanded to Grey Power, Gay Power, and Woman Power. Then in the early 1990s we witnessed another surge of movements toward independence: this time within countries such as the former Soviet Union and Czechoslovakia. People began to worry about segmentation of society.

But trends in the opposite direction became gradually visible in the 1980s. The formation of the European Common Market was intended to increase economic interaction and mutual benefit without destroying the heterogeneity of cultures and languages in Europe. Less publicized was the massive migration of people in Europe; first from south to north, then from east to west. The first migrations from Turkey, Yugoslavia, and other Southern European countries to Germany and Sweden continued for several decades and were a demand-pull phenomenon: Factories in Germany and Sweden needed factory workers. The number of migrants was considerable, but not threatening to the cultures of the host countries. But the post-Perestroika migration from east to west is beyond control. There simply are not enough jobs, housing, schools, and medical facilities to accommodate even a fraction of them. Drastic social and legal changes are inevitable.

With some time lag, Japan has faced and is facing the same problem. Japan needed engineers and factory workers, and many from China, Taiwan, Iran, and Southeast Asian countries filled the needs, often illegally.

Labor shortages still exist in some categories of work, and the Japanese immigration law has undergone successive modifications to legalize foreign workers.

Whatever the circumstances, one trend is inevitable: All industrialized countries are becoming multi-ethnic and multicultural. And the "original" inhabitants of these countries, for example "Native Swedes" or "Native Japanese" in contrast to foreigners, are individually heterogenizing themselves, choosing and taking up aspects of foreign cultures. Even though some still believe that international contacts will lead to homogenization, the reverse is occurring, imperceptibly at first, but more and more visibly as we move toward the 21st century.

Fallacious Assumptions Held in the 20th Century

Some of the assumptions held in social sciences and psychology are incorrect. Examples are: (1) Each culture is perfect and it is better not to change it; (2) all "normal" individuals in a given culture are acculturated and are epistemologically and psychologically homogeneous; (3) babies are born with blank minds, to be filled with culture; (4) a culture is a mentally healthy environment for all its normal members; (5) rapid social change is traumatic to all persons; (6) cross-cultural or cross-national migration increases anxiety; and (7) contact with many cultures will make the individual lose his/her identity.

These fallacious assumptions stem from epistemological errors made in the 20th century. Incorrect epistemologies were also sources of various political and social phenomena such as the colonialism which began in the 16th century; the isolationism, separatism, and regionalism of the 20th century; and the seclusionistic aspects of the hippy movement in the 1960s. The interactive and interwoven cultural and individual heterogeneity of the 21st century will require a new epistemological framework, which will be our next topic.

Different Epistemological Types

Modern physicists and computer scientists have constructed different types of logic. But these logics, though new to scientific theories, had long existed in the biological, physical, and social worlds. In some of the human cultures, they have been used since prehistoric times. But for several centuries before the mid-20th century, they had been excluded from science and philosophy. There are many logical types, but the boxed chart in Table 1 details four which not only are illustrative of some scientific theories but

Table 1. Epistemological types

H-type	I-type	S-type	G-type
homogenist	heterogenist	heterogenist	heterogenist
hierarchical	isolationist	interactive	interactive
eternal	temporary	stabilizing	change-amplifying
zero-sum	negative-sum	positive-sum	positive-sum
competitive	uniquing	cooperative	cogenerative
classifying	randomizing	contextual	context-generating
sequential	haphazard	simultaneous	simultaneous
universalist	individualist	mutualist	mutualist
opposition	independence	absorption	exploration
boundary	seclusion	no separation	flow
specialization	specialization	convertibility	convertibility
one truth	subjective	poly-objective	poly-objective

NOTE: **H** stands for *hierarchy* and *homogeneity*; **I** stands for *isolationism, individualism,* and *independence*; **S** stands for *stabilizing*; and **G** stands for *generating*.
CAUTION: (1) There are more than 4 types; (2) There are mixtures between types; (3) The 4 types do *not* fit in a 2 by 2 table. They are more like the four corners of a tetrahedron (a pyramid shape with a triangular bottom); and (4) S and G are *not* between H and I. Positive-sum cannot be between zero-sum and negative-sum.

also turned out to be the most frequently found epistemological types among individuals in most of the cultures.

In terms of science and technology, self-learning neural net computers are of G-type. The second cybernetics (Maruyama, 1960; 1963) using change-amplifying causal loops is also of G-type, while the first cybernetics (Wiener, 1948) for stabilization using change-counteracting causal loops was of S-type. Shannon's information theory (Shannon & Weaver, 1949) of coding for maximum use of channel capacity was of I-H-S combination. The 19th century thermodynamics was of pure I-type. Most of the sociological, anthropological, political, and psychological theories talk about causal relations *without causal loops*; they are of H-type. Econometrics considers causal loops, but focuses on equilibrium or cycles. It is of S-type because cycles are an equilibrium with time-delayed feedback loops. Economists ought to consider causal loops, but when they make statements on actions to be taken, such as the setting of interest rates, reserve ratio, or investment rates, they tend to forget about causal loops and fall into H-type thinking.

In a causal loop, the causal influence from one element goes through other elements and eventually comes back to itself, either counteracting or amplifying the original change, depending on the polarities of the influences along the loop as well as the time delay phase shift (Maruyama, 1963). Among the variables there may be several causal loops with different characteristics, and the behavior of the set of variables is therefore very complex.

The Aristotelean logic, which was of H-type, was the standard logic in European sciences and philosophy. It prohibited "circular reasoning," and prevented scientists from examining causal loops which were abundant in social and biological, and even in complex physical processes.

Individual epistemological heterogeneity existed in every society. There were epistemological rebellions from time to time. The nominalists of the mediaeval age are an example of one who advocated an I-type logic. More recently, Søren Kierkegaard of the 19th century was of I-H type. Martin Heidegger and Jean-Paul Sartre of our century were of H-I and I-G types, respectively. Many individuals with non-dominant epistemological types became artists to express their minds. Picasso and Stravinsky, who were of G-type, are examples.

Fortunately, the influence of Aristotelean logic was limited mainly to Europe and North America. In many of the African cultures (Camara, 1975), G-type logic was practiced. In Japan, the prehistoric Jomon culture which began 11,000 years ago was of G-type (Maruyama, 1980), followed by Yayoi culture of S-type which began 2,300 years ago. Later, 1,500 years ago, an H-type culture arrived from Korea which became known as Yamato culture. Today the three epistemological types are mixed and co-exist in Japan, in different proportions in individuals. In Korea, H-type is still quite strong, and in Indonesia, S-type is much stronger than in Japan.

As was the case of the Nominalists in mediaeval Europe, rebellions against H-type *usually* take the form of I-type. The hippes of the 1960s who rebelled against the dominant H-type fell into an isolationistic logic. So did many ethnic movements of the 1960s and regional separatist movements of the 1990s. This occurred not only in political and social spheres, but also in European art. European architects and music composers, in their attempt to escape the H-type design principles (See Table 2 below), resort to I-type principles, rather than S-type and G-type principles, which have been cultivated in Japanese architectural, landscaping, and floral designs (Maruyama, 1981) for several centuries.

Against H-type political and social systems, the rebellions of the past three decades took I-type forms. Now there is a new anxiety in Europe, caused by new massive migrations westward, which adds to the continuing migrations from the south. This time it is not an oppression from powerful

Table 2. Aesthetic and spatial design principles in the four types of logics

	H-type	I-type	S-type	G-type
Aesthetic	Beauty in unity by similarity and repetition, arithmetic proportion, and geometric regularity. EXAMPLE: Gothic cathedral, Baroque music.	Beauty consists in randomness, caprice, and unexpected surprises.	Beauty consists in avoidance of repetition. Harmony of dissimilar elements which enhance individuality of each element. EXAMPLE: Some of the Japanese gardens and floral art.	Changing harmony of diverse elements. Designed for simultaneously multiple as well as changing interpretations. Deliberate incompleteness to allow for evolution. EXAMPLE: Some Japanese gardens and floral art, Katsura Palace, Picasso and Stravinsky.
Spatial	Space is a transparent mass, with boundary, identity, and specialization. House separates the indoors from the outdoors.	Insulated from other spaces.	No boundary. Partition between rooms can be removed. Outer shell of the house can be removed to let the outdoors come inside.	No boundary. Space is convertible to many functions. A house is a base for interaction with environment and with other households.

governments, but rather, poor, powerless foreign individuals who are seen as a threat. And the reactions sometimes take an H-form, such as Neo-Nazism, directed toward powerless individuals. Similarly, the revival of Ku Klux Klan and other racist activities in the U.S.A. is caused by rising unemployment, which is not an intentional scheme by the government but is a result of a loss of international competitiveness in the U.S.A.'s business firms. The H-type and I-type are two sides of the same coin. Is it possible to get out of the opposition between the two types?

The answer lies in two trends: (1) self-heterogenization of each individual (Maruyama, 1973; 1994b); and (2) rediscovery of hidden non-dominant epistemological types.

Self-heterogenization comes from increased accessibility of different cultures, lifestyles, entertainments, foods, and languages to individuals.

While living in one place, it has become easier to obtain foreign books, video cassettes, foods, and other commodities, information, or knowledge. One can choose them, turn them on and off (Maruyama, 1985), and make one's own combinations. One is an active pattern-maker, not a passive victim of one radio station or a single newspaper, as it was in the early days of mass media technology. Nowadays there are many television channels from which to choose, including programs from foreign countries.

On the other hand, rediscovery of hidden non-dominant epistemological types has hardly begun, but will be in full development sooner or later, depending on the speed of diffusion of this concept which is already used in international business management (Maruyama, 1992; 1993; 1994a). We will return to this topic again later in this chapter.

☐ Heterogeneity of Individual Epistemological Types that Cut Across Cultural Boundaries

The Fallacy of the Assumption of Normal Distribution

Epistemological types are also called "mindscape types" (Maruyama, 1980; 1992). Unlike some physical quantitative characteristics such as height and weight, which may follow normal distribution (bell-shaped curve), mindscape types do not follow normal distribution.

Many of the researchers have forgotten two basic considerations of statistics: (1) that a normal distribution is obtained when fluctuations are random in addition to being *independent of one another* (such as the number of heads or tails when a coin is tossed many times); and (2) that the quantities called "mean" and "standard deviation" can be calculated and printed out regardless of whether the distribution is normal or non-normal.

Individual epistemological types are a result of complex biological and social interactions (Maruyama, 1960, 1963) which are the opposite of random and independent events. It is *illogical to expect* that the individual mind is normally distributed in each culture, subculture, or any social entity. The mathematically defined quantities "mean" and "standard deviation" do not depend on normalness of distribution. They can be calculated regardless of the shape of the distribution curve. Many people assume that if the computer prints out the mean and the standard deviation, the distribution must be normal (bell-shaped), even though some slightly more careful researchers suspect that if the standard deviation is too large, the distribution curve may have several peaks (many humps). But even these researchers tend to hold the attitude that a distribution is normal unless proven to be otherwise, and go on with "business as usual" (i.e., assuming that the distribution is normal).

According to such a reasoning, if a statistically significant difference is found between Culture X and Culture Y, then all persons in Culture Y are displaced with respect to all persons in Culture X, even though there may be an overlap between the two bell-shaped curves and, therefore, some individuals in Culture Y are similar to some individuals in Culture X. The situation can be illustrated in the following metaphor. Ship X contains all persons of Culture X, and Ship Y contains all persons of Culture Y. The shape of the ships depends on the standard deviation (SD): long and narrow for a large SD; short and wide for a small SD. The bigger the population, the more crowded. On each ship, most people are in the middle, with fewer toward the stern and the bow. If the mean of Culture X and that of Culture Y are the same, then the two ships are positioned parallel to each other in such a way that the middle point of Ship X and that of Ship Y line up side-by-side. If the means of both cultures are different, then one ship is ahead of the other ship but the stern of one ship may overlap with the bow of the other ship. In that case, some persons in Culture X have the same score as some persons in Culture Y. In fact, this is the way the believers in normal distribution explain the fact that some persons in a group have the same test score as some persons in another group. If the means of two cultures are different, then everybody in a culture is displaced in reference to the other culture, because one ship as a whole is ahead of the other ship, even though there is some overlapping between the two ships. This way of thinking induces the idea that everybody in Culture X is *basically* different from everybody in Culture Y; for example, that every person in a culture has a smell specific to that culture which is different from the smell of those in other cultures: All Germans smell like Sauerkraut and all Italians smell like garlic bread, even though some Germans may eat garlic bread and some Italians may eat Sauerkraut. This way of thinking fosters and reinforces cultural and social stereotypes.

On the contrary, mindscape types do not follow normal distribution in any culture. Moreover, they are found across cultural boundaries: Any type that is found in one culture can be found in other cultures, as illustrated on the following heterogram. Cultural differences consist in the way some type becomes dominant and suppresses, transforms, ignores, or utilizes other types. This heterogram conceptualization is contrasted with the incorrect assumption of normal distribution (see Figures 1 and 2).

A Psychological Test

The existence of individual epistemological types that cut across cultural boundaries was known to the author in his numerous case studies since the 1950s (Maruyama, 1959; 1961; 1973; 1974a; 1974b; 1977; 1978a; 1980; 1981). Though there can be many mindscape types (epitemological types) and their mixtures, a relatively small number of them and their mixtures account for more than a half of the population in most of the cultures. The author sometimes used three types (Maruyama, 1974b), four types (Maruyama, 1978a; 1980; 1981) or five types (Maruyama, 1977).

In 1976, while attending a biology conference at the University of Colorado, the author went to the psychology department during a coffee break and found that O. J. Harvey had been doing a study of epistemological types, using large-scale statistical sample, over the course of a few decades. He and I compared our findings and were surprised that his first, second, and fourth types were almost identical with my H, I and G types, although his third type was different from my S-type. He found that about one third of university freshmen were of H-type, another third were of the other three types or mixtures of the four types, and the rest incorporated types other than the four. We were almost shocked, pleasantly however, by the agreement between the results of his studies using large-scale statistical methods on university students and those of my case studies on scholars and professionals in several countries. This encouraged and motivated me to devise psychological tests which can be used in many countries and at several age levels. Harvey's test was a verbal test, similar in structure to the F-scale test developed by Adorno and Sanford (1950). Mine would need to be nonverbal tests, in order to be useful at all age levels (including children) and in many cultures. However, for complex reasons, I had to move around from country to country in the 1970s and 1980s (Maruyama, 1978b). It was in the early 1990s that I finally had time to work on my psychological tests. I wanted to begin with a simple test. I decided to devise an aesthetic preference test in terms of spatial composition because I knew that the concept ofbeauty was related to

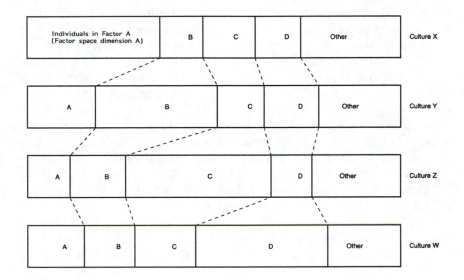

FIGURE 1. Heterogram of individual heterogeneity across cultures (transcultural individual types).

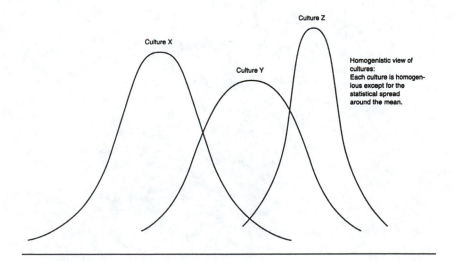

FIGURE 2. Homogenistic view of cultures (incorrect assumption of normal distribution).

mindscape types (Maruyama, 1981): H-type individuals tended to prefer hierarchical, symmetrical, and repetitious composition, while nonredundant (nonrepetitious, nonsymmetrical) designs tended to be preferred by G-type individuals. Another reason was that aesthetic preferences would be less subject to political pressures than other aspects of mind, even though political suppression of aesthetic styles occurred in some countries (Deshmukh, 1981; Konečni, 1995). An example of nonredundant design is given below (see Figures 3, 4, and 5).

At an earlier stage of the development of the psychological tests using these patterns, the author, with cooperation from Professor Jean-Luc Capron of Belgium and Dr. András Farkas of Hungary, made a test run using sixteen patterns shown below in Figure 5. Because the test was given in Tokyo, Brussels, and Budapest, the author named the test "TOB Test #1" to be followed by subsequent improved tests.

TOB Test # 1 was meant to be a test run for more complicated tests to follow. Therefore it was run with a small number of subjects: 29 Japanese, 21 Hungarian, and 20 Belgian subjects took the test. The methodology of

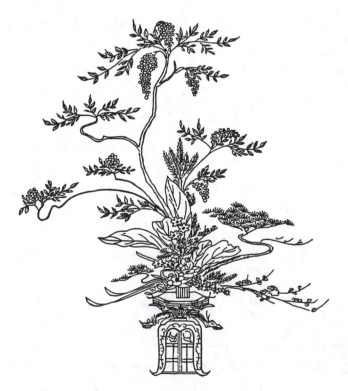

FIGURE 3. Example of S-type design (Japanese floral art).

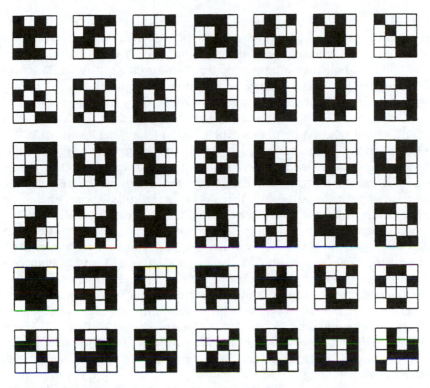

FIGURE 4. The 42 patterns used in the TOB test.

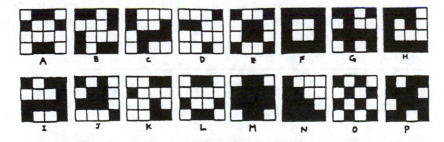

FIGURE 5. The 16 patterns used in an earlier version of the TOB test.

analysis which I devised consisted of two steps: (1) first, make a correlation matrix of the patterns, factor-analyze it, and define a factor space; (2) then cluster-analyze the individuals in the factor space. After giving the test, we found that some patterns had symbolic or representational meanings while other patterns were free from contamination by meanings. In the test, in addition to scoring each pattern on a 7-point scale between adjective pairs such as beautiful/ugly, interesting/boring, the subjects were to indicate whether the pattern had meaning, and what the meaning was. Examples of the meaning given by the subjects were: Nazi, Red Cross, bird, dog, windmill. Symbolic meanings varied from culture to culture while representational or pictorial meanings were common to all cultures. Therefore, when we identified the factor space, we made the correlation matrix of patterns in three ways: (a) patterns without meaning; (b) patterns with meaning; and (c) mixture of meaningful and meaningless patterns.

Furthermore, just to see whether the methodology uncovers any individual clusters across cultures, we first took only a single adjective pair—beautiful/ugly—and constructed a correlation matrix of the 16 patterns. Then we divided the patterns in three ways as indicated above, and chose some patterns from each way. We combined all subjects from all countries to generate a factor space from the correlation matrix of the patterns in each way using the scores on beautiful/ugly scale, and cluster-analyzed all subjects together. The results are shown in Figures 6, 7 and 8. Four distinct clusters emerged across cultures for patterns which were free from contamination by meanings. And as expected, for patterns with meanings, some clusters emerged which were present in some cultures but absent in others. It was a pleasant surprise for us that the simple TOB Test #1, even with a small number of subjects, already confirmed at statistically significant levels the existence of individual types across cultural boundaries (statistical details are given in Maruyama, 1995). However, the individual clusters found in this test did not correspond to mindscape types. In order to refine the test, we needed to include more patterns and increase the number of subjects. Therefore, we devised TOB Test #2 with 42 patterns (Figure 4). We may add several more patterns (Figure 9).

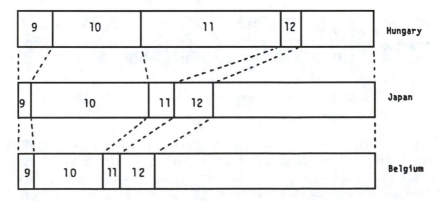

FIGURE 6. Individual clusters for patterns without symbolic or representational meaning (for patterns C, D, K): The numbers are used as cluster names.

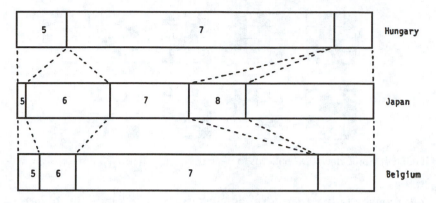

FIGURE 7. Individual clusters for patterns with symbolic or representational meaning (for patterns B, G, H, J, P): The numbers are used as cluster names.

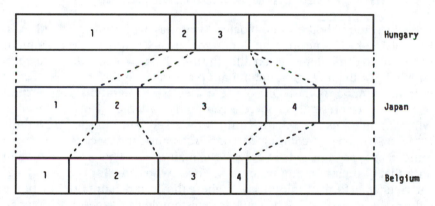

FIGURE 8. Individual clusters for mixed patterns (for patterns C, D, F, H, K, P): The numbers are used as cluster names.

The author has given TOB Test #2 to 70 Japanese and 10 non-Japanese subjects in Tokyo. Professor Anatoly Zankovsky has given the test in Moscow, and Aachen in Gemany; Professor Tamal Fatehi has given the same test in Azerbaijan. Professor Zankovsky has input the test scores. The analysis is in progress (Maruyama, 1998b). TOB Test #2 was also given to 35 Hungarians in Budapest and 35 Belgian and foreign subjects in Brussels. Using the scores from Tokyo, Brussels, and Budapest only, 13 factors were found among 42 patterns. However, perhaps because the number of factors was large and the individual scores became scattered in a large space with too many factors, distinct clusters could not be identified. Another possibility is that individual scores are distributed

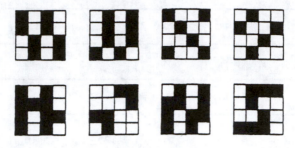

FIGURE 9. Some new TOB patterns to be included in future TOB tests.

continuously, rather than forming clusters. We are looking into various possibilities.

☐   Cases of Selection of Cultural Milieu

Any given individual epistemological type may be found in all cultures. However, which type may be dominant (mainstream) or nondominant (nonmainstream) depends on the culture. There are various strategies which the individuals of nondominant types may employ in order to cope with the dominant types. One of the strategies is emigration. This portion of the chapter presents a concrete example of a large factory in Sweden where immigrants from many countries worked. Most of the immigrants came to Sweden for economic reasons. But some came because their own mindscape type matched better with the mainstream type in Sweden than with that of their own home country. Those who came for economic reasons tended to form ethnic enclaves where they could maintain their home cultures, whereas those who came for epistemological type-matching had no need to form an ethnic enclave, because all of them had the same epistemological type which corresponded to the mainstream type in Sweden. Furthermore, some of those who came for economic reasons found their own type compatible with the Swedish mainstream type, and moved away from ethnic enclaves. In the 1970s and 1980s, large factories in Sweden and Germany were noted for their multi-ethnic employee mix. In Sweden, there were many immigrants from Finland, Yugoslavia, Turkey, Assyria, and other South European, African, Asian, and South American countries, most of whom became permanent residents and citizens of Sweden. In Germany, there were many "guest workers" (temporary workers) from South European countries. At the same time in France and Belgium, workers from Northern and Western Africa were increasing. In the early 1990s, there was an influx of former East German workers to western parts of Germany, some of whom commuted daily from the Germany to the West. Some Russian workers arrived in Poland, and there were also labor migrations between China and Siberia.

Some countries, such as Sweden and Germany, have had a great deal of experience in multi-ethnic employee mixes resulting from world-wide labor migration. Other countries, such as Singapore, have had labor flow from nearby countries only. Some have had very little foreign labor force, such as Japan, Korea, and Iceland.

In this sense it is useful to discuss the experience of a leading manufacturing firm in Sweden, at which I conducted very long interviews with 36 employees from 10 countries. The composition of the 36 interviewees is as follows: Sex: 20 male; 16 female. Birth place: Sweden, 8; Denmark, 1; Finland, 11; Yugoslavia, 9; Turkey, 2; Portugal, 1; Algeria, 1; Zaire, 1; Pakistan, 1; Chile, 1. Number of years in Sweden: Lowest, 5 years; highest, 21 years; median, 13 years. Number of years in the factory: lowest, 1 year; highest, 17 years; median, 7 years.

Most of the interviewees from Europe spoke Swedish well, and the interviews with them were conducted in Swedish, except for one Danish worker with whom Danish language was spoken. The interviews with the Algerian and the Zairean were conducted in French, and those with the Pakistani and the Chilean were in English. I spoke all these languages myself, and no interpreter was needed. The interviews were conducted in a small room inside one of the factory buildings. The duration of the interviews varied from 25 to 90 minutes. A conversational style was used, and the interviewees could bring up any topic of their own relevance.

Problems mentioned frequently in the interviews were: (1) attitude and perception between ethnic groups; (2) assignment discrimination on the job; (3) discrimination in applicant acceptance; (4) xenophobia among young Swedish employees; (5) inefficient or impossible task combinations at each spot on the assembly line; (6) Swedish language lessons taught by literature specialists instead of technical specialists; (7) discriminatory medical care; (8) improvements which can be easily made but are neglected, such as adjustable hoist level on the assembly line; (9) other physical conditions such as poor ventilation and excessive illumination; and (10) frequency of change between the day shift and the night shift.

The interviewee from Denmark was an example of a person who had felt mismatched to his home culture, but matched to the Swedish culture. As I have lived in both Denmark and Sweden for several years, let me summarize some of the differences I observed between the two cultures as a background information.

In the Danish culture, the main purpose of interpersonal communication is maintenance of familiar atmosphere and affect relations. For example, a small group of friends often sit together in the same cafe, eating the same pastry week after week, telling the same or similar gossips. Subtle variations are considered interesting. Let's say that everyone in the group knows that Mr. X ties his left shoe first, then his right shoe. One day he reverses the sequential order. This becomes big news. Less subtle information is avoided because it may disturb the familiar atmosphere. It is impolite to explain things, because such an act assumes that the listener is ignorant. It is also impolite to ask questions regarding anything beyond immediate personal concern, because the respondent might not know the answer. It is often considered aggressive to introduce new ideas. One prefers to repeat the same old jokes. Discussing politics or economics is taboo except in marginal enclaves which are niches for those who avoid the mainstream mindscape type. Safe topics of intellectual conversation are art, literature, and music, on which you can disagree without embarrassment because people are expected to have different tastes.

In contrast, in Sweden, the purpose of daily interpersonal conversation is the transmission of new information or frank expression of feelings. One prefers to remain silent unless he or she has an important message, while in Denmark one must keep talking. In a psychiatric comparative study, Hendin concluded that Swedes were performance-oriented while Danes were affect-oriented (Hendin, 1964). The dominant mainstream mindscape type in Sweden is of H-type, while an S-type characterizes the Danish culture. Other types either form their own enclaves or emigrate. Peter-Freuchen, a Danish explorer, said that all Vikings had left Denmark.

The interviewee from Denmark was happy with his job. He even preferred to talk in Swedish, even though I began the interview in Danish. At the time of the interview, he was a foreman of 19 workers, of whom 11 were Finnish, 6 were Swedish, 1 was English, and 1 was Greek. There were 3 women among the Finns, and the Greek worker was a woman. The interviewee said, "Danish workers in this factory can be divided into two categories: those who like to work in Sweden, and those who do not. The latter return to Denmark after a short time. The former have been working here for many years."

Individual differences were found in several other aspects. For example, many of the Finnish workers who worked in sections where they were the ethnic majority said that they would rather mix with Swedes in order to learn Swedish language.

Differences in preferences regarding job rotation revealed mindscape-type differences. Most interviewees were accustomed to rotating within one section and wanted to do so, but a small number of interviewees wanted to be rotated to different sections because it would be more interesting. One deterring consideration was that a change between sections sometimes entailed a loss of accumulated pay increments: if one were to change sections, he or she would have to start all over again from a lower payscale.

The problem of workers' lack of opportunity to be exposed to other sections where they might find a better mindscape match, which was experienced as a deprivation, will be discussed in the following section.

☐ New Directions of Counseling, and Educational and Vocational Equal Opportunity for All Logical and Epistemological Types

Suppression of Epistemological Types

In each culture, it is possible to find all the individual epistemological types that are found in other cultures. Cultural differences consist in the way one type becomes dominant and suppresses, transforms, ignores, or utilizes other types.

One whose epistemological type is nondominant can use several strategies for survival: One can (a) make niches to avoid the dominant type; (b) camouflage one's own type; (c) switch back and forth between one's own type and the dominant type, depending on the situation; (d) repress one's own type into the unconscious, whereby the repression may be either reversible (one can regain one's own type under favorable conditions) or irreversible; (e) rebel; or (f) emigrate. In some rare cases, a nondominant type may acquire high prestige. In such cases, false self-presentation as the dominant type may occur.

Because of strategies (b), (c), and (d), in statistical surveys the number of individuals observed as belonging in the dominant epistemological type may appear to be larger than if the camouflaged and repressed types are taken into consideration.

An important implication is that the surface appearance of homogeneity in each cultural or social group or subgroup is attained at great psychological costs on the part of individuals of nondominant epistemological types. This is a mental health implication. The second is a civil rights implication. In education and in intellectual professional work, individuals of nondominant epistemological types are highly disadvantaged, and often remain unemployed or misemployed, which further leads to mental health side effects. Equal opportunity for all epistemological types must be legally established and practiced.

Counseling for Individuals

Counseling for social adaptation may be necessary in cases of antisocial behavior, withdrawal, or alienation. However, a new direction of "selection of sociocultural milieu" must be considered at the same time, because anti-social behavior, withdrawal, and alienation may be caused by a mismatch between the individual's epistemological type and the mainstream type in the sociocultural group.

As we have seen, individuals of nondominant epistemological types may use various coping strategies. Niche formation is a collective withdrawal. Camouflaging and switching are adaptive behaviors but entail psychological stress. Repression is mentally unhealthy. Rebellion may be successful or unsuccessful. Emigration from one sociocultural milieu to another is a new solution. In order to implement this method, the individual must first be exposed to several different sociocultural milieux. The role of the counselor in this case is to preselect some possible sociocultural milieux where the counselor believes the individual has a likelihood of attaining an epistemological match. For this purpose, it is necessary for the counselor to be familiar with several sociocultural milieux.

As for individual identity formation, the counselor may suggest self-heterogenization instead of pursuing a homogeneous identity or adhering to one ideology (in Erikson's sense) or one ethnic minority group.

Counseling for Organizations

Quite often an organization has several suborganizational milieux. For example, the factory in Sweden had a variety of suborganizational milieux. In spite of this, many employees are stuck with one milieu. The counselor can advise the organization to provide opportunities for its employees to experience other suborganizational milieux. To illustrate concretely: Large ethnic groups, such as Finns and Yugoslavians, formed their own ethnic communities outside the workplace, and isolated themselves from one another. On the other hand, members of small ethnic groups did not have their own communities. The factory did organize social activities for the employees such as excursions. When I asked about the usefulness of such programs, members of the large ethnic groups said that they had their own activities and did not need factory-sponsored programs. Conversely, the sole Pakistani employee, who was lonesome, said that he could not make new friends on the factory-sponsored trips because the participants stayed with those they already knew.

In this factory, each job spot on an assembly line is called a "balans." The word also means the combination of 10 or 15 tasks assigned to the job spot, such as insertion of a wire into a hole, tightening a nut, etc. An assembly line or a group of assembly lines is called a "bana." There are systematic rotations of workers between balanser (plural of balans) within a bana at fixed time intervals such as one hour, two hours, one day, etc., depending on the nature of the bana. However, the workers were not usually rotated between banor (plural of bana). Therefore, each bana becomes a social unit within which the workers worked closely together and understood one another's work. In each bana, some ethnic group tended to be in the majority. This was not primarily because of ethnic discrimination, even though banor consisting of dirty or strenuous work were avoided by northern Europeans.

The uneven ethnic distribution was caused by two reasons: (1) the new employee's desire to work in the same bana as a friend; and (2) coincidence of establishment of a new bana with the time of the arrival of some ethnic group from a foreign country.

In some cases there was ethnic discrimination. Several ethnic minority workers said in the interviews that when their countrypersons tried to get a job in the factory, they were told that there were no job openings, while the factory kept hiring Swedes. This happened in the early 1980s when Sweden began to experience unemployment.

In many cases new employees preferred to work in a bana where their friends worked, this contributed to the formation of ethnic clusters, but many of the Finnish workers who worked in banor where they were the majority said in the interviews that they would rather mix with Swedes in order to learn Swedish language. We may also recall that Danish workers who stayed in Sweden preferred the Swedish culture to the Danish culture, and had no tendency to form a cluster of Danes.

The irony is that if a factory lets individuals choose their ethnic mix in order to maximize the opportunities for individually different mindscape-type mixes, the result may be loss of individual mindscape types if some ethnic group requires in-group conformity. The firm can devise ways to free individuals from such intragroup pressures.

The counselor can help a firm devise ways to provide the employees with opportunities to be exposed to various suborganizational milieux and to the mindscape types of other employees. A suggestion, for example, is to hold frequent art exibitions or to continually display the paintings, photos, or other decorations made by employees in the workplace as a way to get to know one another's mindscape types, in addition to brightening the workplace. Amateurish, informal, and inexpensive self-made art products are a better form of mutual communication than are formal, selective exhibitions. It is important to change the displays often to symbolize constant creativity and to enable many people to participate. Another variation is to have work sections, not ethnic groups, compete to see which section can decorate its space more beautifully with the artwork of its members. It will be a cooperative effort within each section. A requirement is that in each section, every person must contribute one work of art. This method is effective where individual competition is unacceptable but group competition is encouraged. Under the guise of group competition, individual mindscape types can be expressed using this method, and viewers from all sections can identify individual mindscape types.

Counseling for Educational Systems

Currently, most of the education systems in North America and Europe, as well as in such places as Singapore, Korea, and Japan are based on an H-type mindscape. Learning is classificational, sequential, and hierarchical. To know is to classify. To define is to classify. To learn is to proceed from chapter one to chapter two. To reason is to deduce from the general to the specific. In order to counteract the H-type mindscape, some educational systems use relational, simultaneous, and interactive methods, such as "on-the-job training" in which many things happen at the same time and one must act relationally and interactively. S-type and G-type methods are relational, simultaneous, and interactive. Some educators use inductive methods rather than deductive methods. But in order to learn with such methods, a child must go to special schools, mostly private. Thus educational equal opportunity does not exist for S-type and G-type individuals. As the child advances to higher education and later to professional life, the situation may get worse. In order to get a good grade, to get a scholarship, to obtain a research grant, to get a dissertation approved, to be published, to obtain a job, and to be promoted, one must strictly adhere to the mainstream methodology and theory (Maruyama, 1998a). Now we are in a top-heavy, job-scarce era. In order to survive in it, a great deal of obsequity and allegiance to the established theory and methodology are required. Nondominant types do not survive unless they camouflage themselves.

It is difficult for a counselor to change the higher educational systems. But elementary educational systems might listen to counselors. As examples of alternative methods of learning, let us consider cartoonized educational materials and variable speed video tape playback. I must insert here some background information. In recent years, sophisticated educational materials using high-quality cartoons have become widely available in Japan. History, social science, and even biology and physics can be studied through cartoons, which are often drawn with scientifically accurate details as well as artistic refinement. Another piece of background knowledge necessary for appreciating the importance of visual materials is the following. From the point of view of the mathematical theory of communication, picture-coded systems have several advantages: (1) The amount of information that one page of a well-prepared picture can contain is many times greater than that of one page of written text; (2) pictorial input into the brain is simultaneous, but verbal input is sequential and time-consuming; and (3) if a relation shown in a picture has to be translated into verbal statements, the complex relation must first be broken down into segments and coded into statements which the recipient must reconstruct into a picture. Much distortion occurs. Suppose you describe someone's face over the phone, and the other party reconstructs an image of the face from your statements. The reconstruction will be very inaccurate. Furthermore, computer graphics has elevated pictorial communication to a much higher level than that of written communication.

Data from book rental stores in Japan indicate that many youngsters can read as many as 20 cartoonized books a day. Video tapes can be viewed at stores which charge one or two dollars per 30 minutes for the use of a VCR player but provide an unlimited number of tapes free. Many children accelerate the playback speed in order to save money, and they can view in 30 minutes several tapes, each of which takes 60 to 90 minutes at normal speed. Moreover, they can remember all the details of the stories. An important aspect of this viewing is that the children interact with the machine, accelerating and slowing down depending on what is happening in the story. This active interaction distinguishes their video viewing from passive television watching. Counselors can suggest such new methods of learning and teaching to educational systems.

Civil Rights Implications

Equal opportunity in terms of race, sex, and age has received much attention, and some improvement has been attained. But equal opportunity for nondominant epistemological types has not yet been advocated. It is an unrecognized urgent problem. Statistically, only about one-third of the population is of pure H-type, but they dominate the educational and professional systems. Direct lack of educational, vocational, and professional opportunity as well as indirect psychological stresses are costing our society economically and psychologically.

☐ References

Adorno, T. W. & Sanford, N. (1950). *The authoritarian personality*. New York: Harper.

Camara, S. (1975). The concept of heterogeneity and change among Mandenka. *Technological Forcasting and Social Change, 7*: 273–284.

Deshmukh, M. F. (1981). Art and politics in turn-of-the-century Berlin: The Berlin secession and Kaiser Wilhelm II. In G. Chapple and H. H. Schulte (Eds.), *The turn of the century: German literature and art 1890–1915*. Bonn, Germany: Bouvier Verlag.

Harvey, O. J. (1966). *Experience, structure and adaptability*. New York: Springer-Verlag.

Hendin, H. (1964). *Suicide in Scandinavia*. New York: Grun & Stratton.

Konečni, V. J. (1995). Politika i sotsialnaya ekologiya arkhitekturi [Political and social ecology of architecture]. *Kulturologicheskiye Zapiski* (Russia) April/May 1995 issue.

Maruyama, M. (1959). Critique de quelques idées très répandues au sujet des rapports entre les cultures et la santé mentale [Critique of some widely held assumptions on the relationship between culture and mental health]. *Revue de Psychologie des Peuples, 14*, 273–276.

Maruyama, M. (1960). Morphogenesis and morphostasis. *Methodos* (Italy), *12*, 251–296.

Maruyama, M. (1961). Communicational epistemology. *British Journal for the Philosophy of Science, 11*, 319–327; *12*, 52–62; 117–131.

Maruyama, M. (1963). The second cybernetics: Deviation-amplifying mutual causal processes, *American Scientist, 51*, 164–179; 250–256.

Maruyama. M. (1973). Human futuristics and urban planning. *Journal of American Institute of Planners, 39*, 346–357.

Maruyama, M. (1974a). Hierarchists, individualists and mutualists: Three paradigms among planners. *Futures, 6*, 103–113.

Maruyama, M. (1974b). Paradigmatology and its application to cross-disciplinary, cross-professional and cross-cultural communication. *Cybernetica, 17*, 136–156; 237–281.

Maruyama, M. (1977). Heterogenistics: an epistemological restructuring of biological and social sciences. *Acta Biotheoretica, 26*, 120–136.

Maruyama, M. (1978a). Heterogenistics and morphogenetics: Toward a new concept of the scientific. *Theory and Society, 5*, 75–96.

Maruyama, M. (1978b, November 20). Seven moves in seven years. *Chronicle of Higher Education* (p. 18).

Maruyama, M. (1980). Mindscapes and science theories. *Current Anthropology, 21*, 589–599.

Maruyama, M. (1981, October). Denkmuster: Metaprinzipien der umweltgestaltung [Mindscapes: metaprinciples of environmental design]. *Garten und Landschaft*, pp. 806–815.

Maruyama, M. (1985). The new logic of Japan's young generations. *Technological Forecasting and Social Change, 28*, 351–364.

Maruyama, M. (1992). Changing dimensions in international business. *Academy of Management Executives, 6*, 88–96.

Maruyama, M. (1993). Mindscapes, individuals and cultures in management. *Journal of Management Inquiry, 2*, 140–155.

Maruyama, M. (1994a). *Mindscapes in management: Use of individual differences in multicultural management*. Aldershot, England: Dartmouth Publishing Co.

Maruyama, M. (1994b). Interwoven and interactive heterogeneity in the 21st century. *Technological Forecasting and Social Change, 45*, 93–102.

Maruyama, M. (1995). Individual epistemological heterogeneity across cultures and its use in organizations. *Cybernetica, 37*, 215–249.

Maruyama, M. (1998a). Academic concept inbreeding, failure of interbreeding, and its remedy by outbreeding. *Human Systems Management, 17*: 89–91.

Maruyama, M. (1998b, August). Heterogenistics and heterogram analysis. Paper presented to the Congress of the International Association of Cross-cultural Psychology, San Francisco, CA.

Shannon, C., & Weaver, W. (1949). *Mathematical theory of communication, Urbana*, IL: Univ. of Illinois Press.

Wiener, N. (1948). *Cybernetics*. Paris: Hermann et Cie.

CHAPTER

Frederick T. L. Leong
Azara L. Santiago-Rivera

Climbing the Multiculturalism Summit: Challenges and Pitfalls

This chapter discusses several challenges and pitfalls in the movement toward multiculturalism. It is proposed that Kurt Lewin's theoretical formulations on the utility of a force-field analysis in understanding personality can be extended to that of social and scientific movements. Using these concepts extended from Lewin's framework, it will be illustrated how certain prevailing and countervailing forces are at work in shaping multiculturalism as a social movement. Borrowing concepts from social and organizational psychology, the authors go on to describe a number of the countervailing forces that serve to hinder the advancement in multiculturalism in psychology and counseling. For example, the false consensus effect, attraction selection-attribution (ASA) framework, and psychological reactance concepts are presented as countervailing forces against the expansion of the multicultural movement. Implications are discussed as they relate to graduate training in psychology and the advancement of the multicultural perspective in the counseling and counseling psychology fields.

In the lead article of a special issue of the *Journal of Counseling and Development*, Paul Pedersen (1991) proposed that we are moving towards "Multiculturalism as a fourth force in psychology" following the three major forces, namely psychodynamic, behavioral, and humanistic. While it is true that culture is beginning to play an increasingly important role

---

An earlier version of this chapter was presented by the first author at the International Congress of Psychology, Montreal, August 16–21, 1996.

An Extension of Lewin's Force Field Analysis to Social Movements such as the Multiculturalism Movement

Lewin's Model of Personality	Proposed Model of Social Movements
Life-Space	Social-Space
$B = f(P, E)$	$SM = f(P, C)$
Personal Typology	Social Typology
Psychic Energies	Social Energies
Locomotion	Expansion or Constriction
Personal Equilibrium	Social Equilibrium
Personality Dynamics (Forces & Tensions)	Social Dynamics (Forces & Tensions)
Driving Forces Restraining Forces	Prevailing Forces Countervailing Forces
Individual Needs, Valences, Vectors	Individual Needs, Valences, Vectors + Organizational Level & Institutional Dynamics

---

in psychological research and theory building, we believe that multiculturalism is far from becoming a dominant force in psychology. One need only review some recent introductory psychology textbooks and role of the cultural dimension in graduate psychology curricula to see that multiculturalism is far from taking center stage in our field. As psychologists committed to the study and understanding of cultural differences and similarities, we are also interested in increasing the attention paid to the cultural dimension in psychology. However, we believe that the movement towards affording culture the appropriate recognition in our field is a long and tedious journey which has just begun. We also believe that this journey is an uphill one and that we are embarking on a difficult climb to the top of the multiculturalism summit. The nature and difficulties inherent in this uphill climb will form the basis of our chapter.

Using a Lewinian force-field analysis, this chapter presents several challenges and pitfalls in the movement towards multiculturalism. Borrowing from Lewin's famous formulation that behavior is a function of the interaction between the person and his or her environment (i.e, $B = f(P, E)$), it is proposed that some of his conceptualizations can be extended and applied to higher level phenomena. Whereas Lewin was primarily interested in an individual's personality and behavior, his concepts can be readily applied to social movements as well, such as our present topic, the movement towards multiculturalism in counseling and psychology.

The text box illustrates our proposed model of social movements which parallels Lewinian concepts. For Lewin, a person and his or her psychological environment would be contained in an individual *life space*. Our parallel is the social environment's *social space* which contains a variety of social institutions and social movements. Similar to Lewin's concept of psychical energy and tensions within an individual's personality dynamics, our concept of social space also consists of various social energies and tensions between the various social institutions and social movements. Just as the psychic energies propel and restrain the locomotion of the individual, the social energies of our proposed model facilitate and hinder the advances or retreat of our social movement. Similar to personality dynamics, our social dynamics would alternate back and forth between states of equilibrium and disequilibrium depending on the balance of the forces between the social institutions and social movements.

Therefore, the advances of a movement like multiculturalism in counseling and psychology can be studied and understood in view of this force-field analysis that delineates the prevailing and countervailing forces. Similar to Lewin's famous equation, our present equation is SM = f (P, C) where the advances and development of a social movement would be a function of the prevailing and countervailing forces. These prevailing and countervailing forces are similar to Lewin's driving and restraining forces in his analysis of personality dynamics. Like Lewin's theory, these forces come from individual needs and valences (value for a particular person). However, since our force-field analysis is of social space and social movements, group-level and institutional dynamics also come into play, in addition to individual needs and valences. For instance, once an institution has been founded, it tends to develop a life of its own, independent of its original function, and will seek to maintain and often expand its roles and activities. In the United States of America (herein, U.S.A.), the Congress and the Social Welfare System are two such examples. Moreover, Thomas Kuhn's *The Structure of Scientific Revolutions* (1970) exemplifies the group-level dynamics in the analysis of science as a social movement.

The prevailing forces that are pushing the multiculturalism movement forward are well-known. First, there is the increasing globalization of businesses, with a rise in multicultural corporations and other organizational shifts such as the formation of the European Union. Second, there has been a steady increase of immigrants and refugees moving from less developed to more developed countries. Third, many of the more recent immigrant populations are reproducing at much higher rates than the earlier, older, and more established immigrants. Finally, there has been an increase in travel to and from different countries for a variety of purposes such as studying abroad and tourism. These and other factors have created a situation where more and more people of different countries come in contact, promoting cultural interchange at a much higher rate than in previous generations. It is in the context of these developments that multiculturalism has developed an increasingly central role in our economic, political, educational, and professional activities. Taken together, these prevailing forces have created a set of conditions conducive to the development of multiculturalism. This movement has been characterized as the rise of the cultural pluralism perspective which had its early roots in education (e.g., Epps, 1974; Krug, 1977) and eventually spread to counseling and psychology.

We will now turn our attention to the counteracting forces rallied against the multiculturalism movement in counseling and psychology. Given that the present model is focused on an analysis of social space and social movements, it follows that many of the concepts used come from the field of social psychology, which has devoted considerable attention to such phenomena.

☐ Ethnocentrism

From the field of cross-cultural social psychology, the problem of ethnocentrism as a fundamental human tendency serves as a major countervailing force. A quote from Triandis' (1994) textbook, *Culture and Social Behavior*, provides us with a working definition:

> "We are all ethnocentric, some of us more than others, especially if we have not tasted another culture. How could it be otherwise? Most of us know only our own culture, and it is natural that we will consider it as the standard against which to judge others. The more another culture is like our own, the "better" it is. That is the essence of ethnocentrism" (p. 249).

Hence, ethnocentrism is a natural human tendency and it consists of using our own culture as a standard for evaluating others. How does ethnocentrism serve as a countervailing force against multiculturalism? Once again, Triandis (1994) proposed that "Ethnocentrism and cultural distance work together to create perceived dissimilarity. Dissimilarity results in conflict, and conflict results in negative stereotypes. As a result, people make nonisomorphic attributions and experience the relationship as one in which they have no control. They feel culture shock, and they feel hostility toward the other group" (p. 249).

The end result of ethnocentrism is increased cultural distance and cultural stereotypes and misunderstandings. Furthermore, Brislin (1993) has pointed out, "When people make ethnocentric judgments about culturally diverse others, they are imposing the standards with which they are familiar given their own socialization . . . Ethnocentric judgments, then, are based on feelings that one's own group is the center of what is reasonable and proper in life. Further, the term implies that others can be judged according to one, central set of standards. An implication of the judgments is that one group is clearly better, even superior, than the other since its members practice proper and correct behaviors. As might be expected, the group considered better or superior is the one to which the person making the ethnocentric judgments belongs" (p. 38).

It is proposed that since the field of counseling and psychotherapy in the U.S.A. is dominated by European Americans, the ethnocentric viewpoints of this majority will continue to prevail over the call for multiculturalism. It is true that the increasing cultural diversity of the U.S. population is making many social scientists and mental health professionals pay attention to these demographic trends. Yet, acknowledging these demographic trends and acquiring additional skills to work with these "special populations" is a far cry from adopting multiculturalism as a central tenet in one's approach to counseling and psychotherapy. For example, in the U.S.A., the APA Division of Counseling Psychology (Division 17) commissioned a group of counseling psychologists to develop a set of cross-cultural counseling competencies in view of the demographic trends just mentioned. The committee, chaired by Derald Sue, presented the findings in a position paper published in the division journal, *The Counseling Psychologist*, in 1982 (Sue et al., 1982). Ten years later, in 1992, there was a symposium at the APA conference to discuss the status of that paper. Unfortunately, very little had been done by the division in that ten year period, except to publish the position paper. At present, Derald Sue has concluded that members of Division 17 are not very receptive to integrating the multicultural perspective within the Division. Consequently, the position paper has been sent to the American Counseling Association (ACA) for consideration. Hence, one could conclude that members of Division 17 who are in positions of power were well-intentioned (i.e., they approved the committee and published the findings), but ethnocentrism ensured that no real changes took place. Although this is our interpretation of the situation, we believe that few cross-cultural psychologists would predict that ethnocentrism will diminish significantly in the near future.

☐ False Consensus Effect

From the field of social cognition, the false consensus effect may serve as a another constraint and a countervailing force. According to Fiske and Taylor (1991), "The false consensus effect, or self-based consensus effect, is the tendency to see one's own behavior as typical, to assume that under the same circumstances others would have reacted the same way as one self " (p. 75). The authors describe a study conducted by Ross, Greene, and House (1977) which demonstrates the occurrence of this phenomenon. In this study, college students were asked to walk around campus wearing a sign that read "Eat at Joe's." Some of these students agreed to wear the sign, while others did not. Those who agreed were then asked to determine the percentage of other students who might also agree to wear the sign. The same was asked of those who declined to wear the sign. The results showed that both groups of students (i.e., agreed vs. declined) believed that at least 60% of their peers would side with them. Since then, a significant number of follow-up studies have clearly demonstrated this effect.

Fiske and Taylor (1991) also offer several possible explanations for the false consensus effect. They argue that people tend to seek out others who are like themselves in such aspects as behaviors, attitudes, and beliefs. As such, when an individual reaches conclusions about what others believe, the people who come to mind are those same individuals who are thought to be similar. Fiske and Taylor go on to explain that this perception can lead to "overestimating" the extent to which others share in the same attitudes and beliefs. An alternative explanation is that an individual's opinion about something may be so central that it increases the likelihood of thinking that others share the same opinion.

Despite the growing number of racial and ethnic minorities in the U.S.A., the majority of the population for the next few decades will remain as European Americans with an understandably Eurocentric perspective. The same would be true of the mental health profession. In view of the false consensus effect, it is not inconceivable that these Eurocentric perspectives and values will continue to dominate in both the mental health profession and in U.S. society in general.

☐ Attraction-Selection-Attrition Framework

Another countervailing force against the development of multicultural-ism is the Attraction-Selection-Attrition (ASA) framework presented by Schneider (1987). According to Schneider organizations develop a partic-ular culture or climate because they undergo a process he labeled as the ASA cycle. Through the processes of attraction (i.e., who chooses to join the organization), selection (i.e., who is admitted into the organization), and attrition (i.e., who chooses to leave the organization), organizations eventually develop a very distinctive character. Through the ASA cycle, or-ganizations also become very homogenous and resistant to change, which Schneider considers dysfunctional.

According to Schneider (1987), the ASA cycle accounts for how or-ganizational climates and cultures develop and also for the difficulty in organizational change. He has provided more evidence supporting the ASA cycle in organizations in a recent update (Schneider, Goldstein, & Smith, 1995). For instance, in their review of relevant studies, there is evidence to suggest that organizations define the characteristics of people who enter them, thus supporting the homogeneity hypothesis.

There are several social psychological processes which support the development and maintenance of the ASA cycle. The first component of ASA which creates this tendency towards homogeneity and resistance to change in organizations is the "group-think" phenomenon described by Janis (1972). Another important component supporting the ASA cycle is Byrne's (1971) similarity-attraction model. According to this model, we are more likely to like and be attracted to individuals who are similar to us in attitudes, beliefs, and values than those who are dissimilar.

☐ Psychological Reactance

The theory of psychological reactance (Brehm, 1966; Brehm & Brehm, 1981) provides another countervailing force against the development of multicultural thinking among counselors and psychologists. According to Brehm (1966), psychological reactance is a motivational force to regain or restore lost freedoms or to counter threats or attempts at reducing our freedoms. To the extent that a change in how we think about our work requires giving up the established and familiar ways (i.e., monocultural versus multicultural) and serves as a threat to this freedom of "business as usual," then the multiculturalism movement is likely to arouse this motivational force of psychological reactance.

Many counselors and psychologists, although they may not admit it publicly, will resent the multiculturalism movement and perceive it as an attempt to "force" them how to think and behave in a certain way with clients and colleagues who are culturally different from them. Indeed, this psychological reactance to new movements in psychology is the basis of the "backlash phenomenon." The backlash phenomenon has been discussed in regard to the women's movement and will no doubt occur for the cultural diversity movement as well. Part of the problem is that the multiculturalism movement has been closely associated with the whole issue of "political correctness." There is already evidence of a backlash against this whole issue of political correctness—so much so, that there are TV programs with titles like "Politically Incorrect."

It is inevitable that psychological reactance will be aroused among some individuals when a new movement is introduced that requires a change in attitudes, cognitions, and behaviors that have become habitual. The challenge for the multicultural movement is not to avoid arousing this psychological reactance, but to become aware of its existence and develop ways of countering it. More specifically, there is a need to study and examine this process of psychological reactance to multiculutlralism in order to more fully understand it and devise strategies for dealing with it.

☐ Beliefs versus Values

From the study of the psychology of science, the distinction between beliefs about science, versus values within science, makes advancing the multiculturalism paradigm within counseling and psychology akin to scaling Mount Everest. Following the lead of Arthur Kleinman, we assume that the scientific enterprise is a cultural institution. Kleinman, a Harvard psychiatrist and anthropologist, has eloquently argued that the mental health profession is a cultural institution and can therefore be studied from a cultural perspective, for example, with an analysis of its dominant values and customs. In the same way, the scientific profession is also a cultural institution with dominant values and customs. Therefore, we should be able to study the rise and fall of different movements within scientific fields like psychology from a cross-cultural psychological perspective.

Michael Bond (personal communication to first author, 1994) recently pointed out that the field of cross-cultural psychology makes an important distinction between values and beliefs. Values are our conceptions of that which is desirable, whereas beliefs are our conceptions of that which is true. Cross-cultural psychology has expended a considerable amount of effort to study values, and only recently has begun the systematic study of beliefs. It is proposed that another major countervailing force which has been rallied against the multiculturalism movement in counseling and psychology is the Values-Belief Fallacy. This fallacy consists of individuals who operate with their values as if they are beliefs. As such, we propose that psychologists, as scientists, are also vulnerable to this fallacy. As members within the cultural institution called "the scientific community," they ascribe to certain values, such as logical positivism and the importance of experimentation, as the primary form of epistemology, as contrasted with other values such as constructivism and the importance of existential phenomenology.

Values are, by their very nature, hierarchical—one mode of being and doing is preferred over another, and is eventually viewed as superior. This process of the "deification of values" may eventually lead to another major problem. While values are powerful cultural determinants of behavior, they are at least recognized as cultural choices, and are more malleable, since preferences can evolve and change. Beliefs, as conceptions of that which is true, are much more powerful as determinants of behavior, and are extremely resistant to change. Milton Rokeach's *The Three Christs of Ypsilanti* (1981) is an early social psychological study of the power of religious beliefs, and serves as a good example. A more contemporary example is the war in Bosnia. The Serbs and Bosnians are not fighting because of their cultural values (e.g., how one should live and how one should worship God); otherwise there would be wars all over the world. An alternative reason is that each side *believes* the other side is the enemy that needs to be destroyed.

As recent history has demonstrated, these beliefs are extremely resistant to change. Therefore, many psychologists, as scientists, are operating as if the values of science are personal beliefs. They do not just value experimentation as a way of discovering the truth; they believe that it is *the only way* to discover the truth. Many of our colleagues in psychology believe that they are discovering universal laws of behavior and believe that cultural differences are nuisance variables at worst, and extraneous variables at best. Many of them do not believe that we need the cross-cultural psychological perspective to take a central place in our profession. Two examples are provided in support of this position. Within the American Psychological Association (APA), it took until the formation of the Society for the Psychological Study of Racial and Ethnic Minority Issues in Psychology (Division 45) before APA would accept and recognize the importance of racial and cultural differences. Another example is the focus and content of our introductory psychology textbooks. It is well recognized that relatively little attention is given to cross-cultural psychology, with the exception of a few "boxes" and inserts.

☐ Conformity: Minority and Majority Influence

Finally, the analysis of social influence as it relates to the phenomenon of conformity provides another example of a roadblock in advancing multiculturalism. In particular, much of the research on majority and minority influence offers powerful evidence that individuals are motivated to accept the "majority" position (Devine, Hamilton, & Ostrom, 1994). In landmark studies conducted by Asch (1956), it has been shown that people experience considerable stress when exposed to majority viewpoints that deviate from their own beliefs and judgments. As such, these individuals tend to move in the direction of the majority for fear of disapproval.

Likewise, such a movement to conform to the majority view may be due, in part, to the perception that the "influential" group has characteristics that they attribute to themselves. On the other hand, if a group holds a minority view on a particular issue and the perception of that group is indeed negative, most likely the individual will resist siding with that group (Mugny, 1980). Thus, that individual will move toward the majority opinion.

This phenomenon is especially meaningful when examined in the context of a countervailing force. Specifically, if the public majority continues to have ethnocentric views, one would be hard pressed to expect multicultural views or perspectives held by the minority public to swiftly take hold. Moreover, following Mugny's formulations, in a society where negative stereotypic images of ethnic and cultural minority groups prevail, it is unlikely that individuals who are members of the White majority would shift their views and judgments about the importance of multiculturalism.

☐ Implications

Multiculturalism as a movement in psychology is possible; however, it is important to recognize the potential barriers and processes that are likely to inhibit or hinder its advancement. We propose that it is worthwhile to apply Lewin's force-field analysis to the multiculturalism movement in psychology in order to fully understand both the prevailing and countervailing forces at play in this social movement. Using such an analysis as illustrated in this chapter, one can identify the various countervailing forces at work in order to study them more closely and provide strategies for countering them. Once these countervailing forces are identified and understood, one can develop effective methods of reducing their potential effects. In fact, one could argue that graduate training programs in psychology and counseling are settings in which these processes could be targeted for change.

It is well recognized that most of our training programs do not adequately address multiculturalism in their curricula (Stricker et al., 1990). Many proponents of multiculturalism have cogently argued that there are numerous barriers at the institutional, departmental, and individual levels. For instance, Midgette and Meggert (1991) argued that such training programs have undergone very little change in integrating multicultural perspectives in their curricula, primarily due to a "lack of qualified faculty." Others state that the multicultural movement has been stifled due to insufficient institutional support, creating systemic barriers (Hills & Strozier, 1992; Reynolds, 1995). Might not the countervailing forces described to be operating also hinder the development of adequate multicultural training programs?

It is proposed that attempts to break down these barriers should include a critical examination of these potential countervailing forces that may also contribute to the challenges inherent in implementing multicultural training in psychology and counseling programs. There are powerful forces rallied against the expansion of the multiculturalism movement in counseling and psychology. In order to advance multiculturalism in counseling and psychology, it is important to analyze these and other potential forces, and develop interventions to reduce their effects in the social-space where multiculturalism is vying for recognition and acceptance. In the same way, the good mountain climber prepares for his or her challenging climb up a summit by studying the map and terrain carefully and learning from other climbers, as well as consulting with "guides" when necessary. The good climber also recognizes the contraints generated by the weather, the terrain, and his or her level of physical stamina, and chooses certain routes in order to avoid potential hazards. In summary, the good climber needs to study his or her undertaking carefully and "gets a good lay of the land" and brings along necessary equipment before proceeding up a steep mountain.

☐ References

Asch, S. (1956). Studies of independence and conformity. *Psychological Monographs, 70(9); 416.*

Brehm, J. W. (1966). *A theory of psychological reactance.* New York: Academic Press.

Brehm, S. S., & Brehm, J. W. (1981). *Psychological reactance: A theory of freedom and control.* New York: Academic Press.

Brislin, R. W. (1993). *Understanding culture's influence on behavior.* Fort Worth, TX: Harcourt Brace.

Byrne, D. (1971). *The attraction paradigm.* New York: Academic Press.

Devine, P. G., Hamilton, D. L., & Ostrom, T. M. (1994). *Social cognition: Impact on social psychology.* San Diego, CA: Academic Press.

Epps, E. (1974). *Cultural pluralism and education.* Berkeley, CA: McCutcheon.

Fiske, S. T., & Taylor, S. F. (1991). *Social cognition* (2nd ed.). New York: McGraw-Hill.

Hills, H. I., & Strozier, A. L. (1992). Multicultural training in APA-approved counseling psychology programs: A survey. *Professional Psychology: Research and Practice, 23,* 43–51.

Janis, I. L. (1972). *Victims of groupthink.* Boston: Houghton Mifflin.

Krug, M. M. (1977). Cultural pluralism: Its origins and aftermath. *Journal of Teacher Education, 28,* 5–9.

Kuhn, T. (1970). *The structure of scientific revolutions* (2nd ed.). Chicago, IL: University of Chicago Press.

Midgette, T. E., & Meggert, S. S. (1991). Multicultural counseling instruction: A challenge for faculties in the 21st century. *Journal of Counseling and Development, 70,* 136–141.

Mugny, G. (1980). *The power of minorities.* London: Academic Press.

Pedersen, P. B. (1991). Multiculturalism as a generic approach to counseling. *Journal of Counseling and Development, 70,* 6–12.

Reynolds, A. L. (1995). Challenges and strategies for teaching multicultural counseling courses. In J. G. Ponterotto, J. M. Casas, L. A. Suzuki, and C. M. Alexander (Eds.), *Handbook of multicultural counseling* (pp. 312–330). Thousand Oaks, CA: Sage Publications.

Rokeach, M. (1981). *The three Christs of Ypsilanti: A psychological study.* New York: Columbia University Press.

Ross, L., Greene, D., & House, P. (1977). The "false consensus effect": An egocentric bias in social perception and attribution processes. *Journal of Experimental Social Psychology, 13,* 279–301.

Schneider, B. (1987). The people make the place. *Personnel Psychology, 40,* 437–453.

Schneider, B., Goldstein, H. W., & Smith, B. D. (1995). The ASA framework: An update. *Personnel Psychology, 48,* 747–773.

Stricker, G., Davis-Russell, E., Bourg, E., Duran, E., Hammond, W. R., McHolland, J., Polite, K., & Vaughn, B. E. (Eds.). (1990). *Toward ethnic diversification in psychology education and training.* Washington, DC: APA.

Sue, D. W., Bernier, J. E., Durran, A., Feinberg, L., Pedersen, P., Smith, E. J., & Vasquez-Nuttall, E. (1982). Position paper: Cross-cultural counseling competencies. *The Counseling Psychologist, 10,* 45–52.

Triandis, H. (1994). *Culture and social behavior.* New York: McGraw-Hill.

PART

II

PARTICULAR ISSUES: PRODUCTIVITY WITHIN THE MULTICULTURAL PERSPECTIVE

CHAPTER

Guler Okman Fisek
Cigdem Kagitcibasi

Multiculturalism and Psychotherapy: The Turkish Case

This chapter addresses the issues involved in multiculturalism and its implications for the practice of psychotherapy. Psychotherapy is a deeply multicultural enterprise that can derive great benefit from an analysis that integrates culturally contextual and universalistic approaches. The multicultural aspect of psychotherapy is seen as being inherent in its interpersonal nature. Multiculturalism is also inherent in the more usual concerns with the application of therapies of western origin in non-western contexts, or applications with minority populations in host societies. Issues involved in this enterprise are explored, using work with Turkish clients as a case example. A multilevel contextual systemic perspective is offered as a framework for understanding barriers to mutual meaning construction, as well as the pitfalls of universalistic approaches. A discussion of therapist biases and client expectations follows. The chapter concludes with some suggestions for multiculturally sensitive psychotherapy and a plea for systematic study of contextual constraints on human experience.

During the last decades there has been an increasing appreciation of the importance of culture in psychological inquiry. This is notable given the long tradition of a narrow focus on the individual out of context. Most research in mainstream psychology is still going about its usual business. Nevertheless, the developments in cultural and cross-cultural psychology over the past quarter century are beginning to challenge the established traditions of psychological research/applications albeit not yet strongly enough to shake them (Bond, 1988; Lonner, 1989).

75

The main issue in these recent developments involves situating psychological phenomena in their cultural contexts. This appears "obvious" since "it is rare (perhaps even impossible) for any human being ever to behave without responding to some aspect of culture" (Segall, Dasen, Berry, & Poortinga, 1990, p. 5). However what appears obvious turns out to be less so when an attempt is made to integrate culture into psychological analysis (Van de Vijver & Hutschemaekers, 1990). This is because, as a rather diffuse, all-inclusive entity, culture presents a problem in research: It cannot serve as an explanation or an independent variable. Secondly, the question of how to study behavior in culture presents a conceptual and methodological problem, mainly in terms of whether to examine phenomena from within (emic) or from without (etic). The emic and the etic approaches have their parallels in the idiographic and nomothetic approaches in psychology, going back to Cronbach's characterization of "the two disciplines of scientific psychology" (1957). They are also similar to the hermeneutic versus positivistic perspectives in anthropology and the indigenous (or relativistic) versus the universalistic orientations of "cultural" versus "cross-cultural" psychology, respectively.

The common element in the idiographic, hermeneutic, emic, indigenous, relativist, cultural approaches is an emphasis on the uniqueness of phenomena in each cultural context because they derive their meanings from these contexts. Thus the unique individual (person, culture, etc.) is to be studied from within, in its own right, defying comparison. In contrast, the nomothetic, positivist, etic, universalistic, cross-cultural approaches study the "typical," not the unique, which can be compared on the basis of a common standard or measure. An underlying similarity is assumed, which renders comparison possible.

Our position in this chapter is that the two approaches can be, and should be, complementary, as proposed earlier (Kagitcibasi, 1992; 1996a). A comparative approach does not preclude a contextualistic orientation, for contexts are not necessarily unique; they can be compared. Culturally sensitive theory and applications can combine cultural contextualization with relevant universalistic standards, avoiding the pitfalls of both rigid absolutism and rampant relativism. Attempts toward discovering underlying reasons for behavior, situated in context, can provide insights into understanding what accounts for the observed similarities and differences among peoples. Thus, integrative functional analyses are called for.

The above conceptual issues provide the background for our discussion of the more specific topic of multicultural psychotherapy in this chapter. Before commencing on that discussion, however, we consider *why* the study of culture, and in particular multiculturalism, has surfaced recently in both research and applications. The reasons are to be found, at least in part, in the recently increasing prominence of ethnicity and ethnic differences in Western societies and particularly in the United States of America (herein, U.S.A.). With international labor migration, the formerly unicultural societies in Europe have also become multicultural. These changes, bringing with them pervasive human problems of discrimination, prejudice, ethnic conflict, etc., have challenged psychological applications, if not psychological theory. Thus, in dealing with intergroup conflict and prejudice, acculturative stress, immigrant adjustment, school failures, and minority problems in general, the applied psychologist/social scientist has had to confront "culture." In particular, multicultural counseling and clinical work has had to develop in response to the rising demand.

Such awakening to culture in the context of ethnicity has necessarily opened the way to a more global cross-cultural perspective in the West. Contemporaneously with these developments, psychologists in other parts of the world have also started questioning the ethnocentric stance of much of American psychology exported to the world. Of special significance has been the great economic growth in the Pacific Rim, providing the only example of economic wealth without an individualistic culture, which does not quite fit the modernization theory assumptions of individualization leading to cultural convergence toward Western patterns. Thus cultural diversity at all levels has become more apparent, influencing psychological thinking and discourse.

The implications of these changes for theory and applications are immense. Many questions need answers such as, "How does the family respond to socioeconomic changes in collectivist cultures?" "Are there points of convergence in response to changing lifestyles?" "How does the definition of the self differ in different cultures?" And, "What is the role of counseling/clinical psychologists in dealing with selves/families in different cultures (ethnic groups)?" The last question will inform our discussions to follow, both in terms of the theoretical underpinnings of multiculturalism and its implications for practice.

☐ Multiculturalism in the Context of Psychotherapy: The Turkish Case

This section aims to cover the application of multiculturalism in the enterprise of psychotherapy, with Turkish culture providing the context for case examples. We will do this from two different vantage points or aspects, both of which have implications for cultural heterogeneity and the forming of bridges across cultural differences. One aspect has to do with the application of therapies of Western origin in non-Western cultures, and the other involves therapy with an immigrant/minority population in a particular dominant or host culture.

These two issues are actually inseparable from each other in Turkish culture. Psychotherapy as a multicultural enterprise has usually been addressed in the context of a therapist–client pair from different cultures, mostly exemplified as a therapist from the dominant culture and a client from a minority group, as in the case of Turkish immigrants in Europe (Abel, Metraux, & Roll, 1987; Fisek & Schepker, 1997; Pedersen, Draguns, Lonner, & Trimble, 1976). The position taken here is that psychotherapy is a deeply multicultural experience for a therapist–client pair from the same non-Western culture, when they are relating within the framework of a therapy of Western origin. The assumptions and ideologies underlying the sense of selfhood and interpersonal relations in traditional Turkish culture are somewhat different from those underlying prototypic Western depictions of selfhood and relationship. Since psychotherapies are significantly informed by the cultural understandings pervading the contexts in which they were developed, application of therapeutic approaches outside of their frames of reference needs to be carefully investigated.

The need for care is especially evident for two individuals from two different sectors or social classes of a rapidly and nonuniformly changing, heterogeneous culture, such as the one under discussion, in which a therapist from the urban professional elite and a client of rural origin can be virtual foreigners to each other. Consequently therapeutic experience both in the Turkish context and in the immigration context involves transcending cultural differences, in short, seeking therapeutic convergence in a context of experiential divergence. What kind of multiculturalism is inherent in these experiences and its ramifications for the therapeutic enterprise are issues that will be discussed in the following pages. Therapeutic work with Turkish clients will provide the basis for specific examples.

☐ Psychotherapy as a Multicultural Experience: Meaning-making Across Cultures

The therapeutic relationship between any two people is a multicultural enterprise comprising at least two cultures. All therapists trained in whatever school are members of a psychotherapy culture with its own mores and norms, differing from their clients in this respect if in no other. The number of cultures represented can increase greatly however, as in the example of the first author who worked in the U.S.A. as a foreign, white, female, adult therapist with black, male, adolescent clients in a middle-class hospital context. It is clear from this example that reaching mutual understanding under such circumstances demands sensitivities above and beyond the usual therapist sensitivity inculcated in all beginning therapists.

Psychotherapy is primarily a meaning-making enterprise in which the people involved offer their individual understandings to each other and negotiate a shared meaning. Meaning itself is a socially constructed phenomenon; the individual fashions interpretations of experience in terms of schemas evolving from countless previous experiences of mutual meaning negotiation, for which the sociocultural context provides the matrix (Stern, 1995). Thus when two individuals collaborate to jointly create a shared meaning, the differences in their formative experiences and schemas have to be resolved. As Howard (1991) states, "One might see examples of psychotherapy as interesting cross-cultural experiences in story repair" (p. 194). It stands to reason that all social-structural, cultural, and historical variables serving to differentiate individuals are potential barriers across which negotiation, more specifically therapeutic negotiation, has to occur.

While all human interaction is a process of working and reworking meanings, achieved, failed, and reachieved attunements, the therapy process has the added element of deliberation on the therapist's part, to enter into the client's world, to understand it and to help gradually alter elements in it. What does a multicultural perspective bring to this process? It is evident that clear-minded therapist participation in such a mutual meaning-making process can best be accomplished if there is a systematic understanding of the potential contextual barriers to attunement. We feel the multilevel contextual systems perspective outlined below can facilitate such an understanding.

☐ A Multilevel Contextual Systems Perspective

When cultural differences are approached from a Multilevel Contextual Systems Perspective (Fisek, 1995b), the underlying differences in cultural assumptions regarding selfhood and relationship become clearer. The cross-cultural psychology literature includes a number of significant variables which occur systematically and describe variations in individual and social life (Kagitcibasi & Berry, 1989), and which can be summarized under the two key dimensions of "structure" and "relationship," dealing with social organization and interpersonal relations respectively (Fisek, 1995b). As a background for the following analysis, a schematic description of three important levels of experience and organization can be useful in identifying differences between prototypic Western and prototypic traditional Turkish experience.

At the cultural level, *"social structure"* describes societies in terms of a bipolar dimension ranging from a hierarchical/authoritarian structure to a horizontal/egalitarian one (Fiske, 1990; 1992; Hofstede, 1980; Hsu, 1985; 1996b; Roland, 1988). *"Relational ethos"* ranges from individualism/separateness to collectivism/relatedness (Kagitcibasi, 1985; 1996b; Triandis, Bontempo, & Villareal, 1988) in reflecting the preferred mode and extent of interconnectedness (Fisek, 1995b). Much of this kind of thinking in cross-cultural psychology has informed the work on individualism and collectivism (see Kagitcibasi, 1997a for a comprehensive review).

Some recent formulations have provided finer tuning. For example, Triandis (1994) and Singelis, Triandis, Bhawuk, and Gelfand (1995) have differentiated between vertical and horizontal individualism/collectivism. This conceptualization recognizes that both the individualistic and collectivist interpersonal relations can be hierarchical or egalitarian. As for "relational ethos," Kagitcibasi (1996b) has proposed two distinct dimensions: "Interpersonal Distance," ranging from separateness to relatedness, and "Agency," ranging from autonomy to heteronomy. There is a recognition here that autonomy does not necessitate separateness, as is often assumed in psychological theorizing, but that autonomy can coexist with relatedness.

While traditional Turkish culture is represented toward the hierarchical/relatedness end of these two dimensions, prototypic Western culture falls closer to the horizontal/separateness end (Fisek, 1982; 1993; Kagitcibasi, 1990; 1996b). At the family level, structure is seen in the dimension of *"gender and generational hierarchy"* which varies in strength and identifies the boundaries differentiating individuals and subsystems within the family system (Fisek, 1991; 1995a; Fisek & Wood, 1991; Minuchin, 1976; Wood, 1985). *"Proximity"* varying in degree, reflects the density and the emotional reactivity of the relationship network within the family (Fisek, 1991; 1995a; Fisek & Wood, 1991; Minuchin, 1976; Wood, 1985). Again, the prototypic traditional Turkish family with its strong hierarchy and high degree of proximity falls away from the prototypic Western family with its weak-to-moderate hierarchy and low-to-moderate proximity levels (Fisek, 1995b).

At the level of the self, the very definition of selfhood can be seen to differ across cultures (Landrine, 1992; Kagitcibasi, 1990; Markus & Kitayama, 1991; Roland, 1988; Shweder & Bourne, 1984). At one pole of *"self structure"* is the "familial self," an intrapsychic organization that allows the individual to find a niche for selfhood "within the hierarchic intimacy relations of the family," while the other pole contains the "individualized self," an intrapsychic organization which permits autonomous existence and development within a network of "contractual egalitarian relations" (Roland, 1988, pp. 7–8). *"Relational style"* for the familial self involves closeness through connections, an interpersonal given, while for the individualized self it involves closeness through autonomy, an interpersonal achievement. Needless to say, prototypic traditional Turkish and Western selves tend to fall respectively on the familial-and-connected versus individualized-and-autonomous poles of self structure and relational style (Fisek, 1995b). It is possible to extend the idea of the interconnected self beyond the family, though most often the interconnectedness does in fact occur within the family. Thus Kagitcibasi (1990; 1996a; 1996b) construes the more abstract relational self (versus the separated self). In a similar vein, Markus and Kitayama (1991) and Singelis (1994) differentiate the independent and the interdependent self.

An Evolving Multiplicity: Social Change and Immigration Effects

Social and economic change are disrupting the traditional hierarchical patriarchal structure of Turkish society, however relational ethos appears to remain strong (Kagitcibasi, 1990; 1996a). Family level hierarchy appears to be undergoing partial disruption in the weakening of control, but nurturant authority remains strong, and proximity remains relatively high (Fisek, 1991; 1995a, 1995b). At the individual level, such changes might be reflected in a new kind of organization variously called "relational autonomous self" (Kagitcibasi, 1990; 1996a, 1996b), "expanding self" (Roland, 1988), and "individuated/familial self" (Fisek, 1995b). Thus the individual is expected to act on the basis of his or her own predilections in addition to the privileges and duties ascribed due to his or her position in the family, but reliance on emotional interconnectedness remains a central feature of one's experience.

The transition from one kind of structure and relational style to another is neither uniform nor congruent. The effects of industrialization, urbanization, and increased educational opportunity have not affected all sectors of the society equally; while some sectors like the urban elite are seemingly indistinguishable from the prototypic Western type, other sectors remain unchanged, and some even seem to be choosing to return to an even more traditional lifestyle. The structural and relational consequences of the experiences of the urban dispossessed are as yet not even well-known. These statements are just a very rough depiction of the multiplicity evolving in the Turkish culture.

It is interesting that migration is an important factor in the multiculturalization of Turkish experience both intra- and internationally. The internal migrant, that is the recently urbanized peasant, and the external migrant, primarily the "Gastarbeiter" in Germany or the immigrant in Northern Europe, undergo experiences of some similarity, in moving from a situation with well-known parameters to one of multiple unknowns. In this process, quite divergent individual experiences, family forms, and cultural expectations coexist side by side. However, there are dramatic differences in the ease of adaptation to and coexistence with the different host cultures. The internal migrant, relying on relationship through connectedness, attempts to recreate his or her old context in the new surroundings through chain migration, making his or her urban locality a safe haven vis-à-vis the wider society. This allows a gradual acculturation and mutual accommodation since the boundaries with the wider society are somewhat permeable and the terms of existence are only partially imposed by the dominant culture (Fisek, 1995b). Thus the possibility exists for the migrant to integrate into urban life, not so much through assimilation but through the creation of a "common culture which includes differences" (Gokce et al., 1993, p. 350).

Such is not the case for the external migrant (Fisek, 1995b; Fisek & Schepker, 1997). In the foreign context, the terms of existence are virtually dictated by the dominant host culture. The external migrant individual or family cannot make use of the same mechanisms of adaptation as the internal migrant, or with the same ease. Rather, they are faced with the choice of assimilation or ghettoization, neither of which speaks to the ideals inherent in the concept of multiculturalism.

Research demonstrated that the general circumstances of majority–minority relationships in a society are of crucial importance (e.g., Ogbu, 1990). The minority status of the immigrant brings lower standing vis-à-vis the majority, both in terms of numbers and lower power/status in society. Furthermore there is often a confounding of ethnic minority status with lower social class standing. Given these barriers, cultural permeability and allowance of a sense of empowerment are minimal. This is especially the case where the host culture insists on seeing the migrants as guest workers, and not an accepted and integral but different part of the culture. Under these conditions it is difficult to talk about multicultural coexistence (Kagitcibasi, 1987; 1997b). Be that as it may, the foreign context also fosters changes in family and individual experience, so that in both cases traditional structures and relational styles begin to show modifications.

Integrative functional analyses promise to provide insights into why and how changes in familial and interpersonal relational patterns occur. This is particularly the case in the context of social and economic change that internal or international migration entails. In response to changing life styles and new environmental demands, certain changes in human relations take place. However, such changes do not appear to be an overall convergence toward the Western pattern, as assumed by modernization theory, but tend to involve modifications in dysfunctional (maladaptive) patterns along with continuities in functional (adaptive) ones in the new environment (Kagitcibasi, 1996a). Nevertheless, this is hardly a smooth process, with vicissitudes occurring in response to adverse experiences in the context of immigration or ethnic conflict. Given this background, let us look at multicultural experiences of therapy within the Turkish context and within the context of the immigration experience.

☐ Implications for Psychotherapy

While the multilevel systems perspective describes prototypic experience and as such is a generalization, it nevertheless allows us to draw
some inferences regarding the cross-cultural application of psychotherapy. The ideological underpinnings of Western therapies view the person
as an individual, self-contained unit (Sampson, 1988); he/she develops
a sense of self based on interpersonal negotiation with significant figures in his/her life (Roland, 1988). The ideal, mentally healthy person is
independent, autonomous, individuated, internally controlled, responsible for himself/herself and has an inner-based sense of self esteem
(Landrine, 1992; Sampson, 1988). A relationship is an understanding
or contract freely undertaken by two autonomous individuals (Cancian,
1989; Fisek, 1992; 1994). Thus, independence from others, meaning a
separate self (Kagitcibasi, 1996a; 1996b) is considered to be the healthy
prototype and a necessary condition for autonomy.

Psychotherapy is predicated on helping people who have difficulties
achieving the above stated attributes and goals. The trouble is that persons
who fit the traditional Turkish scheme of experience are by definition in
need of therapy according to these inferences, since they do not fit the
above listed definitions! More specifically, strong hierarchy in the family
can be seen as repressive; high proximity can be seen as enmeshment
or fusion; and the familial self experience can be seen as dependency
and constriction, even developmental arrest, from the viewpoint of the
above ideology—all of which require therapeutic change efforts. Thus,
Western-based psychotherapy in reference to such individuals runs the
risk of promoting an exercise in multicultural misdiagnosis, stereotyping,
and devaluation; in short, cultural bias parading as scientific wisdom.

Consider the family of the eight-year-old boy brought to a university
clinic for evaluation for attention deficit problems. Naturally his mother
accompanied him and was also interviewed. However the accompaniment
did not end there; his paternal uncle, paternal grandparents and preschool-
age sibling also came along. The initial reaction of the professionals who
saw this family in the waiting room was "What an enmeshed family!"
However the uncle spontaneously stated that he was the only one available
to give a ride from the family's quite distant residence, and the rest of the
family came along partly to see this part of the city where they had never
been before, and partly to satisfy their curiosity about how these clinics
worked, a quite justified curiosity considering how new and little known
such services are in the country.

Clearly, claims of the universal applicability of psychotherapeutic theory and practice need to be treated with extreme caution. However this is
no call for a "to each his own" type of cultural relativism, for good science

cannot be forged out of isolationist noncomparable practices. This notion is akin to Maruyama's critique of "homogenism," with the same risks to which he refers (Chapter 3 in this volume). Instead, what we need is a much better understanding of the mutually interactive roles of social-structural and relational factors in the formation of a sense of selfhood and community and the implications for psychotherapy. To provide an example, taken singly, strong family hierarchy or high proximity may indeed be deleterious to personal growth, family functioning and social life. But it is precisely the combination of the two factors that allows a sense of autonomous but connected selfhood, where hierarchy provides role-based inner differentiation and proximity fosters intimacy and personal depth beyond roles, thus allowing a healthy individuated/familial self (Fisek, 1995b) or an autonomous-relational self (Kagitcibasi, 1996b) to develop.

What the Therapist Brings to Psychotherapy: Multiple Biases

The therapist, like anybody else, is subject to the biases embedded in his/her particular socio-structural, cultural, and historical contexts, and which influence his/her approach to selfhood and relationships. In addition, however, as a member of a professional psychotherapy culture, he/she may be subject to one of two specific biases which influence how differences are construed. In talking about therapist biases, we will borrow an idea from Hare-Mustin and Marecek (1988) who identify two kinds of bias in approaching gender differences. These sources of bias apply equally well in dealing with cultural differences (Fisek, 1995b).

"Alpha bias" involves an exaggeration of the differences existing between two cultures. For the therapist of a host culture or an elite professional class dealing with a client from a different group, this would mean seeing the differences in behavior, values, and mores between the two cultures as being so great that finding a common ground would be difficult. The consequences of such an approach would be as follows:

Emphasis on differences classifies people in such a way that variability within each group is obscured, especially those due to social class. For example, an educated urban Turk will have more in common with an urban German than with a rural Turk in some ways, but this is obscured by classifying all Turks as being similar and different from all Germans. These dichotomies contain hidden hierarchies so that the ways of one group are valued more than those of the other. For example, when the prototypic Western norm of autonomy is used as a goal for therapy, this devalues the Eastern norm of interdependence that the client holds. Such distancing limits opportunities for meeting on common ground. Alpha bias does have the positive effect of highlighting the valuable aspects of the other culture. However here lies the risk of cultural relativism, which can bring about double standards, where what is good for members of the dominant culture is different for what is good for members of the other group; separate but equal can easily become separate and unequal.

In extreme cases, separation can become outright rejection, as in the case of the 19-year-old anorexic Turkish girl who had been living in Germany for many years. Her family apparently sought help when her weight loss reached a critical point. They were shunted between services and hospitals with statements such as, "Our unit does not have a Turkish speaker . . . we have a Turkish-speaking psychologist but this is an adult unit and she is an adolescent . . . there is a psychiatrist in X city three hours away who speaks Turkish." Finally they were given the phone number of the first author in Istanbul for the family to call and seek a hospital placement there. Needless to say the family members did not speak German!

"Beta bias" involves a denial of the differences that *do* exist between cultures. This bias underlies statements such as "we are all part of the human family," an admirable and partly true statement. The problem is that the underlying assumption of similarity all too often means "similar to me," thus obscuring the unique qualities of the other.

The most problematic outcome of beta bias lies in ignoring the differential impact of the social context, that is, differences in status, power, and resources on individuals. Members of the dominant or host culture and members of the "other" cultures do not benefit similarly for "neutral" procedures, and equal treatment is not always equitable. For example, the neutral therapeutic rule of punctuality to appointments can become a punishing and alienating procedure to someone who is not accustomed to the whole notion of civil contracts, and needs to have the rationale explained. Similarly, the psychotherapeutic rule of confidentiality can be alien to people with a familial self, and therapeutic boundaries need to be explained within their frame of reference. For example, it is not unusual for parents to make appointments for their adult children and expect to be included somehow in the therapeutic process, despite their avowals of understanding the confidentiality rule. Adolescents who may refuse to share any information with their parents often bring friends to sessions as seeming advocates, co-therapists, or "co-clients." Obviously, different construals of confidentiality are involved here and these differences need to be sorted out.

☐ What the Client Brings to Psychotherapy: Culturally-informed Expectations

All clients from all cultures come to psychotherapy with expectations comprising idiosyncratic factors, factors generic to the psychotherapy experience, as well as factors that are more specifically culturally informed. In the context of this discussion we will identify some cases of the latter as they find expression in Turkish culture.

Hierarchic positioning of the self or hierarchic intimacy relations (Roland, 1988) is an important part of the familial self, with two important features which find expression in psychotherapy. One is that of control and authority, which is more salient in more traditional hierarchic relations; while the other is nurturance, which is more salient in more modern relationships. The control aspect is seen in the attitude of respect and idealization toward the therapist (Roland, 1988). However, along with this comes the sense of hierarchic distance which can lead to an inclination to limit self-disclosure in order to protect one's sense of relative autonomy, to keep a sphere of experience free from the influence of authority, just as in hierarchic family relations. The nurturance aspect becomes manifest in a wish for mirroring (Kohut, 1977; Roland, 1988), for being understood without verbal explanations, for caring, for acceptance of one's one-down position, reflective of familial proximity.

The two features together present an almost existential tension between reserved holding onto one's individual autonomy versus allowing oneself to relax in the comfort of being taken care of by a respected authority. For the client with a changing self experience, this tension is overlaid with another source of tension, between ascribed familial identities and individualized developmental trajectories, reflected in psychotherapy as ambivalence, conflict, and estrangement from oneself and from one's context.

A female client—a high school dropout of rural origin, with a fairly conservative extended family network who is trying to develop an individuated sense of identity—described this tension thus: "Going from a crowded family of origin to our small families create trouble. Most young couples like this I know are depressive. The issue is how not to lose the small kinds of support which have great spiritual value, in this move."

□ Conclusion: Some Ingredients of Multiculturally-sensitive Psychotherapy

The following are some of the points of multicultural emphasis that emerge from the above analysis. While Turkish culture provides the specific example, it is our belief that the points made below can carry wider applicability and merit consideration whatever the culture in question:

Openness

Openness is, first of all, openness to one's own biases, the ideologies and assumptions underlying one's own therapeutic or theoretical subculture as well as one's personal culture. Conscious professional bias is more likely to be beta bias, accepting all humanity into an inclusive fold, albeit admitting "individual" uniqueness. However, individual uniqueness all too often obscures structural differences (i.e., differences based on being members of different social classes or cultures). This is something to which romanticized democracy is blind, and to which true multiculturalism should open our eyes. Alpha bias is more likely to work covertly and catch the therapist unawares in unwitting reactions to clients who seem different. To the degree that the therapist is aware of the contextual embeddedness of his/her own biases, it will be that much easier to protect against erroneous labeling, pathologizing, or depathologizing.

Systematic Contextual Awareness

The issue here is again one of meanings—how we construe the meaning of cultural similarity and difference, the language we use in our definitions. If the meanings produced by the alpha and beta biases create a difficulty for the therapeutic enterprise, then we need to develop new meanings, a new way of defining similarity-in-difference and difference-in-similarity. In this endeavor a contextual systematic analysis is useful because the parameters defining similarity and difference lie in the structures and processes that evolve in social contexts. Thus, the therapist has to develop an understanding of the client's context in his/her own words, including current circumstances as well as history.

Working Together

If contextual multicultural awareness is to encompass both the therapist and the client, it behooves the therapist to focus on the language with which he/she construes therapy. To the degree that this language includes "doing therapy, helping, correcting, curing, etc.," it may limit the therapist's ability to hear the client's story freely. To the degree that it involves "working together, talking together, discussing together," the therapist is forced to focus on the reciprocity involved in the process. This attention to language is another safeguard to protect true multicultural sensitivity, as it requires attention to the client's discourse, how it is similar to and different from that of the therapist.

The Turkish language is very rich in transactional verbs denoting reciprocal action (e.g., danishmak, tartishmak, anlashmak—to consult with, to argue with, to agree with). The reciprocal morpheme in these verbs denotes an at least two person reciprocal activity, refuting the possibility of an active agent doing something to a passive other. It would be especially

helpful for the Turkish therapist to attend to these verbs and how they influence the way in which he/she construes Western therapeutic concepts
in his/her language. This is also an aid to multicultural awareness. The key
words here are "attention, awareness, curiosity" (Falicov, 1995, p. 385).
Being curious is the most important prerequisite in a joint endeavor in
communication and discovery; it implies not knowing, wanting to learn
and accepting that the other can help one learn. This attitude leads to the
next step which is to develop a new set of meanings, a new story together.

Joining

Up until now we have talked about the therapist's attitude but here the
issue involves the therapist's acceptance by the client. An important point
in attempting to join a Turkish client and possibly others functioning on
a somewhat familial basis, is to be aware of the importance of hierarchy.
As stated before, the client coming for psychotherapy has owned up to
needing help and being in a one-down position vis-à-vis the therapist, yet
there remain a distancing and a tendency to keep one's own counsel about
certain things, thus placing a barrier in front of open communication.
Calling this behavior resistance without seeing the cultural ingredient in
it would be an example of beta bias and multicultural blindness.

The therapist must first of all be aware of this process and join across
this hierarchic divide by accepting the position into which he/she has
been placed. This means being comfortable with the one-up position,
not promoting false equality, rather, promoting togetherness. The contractual equality of two separate human beings in a contextual vacuum
is a Western phenomenon, and as such is not necessarily believable to
a non-Western client, while acknowledgment of being-with-each-other,
albeit in different positions, may be much more meaningful. A common
phrase used by clients of rural origin and/or lower class standing is "You
people who are educated..." thereby pointing out a reality of social differences which goes beyond professional identities. Therapists who do not
acknowledge this difference are being unrealistic and untrustworthy.

In the Turkish case, the way to join in this context will likely involve
symbolically relying on the ubiquitous discourse of kinship through which
strangers are accepted "as if" they were members of a virtual extended
family (Duben, 1982). This, along with the expectation of nurturance and
of being accepted in a one-down position, permits transcendence of strong
hierarchic boundaries, and allows intimacy while still respecting distance
and differentiation.

Consider the case of the 35-year-old, married returnee to university
life, who was disturbed by a female faculty member's sexually provocative

manner of dress and behavior in class. After much hesitation he prefaced his confession to his 30-year-old female therapist thus: "You are my sister (baci) so I can tell you this," compressing into this statement a world of meanings involving hierarchic intimacy, sexual taboos, and a way to communicate across taboos. Thus, the acceptance of an "as if" kinship position can facilitate communication, trust, and the feeling that the therapist is there for the client beyond the call of professional duty, and so too, the client's humanness is acknowledged. For the culturally changing client, acceptance of his/her ambivalence is important and meaningful only if the therapist communicates awareness of the cultural ingredient in it.

Effectiveness Within Constraints

The goal of psychotherapy in the widest sense is achieving some self-understanding and growth with more effective problem solving. In trying to achieve these goals, the therapist should be aware of the interactive roles of hierarchy and proximity in the family, and the wider context of the client, just as in the therapeutic situation. The democratic values of the psychotherapeutic culture, which hold that hierarchy is potentially dysfunctional and unjust, should not blind the therapist to the very real constraints in the context of the client. Respect for boundaries and their rationale needs to accompany confrontation of unjust hierarchy. In practice this means another source of creative tension, between exploring the possibilities of freedom of movement, and awareness of the limits to change that exist in the circumstances of the client.

☐ Summary: What Kind of Multiculturalism?

We would like to begin with what we think multiculturalism should not be. It should not be blind acceptance of diversity, which ultimately leads to isolationist cultural relativism. This raises the worst danger of alpha bias, a "to each his own" philosophy, which hides inequality and inequity, both within and across cultures. Nor should multiculturalism involve beta bias, a blind glossing over of diversity in a "melting pot of the human family," which in obscuring structural differences also hides inequality and inequity.

True multiculturalism is possible only with the integration of ethnic and other kinds of minorities. Integration, in turn, entails the protection and promotion of both the elements of the migrant's original culture and of the host culture. Pressure toward giving up of the original culture leads to "assimilation," and when the host/majority culture is rejected by the migrant/minority member (or denied him/her), we have separation (Berry, 1990). Yet the ideal of multiculturalism (and integration) carries the risk of accentuating (cultural) differences—the alpha bias. Unless concerted efforts are made to engender an appreciation of these differences, ideally through equal-status interdependent contact opportunities, increased awareness of differences may exacerbate the "us–them" type of thinking and lead to seeing the different one as inferior. Often the victim is blamed, and the problem is seen as located within the minority, yet what is needed is large scale sensitization/training of the majority toward an appreciation of the different, not deficient, cultures and languages coexisting in society (Kagitcibasi, 1997b).

Thus the kind of multiculturalism we are advocating rests on two related concepts: an acceptance if sameness-in-difference and difference-in-sameness, thus we are all members of the human family and are also different from each other, a sort of differentiated integration. The important thing to remember is that differences are due not only to unique and idiosyncratic features but also features that vary systematically with economic, social-structural, cultural and historical, even ecological constraints. It is precisely here that a multilevel contextual systems perspective can help us since it focuses attention on important variables underlying human experience at each level of human organization. These variables simultaneously constrain and open up different possibilities for selfhood and relatedness at each level of organization. Briefly put, multiculturalism means appreciation of the richness of human diversity provided we attempt to systematically understand what that richness entails.

☐ References

Abel, T. M., Metraux, R., & Roll, S. (1987). *Psychotherapy and culture.* Albuquerque, NM: University of New Mexico.

Berry, J. W. (1990). Psychology on acculturation. In R. Brislin (Ed.), *Applied cross cultural psychology.* Newbury Park, CA: Sage Publications.

Bond, M. H. (Ed.). (1988). *The cross cultural challenge to social psychology.* Newbury Park, CA: Sage Publications.

Cancian, F. M. (1989). Gender politics: Love and gender in the private and public spheres. In A. B. Skolnick and J. H. Skolnick (Eds.), *Family in transition: Rethinking, marriage, sexuality, child rearing, and family organization.* Glenview, IL: Scott Foresman Co.

Cronbach, L. J. (1957). The two disciplines of scientific psychology. *American Psychologist, 12,* 671–684.

Duben, A. (1982). The significance of family and kinship in urban Turkey. In C. Kagitcibasi (Ed.), *Sex roles, family, and community in Turkey* (pp. 73–99). Bloomington, IN: Indiana University Press.

Falicov, C. J. (1995). Training to think culturally: A multidimensional comparative framework. *Family Process, 34*(4), 373–388.

Fisek, G. O. (1982). Psychopathology and the Turkish family: A family systems theory analysis. In C. Kagitcibasi (Ed.), *Sex roles, family, and community in Turkey* (pp. 295–321).
Bloomington, IN: Indiana University Press.

Fisek, G. O. (1991). A cross cultural examination of proximity and hierarchy as dimensions
of family structure. *Family Process, 30,* 121–133.

Fisek, G. O. (1992). The feminization and romanticization of intimacy: A Western cultural
phenomenon. *American Family Therapy Association Newsletter,* Summer, 1992, 48.

Fisek, G. O. (1993). Turkey. In L. L. Adler (Ed.), *International handbook on gender roles.* Westport,
CT: Greenwood Press.

Fisek, G. O. (1994). Paradoxes of intimacy: An analysis in terms of gender and culture.
Bogazici Journal: Review of Social, Economic, and Administrative Studies, 8 (1–2), 177–186.

Fisek, G. O. (1995a). Gender hierarchy: Is it a useful concept in describing family culture?
In J. van Lawick and M. Sanders (Eds.), *Family, gender, and beyond.* Heemstede, The
Netherlands: LS Books.

Fisek, G. O. (1995b, October). *Contextual awareness in cross-cultural psychotherapy: The German-
Turkish experience.* Paper presented at the Klinik fur Kinder- und Jugendpsychiatric,
Rheinische Landes- und Hochschulklinik Essen, Essen, Germany.

Fisek, G. O., & Shepker, R. (1997). Kontext-bewusstheit in der transkulturellen Psychother-
apie: Deutsch-Turkische Erfahrung, *Familiendynamik* [Context consciousness in transcultural psychotherapy: German-Turkish experience. Family Dynamics.].

Fisek, G. O., & Wood, B. (1991, August). *Gender: An essential factor in the organization of proximity and hierarchy in families.* Paper presented in the Colloquium on Current Topics in
International Psychology, Seattle, Washington.

Fiske, A. P. (1990). *Structure of social life.* New York: Free Press.

Fiske, A. P. (1992). The four elementary forms of sociality: Framework for a unified theory
of social relations. *Psychology Review, 99,* 689–723.

Gokce, B., Acar, F., Ayata, A., Kasapoglu, A., Ozer, I., & Uygun, H. (1993). *Gecekondularda ailel-
erarasi dayanismanin cagdas organizasyonlara donusumu* [The transformation of interfam-
ily support into contemporary organizations in squatter settlements]. Ankara, Turkey:
Turkish Prime Ministry, Women and Social Science Bureau.

Hare-Mustin, R. T., & Marecek, J. (1988). The meaning of difference. *American Psychologist,
43*(6), 455–464.

Hofstede, G. (1980). *Culture's consequences: International differences in work-related values.* Beverly
Hills, CA: Sage Publications.

Howard, G. S. (1991). Culture tales: A narrative approach to thinking, cross-cultural psychology, and psychotherapy. *American Psychologist, 46*(3), 187–197.

Hsu, F. L. K. (1985). The self in cross-cultural perspective. In A. Marsella, G. DeVos and
F. L. K. Hsu (Eds.), *Culture and the self.* London: Tavistock.

Kagitcibasi, C. (1985). Culture of separateness—culture of relatedness in *1984:* Vision and
reality. Papers in *Comparative Studies, 4,* 91–99.

Kagitcibasi, C. (1987). Alienation of the outsider: The plight of the migrants. *International
Migration, 25,* 195–210.

Kagitcibasi, C. (1990). Family and socialization in cross-cultural perspective: A model of
change. In F. Berman (Ed.), *Nebraska Symposium on Motivation,* No. 37. Lincoln, NE:
Nebraska University Press.

Kagitcibasi, C. (1992). *Value priorities in Muslim-influenced countries: A cross-cultural perspective.*
Paper presented at the 25th International Congress of Psychology, Brussels, July 19–24,
1992.

Kagitcibasi, C. (1996a). Family and human development across cultures. Mahway, NJ:
Lawrence Erlbaum Publications.

Kagitcibasi, C. (1996b). The autonomous-relational self: A new synthesis. *European Psychologist, 1*(3), 180–186.

Kagitcibasi, C. (1997a). Individualism and collectivism. In J. W. Berrry, M. Segall, and C. Kagitcibasi (Eds.), *Handbook of cross-cultural psychology (2nd ed.)*, Boston: Allyn & Bacon.

Kagitcibasi, C. (1997b). Whither multiculturalism? *Applied Psychology: An International Review, 46*, 1(pp. 493–531).

Kagitcibasi, C., & Berry, J. W. (1989). Cross-cultural psychology: Current research and trends. *Annual Review of Psychology, 40*, 493–531.

Kohut, H. (1977). *The restoration of the self*. New York: International Universities Press.

Landrine, H. (1992). Clinical implications of cultural difference. The referential versus indexical self. *Clinical Psychology Review, 12*, 401–415.

Lonner, W. J. (1989). The introductory psychology text and cross cultural psychology: Beyond Ekman, Whorf, and biased I.Q. tests. In D. M. Keats, D. Munro, and L. Mann (Eds.), *Heterogeneity in cross cultural psychology* (pp. 4–22). Lisse, Netherlands: Swets & Zeitlinger.

Markus, H. R., & Kitayama, S. (1991). Culture and the self: Implications for cognition, emotion, and motivation. *Psychological Review, 98* (2), 224–253.

Minuchin, S. (1976). *Families and family therapy*. Cambridge, MA: Harvard University Press.

Ogbu, J. U. (1990). Cultural model, identity, and literacy. In J. W. Stigler, R. A. Shweder, and G. Herdt (Eds.), *Cultural psychology: Essays on comparative human development* (pp. 520–541). Cambridge, England: Cambridge University Press.

Pedersen, P. P., Draguns, J. G., Lonner, W. J., & Trimble, J. E. (1976). *Counseling across cultures*. Honolulu, HI: The University of Hawaii Press.

Roland, A. (1988). *In search of self in India and Japan*. Princeton, NJ: Princeton University Press.

Sampson, E. E. (1988). The debate on individualism. *American Psychologist, 43*(1), 15–22.

Segall, M. H., Dasen, P. R., Berry, J. W., & Poortinga, Y. H. (1990). *Human behavior in global perspective*. New York: Pergamon.

Shweder, R. A., & Bourne, E. J. (1984). Does the concept of the person vary cross-culturally? In R. A. Shweder and R. A. LeVine (Eds.), *Culture theory: Essays on mind, self, and emotion*. Cambridge, England: Cambridge University.

Singelis, T. M. (1994). The measurement of independent and interdependent self-construals. *Personality and Social Psychology Bulletin, 20*, 580–591.

Singelis, T. M., Triandis, H. C., Bhawuk, D. S., & Gelfand, M. (1995). Horizontal and vertical dimensions of individualism and collectivism: A theoretical and measurement refinement. *Cross-cultural Research, 29*, 240–275.

Stern, D. N. (1995). *The motherhood constellation*. New York: Basic Books.

Triandis, H. C. (1987). Individualism and social psychology theory. In C. Kagitcibasi (Ed.), *Growth and progress in cross-cultural psychology* (pp. 78–83). Lisse, Netherlands: Swets & Zeitlinger.

Triandis, H. C. (1994). *Culture and social behavior*. New York: McGraw Hill.

Triandis, H. C., Bontempo, R., & Villareal, M. J. (1988). Individualism and collectivism: Cross cultural perspectives on self–in group relationships. *Journal of Personality and Social Psychology, 54*, 323–338.

Van de Vijvir, F. J. R., & Hutschemaekers, G. J. M. (Eds.). (1990). *The investigation of culture*. Tiburg, Netherlands: Tilburg University Press.

Wood, B. (1985). Proximity and hierarchy: Orthogonal dimensions of family interconnectedness. *Family Process, 24*, 487–507.

CHAPTER 6

Leslie Swartz

Multiculturalism and Mental Health in a Changing South Africa

Notions of culture and multiculturalism in the mental health field in South Africa are changing. Cultural relativism was used as a justification for oppression by the previous regime, with some researchers therefore de-emphasizing difference. Currently, interest in diversity is growing. The racial integration of services poses challenges for culturally-appropriate care. Community-based care, apparently a way of meeting challenges of cultural difference, presents other difficulties. There has been uneven development in understanding indigenous healing in South Africa, a factor which may be explained partly by continuing ideological tensions. Debates around multiculturalism in the mental health field can contribute broadly to the challenge of nation-building.

Studies of culture and mental health in the apartheid era made it clear that the concept of culture as used in South Africa was anything but ideologically neutral (Swartz, 1986; 1987; 1998). Arguments about multiculturalism and cultural difference were used to legitimate shameful apartheid practices. Within the mental health field, inadequate and discriminatory services were justified with recourse to the idea that different cultures had "different" needs in the mental health field. Psychological suffering as a response to iniquitous social and economic conditions (such as the separation of families through the migrant labor system) was often seen by

This chapter is a revised version of Culture and Mental Health in the Rainbow Nation: Transcultural Psychiatry in a Changing South Africa, *Transcultural Psychiatric Research Review*, 33, 119–136, 1996.

mental health researchers as primarily a problem of cultural adjustment. By placing cultural difficulties as central to experiences of exploitation, mental health research was culpable in defocusing from patterns of political and socioeconomic abuse (Swartz, 1986; 1987).

Helman (1994) views culture as a

> "... set of guidelines (both explicit and implicit) which individuals inherit as members of a particular society, and which tells them how to *view* the world, how to experience it emotionally, and how to *behave* in it in relation to other people, to supernatural forces or gods, and to the natural environment. It also provides them with a way of transmitting these guidelines to the next generation—by the use of symbols, language, art and ritual" (pp. 2–3).

The political environment in South Africa necessitates taking on a broad definition of culture, making explicit from Helman's definition that culture also includes relationships of power and change. The notion of cultural difference or multiculturalism, wherever it is used, always has a political and ideological dimension (Lock, 1990). This has become more and more obvious over the past decade internationally, and especially following the break-up of the Soviet Union. But arguably, one of the major contributions (in the 1980s in particular) of South African scholarship in the social sciences was the careful exploration of the political dimensions—not only of the notion of cultural difference, but also of many other terms which may easily be taken for granted (Boonzaier & Sharp, 1988).

Within this context, taking up any position on debates concerning multiculturalism as a fourth force becomes difficult, not because the debate is unimportant within the mental health field, but because of the local ideological consequences of taking up a position. Thinking about multiculturalism in South African mental health care, as I shall show later, inevitably involves thinking about what the constructions of that term would be in different South African contexts or discourses. When Murphy (1977) wrote that "transcultural psychiatry should begin at home," his statement was especially apposite to South Africa, where an examination of the cultural process in the construction of culture is necessary. Any clinical practice which is not culturally and politically informed runs the risk of reproducing cultural stereotypes. In this sense, it may be more appropriate to refer to multiculturalism not as a fourth force but as an overarching approach which bears thinking about however one is working. The infusion of problematic notions of culture and multiculturalism into all aspects of mental health care in South Africa has been established (Swartz, 1985; 1991); in this chapter I focus on more recent developments.

The remarkably rapid political changes in South Africa, culminating in the installation of the African National Congress-led Government of

National Unity in 1994, raise a host of questions about the issues which preoccupied many scholars and mental health practitioners in the apartheid period. What has happened to the notion of cultural difference, now that the government is led by a political party with a longstanding ideological position of nonracialism and inclusivity? (Nonracialism as an ideology involves a commitment to equal treatment of all South Africans, but it goes further than this—it explicitly attempts to break away from divisive policies which emphasized difference.) To what extent are mental health services in the "new" South Africa culturally appropriate and accessible to the entire population? What effect, if any, do there now being 11 official languages have on mental health training and service provision? What are the mental health implications of the rapid transition itself?

These are very broad questions which cannot be comprehensively answered here and which would require a great deal of careful research. In outlining some of the responses of the social sciences and mental health fields in South Africa to the changes of the past decade, I shall, for this chapter, focus not on breadth of coverage of the literature, but rather on some key areas central to understanding the nature of the changes and challenges ahead. I shall also rely more heavily than is usual on personal observation, as the rapidity and complexity of change in South Africa throws up issues and experiences which are seldom documented but which encapsulate important processes. The area on which I shall focus is that of changing ideas about cultural difference and its significance in South Africa. I shall then more briefly consider issues of change in mental health services, with special emphasis on language issues and the training of mental health personnel for the "new" South Africa. I shall also consider the question of indigenous healing in the light of attitudes towards diversity. In focusing on these areas I do not claim to be offering a comprehensive analysis of the mental health challenges facing South Africa—this is not my aim here.

☐ Reclaiming Culture?

Progressive South African anthropology in the 1980s, as I have mentioned, played an important role in pointing out the degree to which terms like 'culture' and 'ethnicity' are socially constructed (Sharp, 1980; 1988; Thornton, 1988). The exposure of these terms as socially constructed, however, as I have pointed out elsewhere (Swartz, 1992), is not the sole aim of these critiques. Authors like Sharp (1988), and Thornton (1988), at that time, aimed not only to problematize cultural relativism as a social construction but also to present universalism (another social construction) as more accurately reflecting reality:

"In the marketplace and workplace, listening to music or watching television, at homes and in churches, people *in fact* experience the same desires, profess the same religions, follow the same leaders, and eat the same
cornflakes, notwithstanding their multicultural condition" (Thornton, 1988,
p.18, emphasis added).

The political importance of statements such as this, at the time of the
intensification of the struggle for a new, nonracial society, cannot be too
heavily stressed. For those interested in the psychological experience of living in apartheid society, however, such statements are profoundly unsat-
isfying in that they rule out of court—as a misperception—the experience
that many people had living under apartheid that there were profound,
possibly unbridgeable gaps between people of different races, or cultures
(cf. Kottler, 1990). Essential though it was for it to be shown that the very
terms "race," "culture," and "ethnicity" were political terms not based
on any respectable "real" ("biological") differences, the terms profoundly
affected, and will continue to affect the construction of South African
emotional life—including the life of desire, emotion, and the following
of leaders. (It is interesting to note in passing here that this momentous
South African anthropological critique of "ethnicity," in tending to gloss
over the individual's psychological experience of "ethnicity," has parallels
with issues in the discipline of psychological anthropology as a whole, as
discussed by Shweder, 1990.)

Against the backdrop of the perceived political necessity of a universalist view of culture in the late 1980s and early 1990s, it is significant
that this period also saw increasing emphasis chiefly by black authors
on the importance of the legacy of the South African black consciousness movement of the 1970s. A volume aimed at giving rightful place to
the contribution of Steve Biko, the activist killed in detention in 1977,
(Pityana, Ramphele, Mpulwana, & Wilson, 1991) stresses throughout the
psychological importance of the assertion of positive black identity and
self-reliance. Black South African psychologists, in the tradition of which
Manganyi (1991) was an early exponent, have been quick to emphasise
the importance of recognizing the psychological centrality of black experience, and of the possibilities that this recognition brings for personal
and political transformation (Nicholas, 1994). In the light of this counter-
point to universalism, it is significant that the most recent publication by
one of the intellectual leaders of the black consciousness movement of the
1970s, a physician-anthropologist, is an autobiography (Ramphele, 1995).
For the purposes of the current argument, the use of the autobiographical
form by Ramphele is important for two key reasons. Firstly, the autobiography is a form which profoundly (and especially as used by Ramphele)
foregrounds both the psychological experience of oppression, and the psychological processes involved in personal and political empowerment. In

this respect, Ramphele's work has links with Manganyi's (1991) earlier interest in biography and autobiography as formats which could usefully address issues both of the exploitation of black people and of their liberation. A second important feature of the Ramphele autobiography is that, though she makes very clear the continuities between her present position (amongst other roles, Ramphele is vice-chancellor of the University of Cape Town, an historically white institution) and her political history, Ramphele is currently viewed by many as politically very much within the inclusivist tradition favored by the African National Congress. What Ramphele is suggesting both through her writing and through her current position as a major player in the health and education fields in a politically nonracial society—a society which refuses to categorize and administrate on the basis of race—is that there is room within a broadly inclusive political dispensation in South Africa for a positive affirmation of differences between people. It is beyond the scope of the present chapter to discuss the heated debates between Ramphele and those who regard themselves as more legitimate custodians of the black consciousness cause in South Africa. The central issue here however is that the possibility of recognizing both the political importance of nonracialism and the centrality of divisions along the lines of race, sex, class, and so on to people's lives, can have far-reaching consequences for the ways in which mental illness is understood in this country, and in how services are structured, as I shall argue later in this chapter.

What may crudely be labelled as a "black consciousness response" to the limitations of nonracial ideology has been paralleled by developments in the approach of some major proponents of universalism in the social sciences. Introducing a set of papers from a major conference in 1993 on the theme of "Ethnicity, Identity and Nationalism in South Africa," McAllister and Sharp (1993) speak of "the ethnic taboo," and note that

"To discuss ethnicity was somehow to legitimate its existence, and thus to legitimate apartheid. It was not politically correct to make it the object of academic scrutiny. There are still South Africans who feel this way, but the tide has turned" (p. 7).

Though there was reference at the conference to the unscientific nature of the definition of "race," and concern on the part of some participants that South Africans should avoid thinking in divisive terms,

"... most participants seemed to accept that it is, as Claude Levi-Strauss and other structuralists would have argued, a universal feature of human mental activity to differentiate and to categorise, to distinguish and to label" (McAllister & Sharp, 1993, p. 8).

Ethnicity as a legitimate object of study, through statements such as these, is very much back on the map of South African social science research. Equally important, other contributions to the conference highlighted some problems which had received less prominent attention during the period in which it was necessary to expose the politics of cultural relativism in South Africa. Thus, Degenaar (1993) explores what he terms the "myth of the nation" (p. 16), and demonstrates the extent to which the idea of an inclusive nation-state is in itself historically and ideologically constructed. Simpson (1993) points out further that "nation-building is far from an unproblematic, unilinear, irreversible process" (p. 17). He refers to the fragmentation evident in the postmodern (and post-Cold War) world as demonstrating not only that the politics of ethnicity have enormous salience currently, but also that the idea that a nation can be constructed simply and permanently in a deeply divided society is an idea which does not take the lessons of contemporary world events into account.

An important area focused on at the conference was that of the politics of Zulu identity (de Haas & Zulu, 1993; Hamilton & Wright, 1993). The question of the future of the KwaZulu/Natal province remains arguably the most pressing and vexing political problem in South Africa today. The continuing appalling rate of violence in that region and elsewhere, strongly related to the politics of ethnic mobilization, is a mental health challenge which has not begun to be addressed adequately (McKay, 1995). In an account of the difficulties facing South Africans in negotiating issues of difference in a context where even mentioning difference some years ago was seen as racist, Kottler (1996) makes reference to the position of Harriet Ngubane (probably best known internationally as a medical anthropologist who studied Zulu healing [Ngubane, 1977]) at the University of Cape Town in the 1980s. On entering a world of anthropologists who were suffused in what Kottler (1996) terms the "similarities discourse," Ngubane refused to deny what were, to her, important areas of difference. The fact that Ngubane is currently a member of parliament for the Inkatha Freedom Party, the party involved in violent conflict at the grassroots level with the African Nation Congress in KwaZulu/Natal, and mobilized around the issue of Zulu ethnic identity, is not irrelevant to the present discussion. It is more important to note, though, that this political route (as opposed to a more centrally nonracial route) has been the one chosen by an academic who has made a significant contribution to the literature on cultural aspects of illness and healing. For whatever reason, Ngubane has made her political home in a party the policies of which do not focus on nonracialism. Kottler (1996) ends her analysis with a call for us to find "a way of speaking about difference without invoking a racialist discourse." The gulf between the hope expressed in this statement and the continuing reality of the difficulties with the notion of difference in

South Africa has implications for mental health services, as will be seen in the following section.

These debates are, of course, not simply local South African ones, as I have mentioned earlier. Cultural difference can be, and has been, used as a resource by minorities in a number of countries, including the United States of America (herein, U.S.A.), to improve their position politically and materially (Thornton, 1988). Attempts in the U.S.A. to incorporate the considerable knowledge available on cultural difference into the *Diagnostic and Statistical Manual of Mental Disorders* (4th ed.) (Mezzich, Kleinman, Fabrega, & Parron, 1996) have been muted at least partly by issues concerning the politics of the professional identity of psychiatry (Good, 1996; Lewis-Fernández & Kleinman, 1995). Movements into naive biologism (as opposed to the many spectacular true strides that biological psychiatry is making) can similarly be related at least in part to responses to an increasingly fragmented social world (Eisenberg, 1995). The fact that by the second half of the next century there will no longer be a white majority in the U.S.A. (Eisenberg, 1996, p. xiii) must have consequences for power relationships, and for how all people, including mental health practitioners, grapple with the idea of cultural difference. Multiculturalism as an attempt to incorporate a few people on the edges of society becomes a very different issue when the numerical majority in the society may be seen as out of step with the dominant norms and ideals of that society, as South African history shows. Looking elsewhere in the world, ideas about ethnicity and ethnic purity are implicated in the devastation of parts of Eastern Europe, Asia and Africa. The global challenge for the ideals of multiculturalism, it may be said, is how to allow for and maintain a space for multiple identities (and multiple nuances in health and social service provision) while at the same time not sanctioning discrimination. Postmodernity also offers challenges to formerly unproblematized ideas about identity—it becomes increasingly difficult to think of identity in any fixed way, especially in a world of creolization, massive population movements, and a world in which technology and the internet are changing how we think about identity, and about community (Bibeau, 1997; Turkle, 1995). The idea of community has also taken on a particular local flavor in South Africa, once again with implications for other countries, as will be seen below.

☐ Integrating Services, Finding Communities

Racial desegregation of psychiatric services in South Africa began in earnest in the early 1990s. In many cases, desegregation of psychiatric services occurred later than the desegregation of general medical services—testimony both to the complexity of psychiatric care and to its particular ideological construction and role. Catchment areas for hospitals have in general been redrawn to cover geographical areas rather than "racial" groups.

The political victory involved in the desegregation of psychiatric facilities has been considerable, especially in the case of the many facilities which became integrated ahead of the new political dispensation in South Africa. But although there has been much discussion about how the process has gone (and, in my experience, much amazement at the smoothness of the changes) there has been little written about the cultural changes engendered by integration of services by race. Observations from a small study of the process of integration of two psychotherapeutic units (Roth & Swartz, 1992) suggest that clinicians involved in the integration process have so much invested in the process that difficulties and challenges may be almost impossible to consider in a sustained way. In the unit studied by Roth and Swartz (1992), it appears that there was an implicit fear that to speak about the challenge of difference was to reinvoke racism and to imply a wish to return to unequal services segregated by race. This fear and lack of attention to the problems of managing difference, notably out of place in a therapeutic milieu the values of which strongly promoted talk about all emotional issues, can be seen to relate very strongly to the ideological imperative, in the progressive South African context, of abandoning a culturally relativist stance in favor of inclusivism. A major problem with this position, though, is that it may well have silenced patients' concerns about identity in a changing environment. It could also, paradoxically, silence talk about the development of a positive black identity (in the black consciousness tradition and as exemplified in the work of Ramphele, 1995) which could be a key resource in the therapeutic process for black patients.

The integration of services has taken many black patients from vastly inferior physical environments in psychiatric institutions to formerly whites-only wards. But this is not necessarily the same as the provision of equal care. Examining the issues of integration of a psychiatric hospital formerly set aside for "colored" patients but now admitting large numbers of African patients, Drennan (1995) notes a number of serious problems. Many of these revolve around language—there is a serious shortage of staff able to communicate with patients, and only one interpreter for an entire hospital. The result is that many patients are treated simply on the basis of the staff's observations of their behavior, a situation which is in the interests neither of the patients nor the staff, and which raises serious ethical questions. It is paradoxical that when hospitals were segregated and catchment areas organized by race rather than simply by geographical boundaries, these patients would have been treated in a hospital further from where they lived but which had available wards in which the nursing staff were able to converse with them. In the process of integration of services, therefore, in a climate in which differences are downplayed for important political reasons, some patients may well now have lost access to care which is linguistically appropriate. An irony of the integration process (having been conducted as it was in the context of shrinking rather than expanding resources) is that in terms of having a qualified person to talk to about their difficulties, some patients may have been better off in segregated wards, appalling though many of those were in terms of physical conditions.

The restructuring of services has consequences at all levels of care. Psychiatric community services are now organized more logically on a geographical basis. Though this is welcomed by the personnel involved, it was noteworthy at a workshop on transcultural issues in psychiatric nursing in 1994 that there have not been the resources available to equip practitioners with the skills to work with linguistically and culturally diverse patient loads. The moral and political imperative to "treat all patients equally" is at odds with the clinical experience of practitioners' being confronted with patients they find difficult, and at times impossible (for reasons of language difference) to understand. In this context, networking with appropriate community resources, an integral part of appropriate community care, also becomes extremely difficult. Clearly, nonracial services make new demands on practitioners accustomed to (and skilled at) working in a segregated system.

The challenges that this situation holds for training of practitioners are considerable. Many training institutions (such as the clinical psychology training wing of the University of Cape Town) have set in place proficiency in an indigenous language as a prerequisite for new trainees. Given the linguistic diversity of the country, however, this cannot solve all the problems of service provision. More focused analyses of linguistic needs and policies are required.

Once again, though, the apparently simple task of adding to services such that there will be culturally appropriate care becomes more complex in application than might have been thought. Swartz and Maw (1996) describe the "bicultural workers project" through which black undergraduate psychology students who are fluent in Xhosa have been trained in counselling skills and act as interpreters in a range of mental health contexts. In a study of this project, Bass (1996) found that though one of the central reasons for its having been set up was to address cultural and linguistic diversity amongst clients, the experience for the student bicultural workers was that participation in the project threw into sharp focus their own position at a formerly "white" South African university. They found a channel, through working on the project and participating in the research, for articulating their sense of alienation from an institution which had a history and inherited structure with which the students had difficulty in identifying. One of the primary lessons of that project was that any intervention to make services more culturally accessible impacts on the service providers themselves and even on the structure of service provision.

This leads to a consideration of changes in professional mental health culture in the light of linguistic and cultural diversity. Swartz, Drennan, and Crawford (1997) suggest that since language skills are so central to mental health care, these should be given a more prominent role in deciding the work of different practitioners. Psychiatric nursing sisters, for example, are far more likely to be able to speak the languages of a wide range of patients than are psychiatrists and clinical psychologists, and it may be advisable to employ nursing personnel in roles formerly defined as not their appropriate professional domain. Redeployment of personnel in this manner has implications for training practitioners, and for the engagement of South Africans in a serious consideration of the role of professional culture in providing access to, but also blocks in, the path of appropriate care.

As is the case in many other countries, the racial and gender profiles of professions strongly mirror the power of those professions. The higher one is in the professional hierarchy from psychiatric nursing, to social work and occupational therapy, clinical psychology, and finally to psychiatry, the more likely one is to be white and male. That this situation needs to change is uncontested, and there have been vigorous attempts on the part of many institutions to train more black mental health professionals. Kleintjes and Swartz (1996), however, have shown that there are considerable obstacles faced by black clinical psychology trainees in an historically "white" university, obstacles similar to those faced by black undergraduates (Bass, 1996). Respondents to the Kleintjes and Swartz (1996) study note that what one of them termed the "colorless zone" of the liberal university silenced talk about race and deligitimated the respondents' experience of feeling alienated from the university. In the training context, then, the necessity of facing issues of difference and not obscuring these in a well-meaning inclusivist policy are clear. This observation has implications for patient care, and for our understanding of being a black patient in a white-dominated mental health service context.

A major shift in health policy in South Africa over the past few years has been towards the primary health care approach as exemplified in the Alma Ata Declaration of 1978. The full implications of this shift for mental health care are profound and will not be dealt with here, but I shall make very brief mention here of some ways in which the move to primary health care interface with issues of multiculturalism in mental health.

The integration of mental health care into primary health care presents both practical challenges and reorientation of professional practice—and especially the practice of primary health care personnel, nursing staff in particular (Pillay, Bhana, Bhagwanjee, Parekh, & Petersen, 1994). Primary mental health care depends as well upon the assessment of "community

needs" (Masilela, Macleod, & Tollman, 1994) and the meeting of these local needs in as accessible and as affordable a manner as possible. This much
is central to the primary health care approach, and is uncontested. In fact,
at a recent conference on mental health policy in Cape Town, the parallel
session workshop on community mental health care was oversubscribed to
the extent that there was insufficient space for participants, and competing
workshops attracted only a handful of participants (Petersen et al., 1997).
Interestingly, the term "community" is no less ideologically constructed
than is the term "culture" (Thornton & Ramphele, 1988). An important
line of inquiry for the future should be the extent to which the notion of
"community" as a more politically acceptable term than "culture" in the
South African context is allowing for old debates in mental health care
to be translated into another language without any fundamental change
of topic. For example, in the past it was possible to discuss different approaches to the use of healing systems by referring to cultural differences;
the same issues would probably be more likely to be discussed now by
reference to community needs. Both the terms "cultural differences" and
"community needs" can however be used as a presumptive way of speaking for the "other." Neither term guarantees (ideologically neutral) access
to people's realities and needs.

   I am not suggesting here that there are not important substantive issues
associated with the attempt to integrate mental health care into primary
health care. It may be the case however that the (socially constructed) idea
of the homogeneous and bounded community which apparently provides
a clear focus for mental health work on a local level may have replaced that
of the homogeneous "culture" which has its own needs. By focusing on
communities rather than cultures, therefore, mental health practitioners
may be avoiding the political issues which are involved in the definition
of both terms, but which are certainly more obvious in the South African
construction of "culture." A further area in which ideological factors play
an important role is in the question of the relationship between professional mental health care and indigenous healing, and I shall consider this
in the following section.

☐ The Question of Indigenous Healing

Since the 1970s at least, there have been many calls in South Africa for
the recognition of the mental health role of indigenous healers. These
calls have tended to be stated in the most general of terms (Swartz, 1986;
1987). With some notable exceptions, they failed to consider the political and resource implications of formal recognition of indigenous healing
as a mental health resource. There has also been a lack of engagement

with the question of the possible tensions between considering indigenous healing as an efficacious method of attending to the mental health needs of individuals and exploring indigenous healing practices as processes of communal social reproduction and regulation. How has the debate on indigenous healing developed in South Africa, and to what extent have the issues of a decade ago been taken up and transformed?

There has been a great deal written about both indigenous healing and indigenous beliefs about illness and misfortune in South Africa over the past decade, and a full review of this literature will not be considered here. One notable change in the literature in this area has been increasing concern with witchcraft-related murders and abuse, which have apparently been on the increase in South Africa (Minnaar, Offringa, & Payze, 1991; Prinsloo & du Plessis, 1989). Evans and Singh (1991) and Minnaar et al. (1991) suggest that witchcraft-related murders may be understood in terms of social stressors and political factors at a time of violent social upheaval. A second continuing strand in the literature on indigenous healing is that of ethnobotany and toxicology, in which substances used by indigenous healers are explored for their organic effects (Joubert, 1989; van Eeden, 1991). By far, the bulk of the literature on indigenous healing in South Africa, however, continues to concern itself with the social and personal healing aspects of indigenous healing, and with the question of the relationship between indigenous healing and biomedicine (Blackett-Sliep, 1989; Bodibe, 1988; 1989; Edwards, 1986; 1987; Mdluli & Msomi, 1989; Motlana, 1988; Nzima, Edwards, & Makunga, 1992; Pretorius, 1989; Zungu, 1992). A remarkable feature of this literature (with some exceptions —notably Motlana, 1988) is that authors are almost uniformly well-disposed to indigenous healing, claiming efficacy and community acceptability of such healing, often without any evidence presented in support of this view. Exhortatory statements to respect indigenous healing, aimed at an implied sceptical reader, and making reference to the cultural congruence between the healer and the community, are common, for example:

> "Traditional healers are greatly respected in their communities as both accept the supernatural world" (Blackett-Sliep, 1989, p. 42).

> "The task of scholars in the therapeutic field should not . . . be that of scoffers and scornful critics of indigenous healing, but rather of serious students of this indigenous healing system" (Bodibe, 1989, p. 299).

> "Contrary to modern Western misconceptions, traditional healing is a complex system of learning far removed from the field of magic and quackery" (Zungu, 1992, p. 24).

This body of literature generally makes no reference to work dealing with problems associated with witchcraft, and when witchcraft is mentioned, it tends to be contrasted with respected and helpful healing, with the implicit educational aim of helping the reader not to confuse the two

(Zungu, 1992). A graphic, very recent example of ways in which indigenous healing is discussed was seen in the events at the recent conference on mental health policy referred to earlier. One of the plenary sessions of this conference was addressed by Chavunduka (1995), himself a respected Zimbabwean indigenous healer and sociologist (see, for example, Chavunduka, 1994; Last & Chavunduka, 1989). In line with the literature reviewed here, the presentation argued for the importance and value of indigenous healing. In the discussion of the presentation, a speaker from the floor raised the question of the abuse of indigenous healing and witchcraft, and some debate ensued. At the end of the conference, one of the few resolutions passed without objection by a plenary session concerned the value and necessity of recognizing the positive role indigenous healing plays in mental health care in South Africa. No resolutions were passed raising concerns about witchcraft or the potential abuse of indigenous healing.

It is important to interrogate this acceptance of indigenous healing, ignoring the debates that did take place, and without the careful analyses that some anthropologists working in southern Africa have given to the issues (see, for example, Green, 1997; Reynolds, 1996). It is at least in part an empirical question whether indigenous healing "works" in South Africa, and I am not in any position to comment on how accurate the claims made for indigenous healing are. Even if all the claims are entirely true, however, there is a structuring of the argument about indigenous healing in South Africa which needs attention. To an important degree, the literature supporting indigenous healing is part of the global dissatisfaction with biomedicine, and an increasingly respectful attitude towards alternative therapies. Farmer (1997) has commented on the tendency in the social sciences to discuss folk healing with uncritical praise, arguing: "If folk healing were so effective, the world's wealthy would be monopolozing it" (Farmer, 1997, p. 355). It is beyond my task here to comment fully on why internationally there is something of a tendency to praise indigenous healing often without evidence for its value, but it is important to note that this praise may be related to what Lucas and Barrett (1995) have termed Arcadian primitivism. Lucas and Barrett argue that the idea of the primitive is central to much cross-cultural debate. There are, however, two images of the primitive which recur in the literature— the Barbaric perspective which "equates primitive society with degeneration, disruption and pathogenesis" (p. 289), and the Arcadian perspective, which "treats primitive societies as pristine, harmonious, and therapeutic" (p. 289). These rather fixed images, the authors argue, tend to influence the ways in which writers in the mental health field view the other.

A fixed image of primitivism—probably of an Arcadian type—may be partly responsible for the fact that if one examines the literature, much of what is currently being said in South Africa about indigenous healing has not changed in any important respect from the literature on the subject from twenty years ago. Although the overwhelming majority of articles are supportive of indigenous healing, though, many are written as if this support is not the general view. It may be the case that the experience of authors who write in this field is out of step with published literature—in other words, that many people are critical of indigenous healing but do not publish their criticisms. Though I have no formal evidence on this issue, my experience of discussion with colleagues is that this possible discrepancy is unlikely to explain the situation fully. Another possible explanation for the widespread lack of movement in the field from what is often a moralistic or exhortatory call to the reader to a more nuanced consideration of indigenous healing may lie precisely in the area of the ideological construction of cultural difference in South Africa. The area of indigenous healing, though it is written and spoken of a great deal, is presented to a large degree as unexplained and mysterious to a predominantly white audience—the image of the Arcadian primitive looms large here. The methods which are used to explore and interrogate the efficacy of other forms of healing tend not to be used, and there is a great deal of *description* of the indigenous healing processes rather than *analyses* of these processes. It may be partly true that the methods for exploring the efficacy of other healing forms are not entirely applicable to the study of indigenous healing (though the work of authors such as Edwards (1986) suggest that this is not necessarily the case). But the literature as it stands reinforces an area of "African culture" as fundamentally unknowable to outsiders. It casts scepticism of the processes of indigenous healing, and the desire to interrogate these processes, as evidence of a morally or ideologically problematic position—in short, a failure of respect for "African culture."

During the apartheid era, it was easy to see how the construction of mystery around indigenous healing which was presented by (mainly white) authors as the "natural" choice of black South Africans could be used to legitimate a situation of lack of equal "Western" services for black services (Swartz, 1986). Such services could be cast as culturally inappropriate for blacks, and the lack of them could be legitimated by the argument that blacks prefer, and are better served by, indigenous healing. Currently, though, when the need for redistribution of services in favor of previously marginalized groups is undisputed, the uncritical and largely static discourse on indigenous healing may be playing another function. In the context of an overarching inclusivist approach informing the debates on the redistribution of mental health resources, indigenous healing remains an exclusively black domain (though it is of course true that some whites do use such services, and not all blacks use them). Indigenous healing becomes an area in which the difficulties surrounding the politics of the universalism/relativism debate can ostensibly be suspended. Indigenous healing is presented in essentialist terms as a black enterprise, and, through the relative lack of serious critical interrogation of the practices, refractory to understanding by Westerners. Indigenous healing, then, can function at this juncture both as a site of assertion of power and resistance on the part of black authors and as an arena in which white practitioners can legitimate their own lack of understanding of many of their fellow-citizens. Indigenous healing, in short, provides a site at which cultural difference is asserted as essential even in the context of an overall inclusivist ideology.

☐ Conclusion

The study of indigenous healing in South Africa serves to remind us that, far from now being ideologically neutral, the mental health field, and specifically the field of multiculturalism and mental health, remains profoundly influenced by ideology. The fact that debates on indigenous healing have not been more developed and possibly remain a site of resistance is telling. This fact speaks of the degree to which a dominant overt inclusivist ideology has not dealt adequately with the experience of alienation and marginalization still experienced by many South Africans in the mental health field.

More generally, I hope that I have shown in this chapter that debates around the issue of multiculturalism, and, indeed, transformation of service provision, are affected by and contribute to more general political issues in South Africa, and elsewhere in the world. Part of the international contribution of South African cultural psychology currently may continue to be able to demonstrate a context in which the political and ideological underpinnings of the entire discipline are more obvious than in some other settings. Post-apartheid society does not provide an ideologically neutral context for multiculturalism. Indeed, it throws up new challenges for locating the construction of culture within an ideological context.

☐ References

Bass, N. (1966). A qualitative exploration of the UCT Child Guidance Clinic's bicultural workers programme: Can formalised mentoring programmes assist in the transformation of South African Clinical Psychology? Unpublished honours research project, Department of Psychology, University of Cape Town.

I am very grateful to Ilse Ahrends for research assistance, to the Centre for Science Development for financial support, and to Paul Pedersen for his patience as editor. The views expressed in this chapter, and the conclusions reached, though, are mine alone, and not those of any other person or organization.

Bibeau, G. (1997). Cultural psychiatry in a creolizing world: Questions for a new research agenda. *Transcultural Psychiatry, 34,* 9–41.

Blackett-Sliep, Y. (1989). Traditional healers and the primary health care nurse. *Nursing RSA, 4,* 42–44.

Bodibe, W. J. M. (1988). The inclusion of traditional healers in a mental health team—a social work perspective. Unpublished M. A. thesis, University of South Africa.

Bodibe, W. J. M. (1989). The inclusion of traditional healers in a mental health team—a social work perspective. *Social Work, 25,* 298–299.

Boonzaier, E., & Sharp, J. (Eds). (1988). *South African keywords.* Cape Town, South Africa: David Philip.

Chavunduka, G. (1994). *Traditional medicine in modern Zimbabwe.* Harare, South Africa: University of Zimbabwe Publications.

Chavunduka, G. (1995, October). Traditional healers: Implications for mental health policy development in Africa. Paper presented at the Regional Conference on Mental Health Policy, Cape Town.

de Haas, M., & Zulu, P. (1993). Ethnic mobilisation: KwaZulu's politics of secession. *Indicator South Africa, 10*(3), 47–52.

Degenaar, J. (1993). No sizwe: The myth of the nation. *Indicator South Africa, 10*(3), 11–16.

Drennan, G. (1995, November). Language services and integration: The emperor's new clothes. Paper presented at the University of Cape Town Department of Psychiatry research day.

Edwards, S. D. (1986). Traditional and modern medicine in South Africa: A research study. *Social Science and Medicine, 22,* 1273–1276.

Edwards, S. D. (1987). The isangoma and Zulu customs. *University of Zululand Journal of Psychology, 3*(2), 43–48.

Eisenberg, L. (1995). The social construction of the human brain. *American Journal of Psychiatry, 152,* 1563–1575.

Eisenberg, L. (1996). Foreword. In J. E. Mezzich, A. Kleinman, H. Fabrega, Jr., and D. L. Parron (Eds.), *Culture and diagnosis: A DSM-IV perspective* (pp. xiii–xv). Washington, DC: American Psychiatric Press, Inc.

Evans, J., & Singh, P. (1991). Muti murders: Ritual responses to stress. *Indicator South Africa, 8*(4), 46–48.

Farmer, P. (1997). Social scientists and the new tuberculosis. *Social Science and Medicine, 44,* 347–358.

Good, B. J. (1996). Culture and DSM-IV: Diagnosis, knowledge and power. *Culture, Medicine and Psychiatry, 20,* 127–132.

Green, E. C. (1997). Purity, pollution and the invisible snake in southern Africa. *Medical Anthropology, 17,* 83–100.

Hamilton, C., & Wright, J. (1993). The beginnings of Zulu identity. *Indicator South Africa, 10*(3), 43–46.

Helman, C. (1994). *Culture, health and illness: An introduction for health professionals* (3rd ed.). Oxford, England: Butterworth-Heinemann.

Joubert, P. H. (1989). Acute poisoning caused by traditional African medicines. *South African Journal of Continuing Medical Education, 7,* 821–828.

Kleintjes, S., & Swartz, L. (1996). Black clinical psychology trainees at a 'white' South African university: Issues for clinical supervision. *The Clinical Supervisor, 14,* 87–109.

Kottler, A. (1990). South Africa: Psychology's dilemma of multiple discourses. *Psychology in Society, 13,* 27–36.

Kottler, A. (1996). Voices in the winds of change. In S. Wilkinson and C. Kitzinger (Eds.), *Representing the other: A feminism and psychology reader* (pp. 57–63). London: Sage Publications.

Last, M., & Chavunduka, G. (Eds.). (1989). *The professionalisation of African medicine.* Manchester, England: Manchester University Press, in association with the International African Institute.

Lewis-Fernández, R., & Kleinman, A. (1995). Cultural psychiatry: Theoretical, clinical, and research issues. *The Psychiatric Clinics of North America, 18,* 433–448.

Lock, M. (1990). On being ethnic: The politics of identity breaking and making in Canada, or *nevra* on Sunday. *Culture, Medicine and Psychiatry, 14,* 237–254.

Lucas, R. H., & Barrett, R. (1995). Interpreting culture and psychopathology: Primitivist themes in cross-cultural debate. *Culture, Medicine and Psychiatry, 19,* 287–326.

Manganyi, N. C. (1991). *Treachery and innocence: Psychology and racial difference in South Africa.* Johannesburg, South Africa: Ravan Press.

Masilela, T., Macleod, C., & Tollman, S. (1994, September). Community-based needs assessment: A crucial component of mental health policy development. In Y. Pillay, A. Bhana, A. Bhagwanjee, A. Parekh, & I. Petersen (Eds.), *Proceedings of the primary mental health care workshop, University of Durban-Westville, September* (pp. 75–81). Durban, South Africa: University of Durban-Westville.

McAllister, P., & Sharp, J. (1993). The ethnic taboo. *Indicator South Africa, 10*(3), 37–40.

McKay, A. (1995, November). *Community intervention for rehabilitation of survivors of torture and violence.* Paper presented at the 7th International Symposium of the International Rehabilitation Council for Torture Victims (IRCT): Caring for survivors of torture: challenges for the medical and health professions, Cape Town, South Africa.

Mdluli, S., & Msomi, D. (1989). The day the nyanga came to call. *Nursing RSA, 4,* p. 15.

Mezzich, J. E., Kleinman, A., Fabrega, H., Jr., & Parron, D. L. (Eds.). (1996). *Culture and diagnosis: A DSM-IV perspective.* Washington, DC: American Psychiatric Press, Inc.

Minnaar, A., Offringa, D., & Payze, C. (1991). The witches of Venda: Politics in magic potions. *Indicator South Africa, 9*(1), 53–56.

Motlana, N. (1988). The tyranny of superstition. *Nursing RSA, 3,* 17–18.

Murphy, H. B. M. (1977). Transcultural psychiatry should begin at home. *Psychological Medicine, 7,* 369–371.

Ngubane, H. (1977). *Body and mind in Zulu medicine: An ethnography of health and disease in Nyuswa-Zulu thought and practice.* London: Academic Press.

Nicholas, L. (Ed). (1994). *Psychology and oppression.* Johannesburg, South Africa: Skotaville.

Nzima, D. R., Edwards, S. D., & Makunga, N. V. (1992). Professionalisation of traditional healers in South Africa: A case study. *University of Zululand Journal of Psychology, 8*(1), 82–93.

Petersen, I., Bhagwanjee, A., Parekh, A., Giles, C., Gibson, K., & Swartz, L. (1997). Community mental health care: Ensuring community participation. In D. Foster, M. Freeman, & Y. Pillay (Eds.). Mental health policy issues for South Africa (pp. 55–68). Cape Town: MASA Multimedia.

Pillay, Y., Bhana, A., Bhagwanjee, A., Parekh, A., & Petersen, I. (Eds.). (1994, September). *Proceedings of the primary mental health care workshop, University of Durban-Westville, September.* Durban, South Africa: University of Durban-Westville.

Pityana, N. B., Ramphele, M., Mpulwana, M., & Wilson, L. (Eds.). (1991). *Bounds of possibility: The legacy of Steve Biko and black consciousness.* Cape Town, South Africa: David Philip, and London: Zed Books.

Pretorius, E. (1989). Skakeling tussen tradisionele en moderne geneeskunde in Afrika. Die dekade sedert Alma Ata [Contact between traditional and modern medicine in Africa. The decade since Alma Ata]. *Acta Academica, 21*(2), 101–129.

Prinsloo, M. W., & Du Plessis, J. H. (1989). Towernaarmoorde, rituele doding en medisynemoorde in Venda [Witchcraft murders, ritual killing, and traditional medicine murders in Venda]. *Tydskrif vir die Suid-Afrikaanse Reg, 4,* 617–624.

Ramphele, M. (1995). *Mamphela Ramphele: A life*. Cape Town, South Africa: David Philip.

Reynolds, P. (1996). *Traditional healers and childhood in Zimbabwe*. Athens, OH: University of Ohio Press.

Roth, L., & Swartz, L. (1992). The integration of two psychotherapeutic units: Staff experiences of the first six months. *South African Journal of Occupational Therapy, 22*(2), 6–11.

Sharp, J. (1980). Can we study ethnicity? A critique of the fields of study of South African anthropology. *Social Dynamics, 6*, 1–16.

Sharp, J. (1988). Introduction: Constructing social reality. In E. Boonzaier and J. Sharp (Eds.), *South African keywords* (pp. 1–16). Cape Town, South Africa: David Philip.

Shweder, R. A. (1990). Cultural psychology—what is it? In J. W. Stigler, R.A. Shweder, and G. Herdt (eds.). *Cultural psychology: Essays on comparative human development* (pp. 1–43). New York: Cambridge University Press.

Simpson, M. (1993). Nation-building: A post-apartheid superglue? *Indicator South Africa, 10*(3), 17–20.

Swartz, L. (1985). Issues for cross-cultural psychiatric research in South Africa. *Culture, Medicine and Psychiatry, 9*, 59–74.

Swartz, L. (1986). Transcultural psychiatry in South Africa. Part I. *Transcultural Psychiatric Research Review, 23*, 273–303.

Swartz, L. (1987). Transcultural psychiatry in South Africa. Part II. *Transcultural Psychiatric Research Review, 24*, 5–30.

Swartz, L. (1991). The reproduction of racism in South African mental health care. *South African Journal of Psychology, 21*, 240–246.

Swartz, L. (1992). Professional ethnopsychiatry in South Africa: The question of relativism. In A. D. Gaines (Ed.), *Ethnopsychiatry: The cultural construction of professional and folk psychiatries* (pp. 225–249). New York: SUNY Press.

Swartz, L. (1998). *Culture and mental health: A southern African view*. Cape Town: Oxford University Press.

Swartz, L., Drennan, G., & Crawford, A. (1997). Changing language policy in mental health services: A matter of interpretation? In D. Foster, M. Freeman, & Y. Pillay (Eds.), Mental health policy issues for South Africa (pp. 160–180). Cape Town: MASA Multimedia.

Swartz, L., & Maw, A. (1996, July). Language accessibility and training in clinical psychology: Experiences at the UCT Child Guidance Clinic. Proceedings of *Communication for the health professions in a multi-lingual society* (pp. 68–82). (Ed. W. Loening), Durban, South Africa.

Thornton, R. (1988). Culture: A contemporary definition. In E. Boonzaier &. J. Sharp (Eds.), *South African keywords* (pp. 17–28). Cape Town, South Africa: David Philip.

Thornton, R., & Ramphele, M. (1988). The quest for community. In E. Boonzaier & J. Sharp (Eds.), *South African keywords* (pp. 29–39). Cape Town, South Africa: David Philip.

Turkle, S. (1995). *Life on the screen: Identity in the age of the Internet*. London: Phoenix.

van Eeden, J. A. (1991). Plante vir menslike behandeling—'n gevallestudie van 'n Xhosa-medisynespesialis [Plants for treatment of humans—a case study of a Xhosa medicine specialist]. *South African Journal of Ethnology, 14*, 43–54.

Zungu, H. (1992). Traditional healers in the work situation. *People Dynamics, 10*, 23–25.

CHAPTER 7

Gunnel A. M. Backenroth-Ohsako

Multiculturalism and the Deaf Community: Examples Given From Deaf People Working in Bicultural Groups

Today deaf people are demanding to be recognized as a cultural and linguistic minority group. Deaf people constitute a unique subculture in society. The Deaf community has had a more difficult time overcoming inferiority stereotyping by the majority culture than other minority groups, since deaf people have been viewed as a disability group. Members of the Deaf community are nowadays defining themselves as a cultural and linguistic minority group, not a disability group. Although individual members of the Deaf community have varying degrees of linguistic competence, they are nevertheless bilingual. Today the perspective of hearing loss is enriched by not only medical aspects, but also psychological aspects and sociocultural aspects. The cultural deficit model—stating that norms and cultural patterns of minority groups varying from the majority groups mostly were deviant and destructive—has been replaced by a bicultural model. The Deaf community has become increasingly pluralistic, suggesting that it gradually will give room for more individualism and gradually less collectivism. Furthermore, the Deaf community has increasingly developed away from the melting pot model where oralism reigned in society coloring education and in deaf people's relation to the professional establishment dealing with questions pertaining to the Deaf community. The multicultural mosaic model can best be applied in today's society since interaction between deaf and hearing people is facilitated by mediating deaf individuals having cultural competence in both the Deaf community and the hearing dominant society. These mediating bicultural people—or multicultural people—attempt to bridge the gap between deaf and hearing people. The Deaf community is gradually becoming multicultural as deaf professionals are working on European and International levels and in various capacities are dealing with questions of interest for the Deaf community, in developing countries, and in the United Nations, where they enrich existing knowledge and furthermore interact and mediate between deaf and hearing people.

The human being, a social animal, develops through interaction with other human beings in a society during a specific historical, cultural, economic, and sociopolitical period. Erikson (1968) maintains that human development depends on human interaction and is influenced by its culture. It was maintained already in the 1930s that human problems cannot be separated from their cultural contexts (Horney, 1937). According to Erikson, human beings are born into a given society, into given social groups, and given cultural norms, and this presents possibilities as well as limitations. Thus the cultural prerequisites are inbedded in the child's developmental possibilities (i.e., potentials are inherent as well as limitations). Erikson stresses the importance of the mother's ability in conveying hope based on the cultural values in the environmental context in which the child is raised. It is imperative that the mother is firmly rooted in her own cultural standards and to the existing hope inherent in her particular culture. Furthermore the definition of hope must be contextually relevant outside the nuclear family (i.e., in society).

Past and current research on culturally different populations is culturebound and this in itself results in a narrow view of the meaning and importance of culture. At worst, research on racial/ethnic minorities has portrayed minorities in the majority society as pathological, maladjusted, or deviant (see Sue, Ivey, & Pedersen, 1996). No culture is better than another. Every culture—hearing culture and deaf culture—generates problems. It is essential to view reality from both perspectives, to understand the difficulties and to realize the potentials. An exaggerated or a rigid upgrading of a certain cultural context—idealization—may hamper personality development and unable us to employ adequate coping mechanisms to handle diversity, changes and crises throughout our life-cycle. Lack of professional cultural competence in the area of deafness bears consequences on many areas, for example education, staff training, counseling, rehabilitation, guidance, and vocational training. It is imperative that we provide a more comprehensive educational program at different levels making professionals more culturally competent and sensitive. As hearing professionals, besides taking a genuine interest in the deaf culture, we need a new way of looking at things and we need to find mutual opportunities for learning. We need to learn from deaf people and deaf people must have a key role in the cultural training of hearing professionals.

Multiculturalism refers to a new perspective in mainstream psychology, characterized as a fourth force complementing the three other major theoretical orientations in psychology; i.e., psychodynamic theory, existential-humanistic theory, and cognitive-behavioral theory, addressing the needs of culturally diverse client populations (Pedersen, 1991). Berry (1991) states that: "Multiculturalism is meant to create a socio-political context within which individuals can develop healthy identities and mutually positive intergroup attitudes...some consider diversity to be valuable and seek ways to maintain or enhance it; those we call 'multicultural' or 'integrationist'..." (p. 24).

There are two kind of multiculturalism which can be interpreted as the melting pot model and the mosaic model. The melting pot model on the one hand, assumes that all cultural groups are influenced by one another, resulting in a more or less favorable cultural identity. In reality this means that everyone has to give up the original culture's myths. In this model, a dominating culture absorbs all minority cultures, allowing them only to influence areas such as art, music, literature, or food. The majority culture requires, and represents, what is regarded as normal. The mosaic model, on the other hand, is founded on an interaction between the majority and the minority cultures which also helps preserve and facilitate the cultural identity of the majority group. Social skills are learned in connection with needs arising from interacting with the dominant culture. Furthermore, mutual respect and motivation are important with regard to collaboration. Links are established by mediating bicultural or multicultural individuals, groups, or institutions (Bochner, 1986). An important criticism of multiculturalism is the argument that maintaining interest in enthnicity merely perpetuates ethnic stratification: multiculturalism may serve only to keep particular groups in their place. Furthermore, it may provide a basis for discrimination (see Berry, 1991). A controversial issue in the training of cross-cultural counseling skills is whether to assume a universalist approach or a culture-specific approach (see Leong & Kim, 1991). Multiculturalism recognizes the complexity of culture and the importance of cultural awareness. Multiculturalism is a fourth force and has gained the status of a general theory complementing the three other forces, namely psychodynamic, behavioral and humanistic theories explaining human behavior. "The multicultural perspective seeks to provide a conceptual framework that recognizes the complex diversity of a pluralistic society while, at the same time, suggesting bridges of shared concern that bind culturally different persons to one another...combining the specific and general viewpoints provides a multicultural perspective" (Pedersen, 1991, p. 7). In the present chapter, multiculturalism is addressing the needs of a minority group—the Deaf community—defining themselves as a cultural and linguistic minority group within a multicultural society. Multiculturalism is used in a broad sense, in that deaf people are regarded as unique individuals, as members from different ethnic/nationality backgrounds, and as members of a separate linguistic/cultural group. Thus individual differences, ethnic differences, and cultural differences are recognized within the Deaf community in the context of the dominant hearing culture.

Americans are more aware of cultural and linguistic diversity than has been the case in the past, and this is clearly stated in curricular and textbook reform, bilingual education, and multicultural educational programs (see Reagan, 1988). Furthermore: "The efforts to make the school a more sensitive, tolerant, and humane place for children from 'dominated' backgrounds, however, have consistently overlooked or ignored the deaf as a dominated cultural and linguistic minority" (Reagan, 1988, p. 1). The Deaf community is trimodial in that three communicative modes: oral, written, and signed communications are employed by its members, Reagan maintains. Most educators teaching deaf people have been hearing people, and the hiring of deaf professionals has been resisted. Educators and educational policy-makers in bilingual and multicultural education, have generally overlooked the fact that they may be seen to be an oppressed and dominated cultural and linguistic minority (Reagan, 1988). Traditionally, the American Sign Language (ASL) functioned as a language of group solidarity (Erting, 1978) serving both to demarcate the membership boundaries of the Deaf community and to prevent hearing people from gaining access to the culture. This is now beginning to change and ASL is becoming a forum for the culture itself, and hearing as well as deaf are being portrayed in a more favorable light (Reagan, 1988). In different social situations within the Deaf community different types of signing will be used (Stokoe, 1970). Embracing multiculturalism in practice is not easy, Sue (1992) points out. Regarding disabled populations, denial of the relevance of cultural diversity ought to be avoided (Marshall, 1996).

The purpose of this chapter is to test the generic application of multiculturalism in the Deaf community by reviewing international research and documentation in the area and by illustrating the multicultural application with results from two Swedish studies. The following are the assumptions upon which the chapter is based: (a) although the awareness varies considerably between deaf people, deaf people constitute a bicultural–bilingual minority group in the majority hearing society (i.e., the two relevant cultures are the deaf culture and the hearing culture and that the two relevant languages here are SSL [Swedish sign language] and Swedish); (b) the Deaf community, as well as the hearing society, is heterogeneous in its composition (i.e., there are within-group differences in the Deaf community); (c) deaf culture can be characterized as collectivistic

(i.e., including individuals with strong ties to each other having the motivation to live up to the norms of their in-group); (d) the social interactions
between the deaf person and his/her deaf versus hearing colleagues are
reflected by the bicultural identity and the bilingual competence the deaf
person possesses; (e) deaf people share many characteristics with hearing
people but also possess characteristics referring to the Deaf community, as
well as unique characteristics referring to the individual deaf person; and
(f) the implications of deaf people's biculturalism and bilingualism has not
sufficiently permeated working life.

☐ Is There a Deaf Culture?

The Deaf community constitutes neither a large nor a particularly visible
minority group in our society and thus, it has been easy to overlook it in
the past (Reagan, 1988). Even though deaf people constitute a minority
group in the hearing-dominant culture, they are also a part of the hearing
culture through their hearing family. As the deaf child grows up, he/she
gradually becomes aware of the deaf culture. Similarly, the parents gradually become acquainted with a "new world" (the Deaf community) or
culture through their child.

"The very nature of culture is that it establishes and defines certain
patterns of behavior that exist in, and are unique to, one group, but are
different between groups. These customs are shared and sanctioned by
the group. Each culture provides a model, a measuring stick, by which the
individual behaviors may be prescribed or restricted ... yet culture is far
more than behavior and custom ... Culture is the collective expressions of
the group's personality—its wishes, values, and ideology ... Cultural roots
are planted in childhood and grow deep" (Tseng & McDermott, 1981,
pp. 6–7). The culture, partly, influences the way the individual copes with
his or her perceptual world, providing cognitive structures (i.e., schemata,
concepts, categories, stereotypes, expectations, attributions, associations,
perceptions) (Taft, 1977). As a great deal of our culture seems to be im-
parted implicitly and non-verbally (Stone & Church, 1973), it is difficult
to study. Culture is transmitted through the family. When cultural competence is achieved in later life it may be called enculturation (Herskovits,
1948; Mead, 1963) and it is a process of conscious and unconscious conditioning (Herskovits, 1948).

The parents are the child's first and most influential environmental factors, as regards to personality, social and intellectual development, and
cultural identity. Stone and Church (1973) maintain that incorporating
culture is not a value-free process: "... there is no escaping the process of
cultural learning. A child can develop only in contact with adults during

a long apprenticeship, and there are no culture-free adults..." (p. 151). The child's first hour of life is of utmost importance for communicative processes and interaction in the family. Psychological research (Mahler, Pine, & Bergman, 1975) has demonstrated that the first hour of life constitutes the child's very first sense of identity. Mothers who have just given birth are emotionally open; this applies even to the most withdrawn of women. Emotional openness provides an enormous possibility for mother and child. This "imprinting process" probably serves to enhance the probability of survival. This primitive sense of identity, this warm and secure symbiosis between mother and child, is most favorable. Deficiencies in interplay between the parents and their hearing-impaired/deaf child may result in disturbed parent-child relationship. Parents' reactions to their deaf or hearing-impaired child has been described as a crisis requiring professional intervention and social support from other parents in the same or in a similar situation (Backenroth, 1983; 1984; 1987). Deaf children with hearing parents are more likely to harbor a secret resentment of hearing people than deaf children of deaf parents (Jacobs, 1974). Hafer and Richmond (1988) underline that learning about deaf culture is a lifelong process for hearing parents. The starting point for the learning should—ideally—begin during their child's preschool years. Furthermore, "Learning about deaf culture at this early stage will help parents accept their child, make a strong commitment to using sign language, and make informed decisions about educational placements. As their chid grows and develops, parents' questions and concerns about deaf culture will change" (Hafer & Richmond, 1988, p. 3). According to Erikson (1968), a developmental psychologist and a social psychologist, in every phase of a child's development there is an inherent psychosocial crisis. Every phase of development—if successfully mastered—offers an ethical value (hope, motivation, purpose, competence, loyality, love, care, and wisdom). Infancy is, Erikson maintains, the period when the child learns whether the world is a good and satisfying place in which to live or a source of misery and frustration. This phase provides the foundation for attitudes of optimism or pessimism to the world in general. Parents' attitudes of unconditional love, trust, and respect are essential for the child's developmental possibilities. An attitude of basic trust encourages the development of a variety of emotional responses facilitating an openness to new experiences and an ability to master reality. It is in infancy that the foundation for the future is laid, upon which subsequent developmental phases may grow. Thus, this phase constitutes a very important period in the child's life. Difficulties occurring later in life emanating from abberations in this phase are, for example, emotional detachment, mistrust, and incapacity for permanent relationships, all of which are of importance when establishing and fostering social relations.

In adulthood, deaf people, like many other minority groups in society, develop mutual support systems and networks of friendships (Higgins, 1979). Deaf people themselves prefer to call these informal support systems and friendship bonds of the deaf community (Jacobs, 1974), the deaf subculture (Quigley & Kretschmer, 1982), and the deaf culture (Freeman, Carbin, & Boese, 1981). Padden & Humphries (1988) use the lower case "deaf" when referring to the audiological condition of not hearing, and the upper case "Deaf" when referring to a particular group of deaf individuals sharing a language and a culture. What are the criteria for membership of the Deaf community? Gregory (1992) emphasizes a common language, a person's acknowledged identification with Deaf people and participation in the life of the Deaf community. Hafer & Richmond (1988) claim that the Deaf community includes deaf, hearing impaired, and hearing individuals—usually spouses or the children of deaf parents. The ability to sign well is by and large an essential criterion. Furthermore, "The deaf community comprises those deaf and hard-of-hearing individuals who share a common language, common experiences and values and a common way of interacting with each other and with hearing people. The most basic factor determining who is a member of the deaf community seem to be what is called 'attitudinal deafness.' This occurs when a person identifies him/herself as a member of the deaf community and other members accept that person as part of the community" (Baker & Padden, 1978, p. 4). Deaf people are linked by their language and by their attitude to it. Community membership is an active and positive attitude towards association with other deaf people (Kyle & Woll, 1985). Not all deaf people participate in the deaf community, as is seen in previous studies (Backenroth, 1986; 1992a; 1992b; 1993). Loneliness is experienced in the deaf community either by a personal or an enforced choice (Backenroth, 1993). In an earlier study (Backenroth, 1989), 12 out of 20 deaf subjects (60%) claimed that self actualization meant, for example, participating in two cultures (i.e., the deaf community and the hearing society).

The Deaf community is not a homogeneous community, but utterly heterogeneous to its character (Nash & Nash, 1981; Kyle, 1990) even though individual members share similar experiences, commitment, and have a common language. There are within-group differences in the Deaf community regarding communication skills, motivation to communicate and choice of communication mode. There are, for example, deaf people who use signing in the Deaf community and with hearing people mastering sign language, and use their voices and utilize their lip-reading capacity when interacting with hearing people who are not in command of sign language. There are also deaf people who use their speech to such a degree that signs only become supporting. And there are deaf people who communicate only in sign language, refusing to utilize both their lip-reading

capacity and their voice. Jacobs (1974) states that the common link between deaf people stems from the fact that they share the same problems
and frustrations in the hearing-dominant society. In the Deaf community
they can relax among other deaf people and communicate in sign language without obstacles. For many deaf people, the association of the deaf
constitutes perhaps the most important area in life, in that it offers the
opportunity to develop social networks as well as derive an existential
meaning (Backenroth, 1991). The Deaf community may, in Bott's (1955)
terms, be characterized as a "relatively closed community" (i.e., corre-
sponding to the Swedish local society). The Deaf community is a small
group and "everybody knows each other." As a consequence, social control
increases. Deaf people's working lives and work situations have changed
in pace with increasing professionalization. However, until the middle of
the 1960s, the primary occupations of deaf people in the United States of
America (herein, U.S.A.) were either shoe repair, upholstery, printing,
factory assembly, teachers, or dormitory supervisors at residential schools.
Deaf people in management was very rare. Social clubs for deaf people
have a diminished role today, due to the accessibility of television, tele-
typewriters and videocassette recorders (see Padden, 1996). An important shift in deaf people's work lives has been from essentially a one-class
community to a split working-class and middle-class community. Another
important shift has been the growth of a professional class in the Deaf community (see Padden, 1996). Different classes of deaf people emerge: "The
anxiety over boundaries is partly class-related. When the Deaf middle class
left the Deaf clubs, they took a certain amount of class anxiety with them,
reflected in the nostalgic ways in which they talk today . . . The 'real' culture, as it was in the old days . . . But the reality is that Deaf clubs attract
far fewer attendees than they did thirty or forty years ago, if they still exist
at all, and their impact on the professional class of Deaf people is more
nostalgic than political or social" (Padden, 1996, p. 95). Barriers in communication between hearing and deaf people lead to difficulties on the
part of deaf people which prevent them from establishing close relationships with hearing people: ". . . they may find it difficult to experience fully
the closeness, acceptance, and shared identity traditionally associated with
family. Many deaf people experience some level of frustration in interactions with hearing family members . . . At school and work the separation
persists" (Foster, 1996, p. 129). Another difficulty is the deaf person's inability to gain access to important information. Knowledge about norms
and values in a culture is, for most people, acquired through natural development. This is not the case for the deaf person: "The communication
barriers many deaf people face over a lifetime of interactions with hearing
people make it difficult for them to acquire the wealth of social and cultural
knowledge which hearing people learn incidentally, through observation

and overhearing the conversation of others" (Foster, 1996, p. 130). An ear-lier study described how a cultural subgroup of deaf people (i.e., a group of mediating deaf individuals), experienced their work situation and social relations together with their hearing colleagues (Backenroth, 1995). The mediating individual is characterized by the capacity to select, combine, and synthesize appropriate aspects of both cultures without losing their cultural "core." Mediating individuals furthermore act as links between different cultural systems. They bridge the cultural gaps by introducing, translating, representing, and interpreting their respective cultures to one another (Bochner, 1981; Furnham & Bochner, 1986). Mediating deaf in-dividuals can be regarded as links between the deaf culture (to which they belong) and the hearing society (in which they are working). Furthermore they could be said to interpret two cultures in a bicultural working group. It may thus not be a random choice that these deaf mediating persons are working in bicultural working groups and in professions requiring social contacts, such as in education, service, information and counseling. Ac-cording to research on mediating individuals (Bochner, 1981; Furnham & Bochner, 1986) the "mediating effect" on the individual is personal growth. The effects on society are also positive resulting in inter-group harmony, pluralistic societies and cultural preservation.

The Deaf community does not attract all people with a hearing prob-lem, as Kyle (1985) noted. Those who acquire a hearing loss want to be part of the majority culture and retain their cultural hearing identity. Furthermore, "For those with early deafness the issues concern the com-munity and communication; for those acquiring a hearing loss the issues are adjustment and awareness for both the individual and those around" (Kyle, 1985, p. 140). The same observations have been made in Sweden. Andersson (1995) stresses that being born with a hearing loss is not the same as living with an acquired hearing loss. It is adequate to speak about two different identities of hearing impairment depending on the onset of the hearing loss. The differences in identities make mutual understanding difficult. Persons with acquired deafness in adulthood are unfamiliar with sign language and are not helped by technical devices developed for those with partial hearing disabilities. They need rehabilitation.

Culture is defined as the collective mental programming of the people in an environment. Culture is not an individual disposition; it encom-passes a number of people who were conditioned by the same education and life experience (Hofstede, 1980). Societies can be classified according to two dimensions (i.e., internal and external homogeneity). Today there are very few culturally homogeneous societies in the world, however it is argued that Japan bears the closest resemblance to a homogeneous so-ciety. On the other extreme we find the U.S.A., which always has been regarded as culturally diverse. Examples of internal homogeneity are, for example, language and class structure (Furnham & Bochner, 1986). The cultural identity in a society is defined by the majority culture, usually separated from the minority groups in society. In some societies/cultures the difference between various groups are not important, whereas in other societies such differences are highly salient (Bochner & Ohsako, 1977). The Catholic–Protestant distinction is more salient in some parts of Ireland than in Australia (Furnham & Bochner, 1986). The distinction between the majority group of deaf—"grass-root deaf" in Padden's terms (Padden, 1996)—including deaf using the genuine sign language, and the elite group of deaf, including deaf people who master the Swedish language as well and who can switch between sign language and Swedish according to the requirements of the situation—is not salient in the hearing society but in the Deaf community (Backenroth, 1991). One of the most significant differences between the different cultures—and one of the greatest obstacles in cultural encounters—is the language. Other factors creating difficulties and confusing both parties are non-verbal communication: how to relate socially to one another, non-manifest rules, values, ideology and philosophy of life. Cultures can be compared and described along various cultural dimensions, for example a combination of different culture-typical phenomena. Some cultural dimensions which can constitute important barriers in contact between different cultures is collectivism and individualism, respectively (Hofstede, 1991; Triandis, McCusker, & Hui, 1990) and horizontal and vertical societies respectively (Triandis, 1995). Collectivism is a social pattern including individuals with strong ties to each other. They regard themselves as part of one or several communities (i.e., in-groups). The members are motivated to live up to the norms and requirements expressed by their in-group(s). The group's goal takes top priority and the cohesiveness between the members of these communities or in-groups is emphasized (Hofstede, 1991; Triandis, 1995). Within community or collective cultures the in-group offers the individual protection and support in exchange for total obedience (Hofstede, 1991). Collectivistic cultures are also characterized by intimate relationships between members of the ingroup (Triandis et al., 1990). These statements seem highly applicable and true with regard to the Deaf community. Imbalance of power is another cultural dimension referring to coping with how to cope with the fact that people are unequal (Hofstede, 1991). A culture's horizontal dimension refers to the fact that people are equal in most attributes, status in particular. Generally speaking, Sweden is assumed to have the character of horizontal-individualistic cultural dimension (Triandis, 1995). Berg & Ekelund (1997) report in a Masters thesis in psychology—studying and their norms and attitudes in the Deaf community influence on the relations to hearing people—that the results from their questionnaire to deaf leaders in Sweden supported the importance of the Deaf community, such as its goals, its cohesiveness, and the loyalty of the group. The interaction patterns demonstrated highly collectivistic ideals. Furthermore, the polarization between deaf and hearing people was much stronger than had been expected at the outset of the study. The answers in the questionnaire had a highly emotional tone and indicated that the respondents had not dealt with their own emotions regarding authorities of different kinds. Berg and Ekelund concluded from the respondents in the study (i.e., deaf leaders) that many deaf people, in spite of the modern society of today, still at times feel oppressed by the Deaf community.

☐ Deafness in Retrospect

Plato (427–347 B.C.) recognized deaf people and their legitimate needs. In the writing "Kratylos," Plato talks about deaf people who make themselves understood by gestures and movements. They expressed light movements through raising their hand. They illustrated a running horse through imitation of the movements of the horse (Eriksson, 1994).

In the past, deaf people have been subject to ridicule, discrimination, or oppression. Sussman (1965) maintains that deaf people have been considered to be a deviant group because they have failed to follow the values, norms, and language of the dominant social group in society. Eriksson (1994) presents deaf people's history, and tells us that during the ancient Greek era, deaf people's position in society was regarded as very difficult. People were subjected to times of unrest and war. Great demands were made on the individual's physical and psychological strength. After birth, disabled children were killed, as deviancy was despised and not tolerated. Aristotle (384–322 B.C.) ranked hearing as the most essential of all senses needed in the learning process and came to the conclusion that deaf people in general were more difficult to bring up. Deaf people had at this time no educational opportunities. During Roman times, deaf people also had a similarly difficult time. The Roman father exercised total control over the destiny of his children. Disabled children were often drowned in the river Tiber. However, Jewish law recognized deaf people's rights. Deaf people who were congenitally deaf and mute lacked rights and responsibilities in society. They could not possess any property. Deaf people who could speak, however, had legal rights. Besides possessing property, they could marry and draw up a will. Jewish deaf people enjoyed a better existence than did any deaf under the Greeks and the Romans. Congenitally deaf people had no rights but at least they stayed alive. According to Mosaic law, deaf people (like other disabled people) were not granted admission to holy rooms or sacred spaces, however they could visit temples (Eriksson, 1994).

Prior to 1750, approximately 99% of the deaf children had no hope in learning to read or write (Sachs, 1990). It is important to remember that educational opportunities were highly restricted with regards to hearing children as well, Andersson (1995) points out. When focusing on the Swedish history of the deaf and the creation of a cultural identity (ethnogenesis), it is important to view this development in a European and international perspective. In the following section, the different steps deaf people took toward becoming a recognized culture in the Swedish society will be presented.

In Europe, education was usually given in private tutorage. Pedro Ponce de Léon (1520–1580 A.C.), a Spanish monk, was first in educating deaf people in Europe. He attempted to teach deaf people to speak. Heinicke (1727–1790 A.C.) created the "German method" or the "oral method" (Kruth, 1996). Basic education and teaching methods for the deaf were lacking. At the end of the 18th century schools for the deaf were established. The first school was established in Edingburgh in 1760 but the most prominent one was established in Paris in 1770 by Abbé de L'Épée (Eriksson, 1994) and it had an enormous influence on deaf education in Europe. L'Épée's approach became central because he regarded deaf people as equals, the only difference being that they lacked hearing. L'Épée's school became highly recognized as a school, of great interest to the entire French nation, and it received royal protection.

At the outbreak of the French Revolution (L'Épée died the same year), diversity came to be seen—instead of human—as deviant and pathological. Establishing boundaries between different groups in society became important. Language education was affected and the French Bourgeoisie set the norm for how the language was to be spoken (Kruth, 1996). Outside of Europe, schools for the deaf were also being established, for example, Hartford in the U.S.A. in 1817 by Gallaudet and Clerc, and in Calcutta, India in 1828 by the Englishman, Nicolls. Eriksson (1994) who was a person with an interest for research in the history of the deaf, besides being the first deaf dentist in Sweden, has written a lot on this subject, and from the perspective of his own deafness. The first congress for deaf teachers took place in 1878 in Paris. In 1889 it was decided that education of the deaf should be compulsory (Eriksson, 1994). The founder of the Swedish education of the deaf was Pär Aron Borg, and he did it as Abbé L'Épée in Paris did: education was centered on the direct needs of the deaf themselves. In 1808 Borg established a private school and vocational training services in Stockholm (Kruth, 1996).

For a long time sign language was regarded as an inferior language (Eriksson, 1994; Kruth, 1996). The Swedish Board of Education was unwilling to meet the needs and requirements of the deaf people. In the 1960s intensive discussions took place with the authorities in Stockholm.

During the 60s and part of the 70s only a few sign language interpreters existed, and this made communication with the authorities difficult (Kruth, 1996). The Swedish National Association of the Deaf (SDR), together with experts, fought for sign language in the schools. It was a long struggle. In 1981 the Swedish government—as the first country in the world—adopted a policy to accept and to recognize deaf people's bilingualism. Today, as part of the teaching faculty at deaf schools, there are university educated teachers who are themselves deaf. When deaf people became recognized as being bicultural, this resulted in sign language being accepted as deaf people's first language and Swedish became regarded as deaf people's second language (Eriksson, 1994).

Andersson (1994) maintains that discrimination and historic oppression of deaf people and their language throughout history are two reasons why deaf people function as a minority in most countries throughout the world. In most European countries and in the U.S.A., deaf people are educated mostly through methods emphasizing speech (i.e., oral methods) rather than through their first language—sign language. The educational level varies a great deal. Even in our times, in many countries, deaf people do not have access to any education at all. During the World Federation of the Deaf (WFD) congress in Japan in 1991, it was estimated that approximately 80% of deaf people in developing countries are still illiterate (Eriksson, 1994).

Hearing impairment constitutes one of the most common disabilities in the U.S.A. (Ries, 1982). The same applies in Sweden (Arnets, 1983). Sweden, with its present population of close to 9 million, has roughly 9,000 deaf or seriously hard-of-hearing people who use sign language. We estimate about 10% of the Swedish population to have a hearing impairment. For about 3–5%, the hearing impairment necessitates a hearing aid (Backenroth & Ahlner, 1997). In England, the percentage of hearing impairment is even higher; about 20% of the normal population is estimated to have a hearing impairment of more than 25dB (Kyle, Jones, & Wood, 1985). The WFD estimates the world's deaf population to be approximately 70 million (see Bergman, 1994). Approximately 95% of the childhood-deaf have hearing parents. Up until the mid-seventies, Swedish deaf education was predominantly oral, and when signs were used at all it was not SLL but signed Swedish, which is spoken Swedish with accompanying signs (Ahlgren, 1994). This meant that speech and hearing training had a dominant position in deaf education, since it was forbidden to use sign language as a school language in deaf schools. One of the consequences of this was that many deaf people developed serious deficiencies in the Swedish language and even in other general knowledge. Oralism was a threat to the deaf identity (Hanson, 1982). In 1972 research in sign language started in Sweden at the Department of

Linguistics, Stockholm University, and was commissioned by the Board of Education (Eriksson, 1994). One unique aspect of Bergman's research was that she included deaf work associates (Kruth, 1996). The first position in the world as Professor of Sign Language was established in 1990 and offered to Brita Bergman (Eriksson, 1994). In 1980, Lars Kruth was conferred the title of Honory Doctor in linguistics at the the Department of Linguistics, Stockholm University.

In 1984, UNESCO declared some recommendations based on a conference on the education of deaf children in Paris, namely: (a) that the deaf child should have access to spoken language as well as sign language; and (b) that sign language should be recognized to have the same status as other linguistic systems. Similarly, the socio-political movements in the U.S.A. facilitated the notion of plurality and multiculturalism and their place in education in the 1980s due to the changing demographics of American students who came from increasingly diverse backgrounds. The "melting pot" metaphor was challenged by the "salad bowl" metaphor of the American society, and the rights of minority groups and women were debated. In education, sociocultural and linguistic issues related to the development of the self-identity and cognitive abilities of members of minority groups received extensive attention.

Since then, great interest in studying the deaf culture and the deaf community has evolved. Sociocultural models are needed to articulate how deaf bilingual bicultural people function in a variety of different ways. In 1988, I. King Jordan became the first deaf president of Gallaudet University in Washington, D.C. The Americans with Disabilities Act (ADA), passed by the U.S. Congress in 1990, brought public interest, as well as international interest, to issues surrounding accommodation of deaf people in the workplace (see Parasnis, 1996).

The majority of deaf children in developing countries still have no access to education (Andersson, 1994). Yerker Andersson, former president of the WFD, believes that the deaf community and the hearing-dominant society will regard deaf people as just any other cultural minority in the future: "I believe that deaf people in most countries eventually regard themselves as a linguistic minority instead of a disability group, as they become more aware of their own mental and physical capacities. They will gradually become more concerned about the preservation and development of their own language. In the future, I believe, deaf people will be recognized as a cultural variation, instead of a pathological group" (1994, p. 10).

Is there reason to believe that a special psychology refering to the deaf has been developed? The controversy over whether or not there is a "psychology of the deaf" deals with the issue of whether deaf people are mainly similar to hearing people or distinctly different in their psychological make-up. The well-known researcher and psychologist Harlan Lane strongly rejects the idea that there is a special psychology of the deaf: "the 'psychology of the deaf' is so gravely flawed by weaknesses in test adminis-tration, language, scoring, content, norms, and subject groups ... Attempts to articulate the psychology of a minority group play in the hands of op-pressors who manipulate them for their own ends ... Hearing experts, commonly ignorant of the language, institutions, culture, history, mores, and experiences of deaf people, could only be guided in the first instance by the stereotypes to which we have all been acculturated" (Lane, 1988, p. 16).

The American psychologist Furth (1977), who works from a psycho-social perspective on deafness and learning, underlines the importance of utilizing tests which really measure intelligence, not merely mirroring dif-ferences in knowledge between deaf and hearing children when compared with each other.

☐ Bilingualism and Deafness

All languages are equally rich and complex. They have the same poten-tial for expression of thoughts and feelings. They are equally efficient as tools of communication. Yet languages are greatly unequal. A status hi-erarchy exists between languages and there is a correspondence between a language's hierarchical rank and the amount of money spent on that language in society. Mother tongue education in a minority language is seen as unnecessary, a luxury, or sometimes harmful. When a minority culture is being socialized by and into its own language, the language is strengthened and enriched. Economical and legal-political factors are cru-cial aspects to take into consideration when developing the importance of the language (Hyltenstam, 1994). The bilingual person handles with two languages in "a delicate pattern of coexistence, cooperation, and compe-tition" (Hakuta, 1986, p. 3). Bilingualism is present in practically every country throughout the world. Most deaf people are deaf-dominant bi-culturals in that they identify primarily with the deaf community, but many of them are also connected to the hearing world and interact with it and hence therefore, are also members of it (Grosjean, 1996). Andersson (1994) maintains that the term bilingualism creates confusion and that the scientific and political definitions in the U.S.A. have failed to take into consideration the role of sign language as a part of bilingualism per se. Signed languages are known to exist in all parts of the world and are expressed in an unknown number of national, regional, and cultural va-rieties. Even though sign language is not international, users of different sign languages can often communicate across language boundaries by us-ing iconic forms of signing, improvisation, and miming (Bergman, 1994). In Sweden, deaf children are exposed to sign language from very early age (e.g., in the family, in preschool, in the schools for the deaf, in the media).

Sign language is regarded as the deaf child's mother tongue although it is for many parents their second language (or even their third, fourth, or fifth language). The deaf child develops and learns sign language according to the developmental stages valid for hearing children learning to speak (Ahlgren, 1994).

One of the most interesting aspects of bilingualism is the fact that two or more languages are manifest and latent within the same person. If the bilingual person is defined as a person who uses two or more languages (or dialects) in everyday life, most deaf people who sign and who use the majority language may be defined as bilingual. However, bilingualism of the deaf remains a poorly understood topic. In general, bilinguals acquire their linguistic competence under different circumstances and use their languages for different purposes, in different domains of life, with different people, and it is because of this that they rarely develop equal fluency in their languages. Researchers are now starting to view the bilingual person as a fully competent transmitter-sender who has developed a communicative competence that is equal, but different in nature, to that of the monolingual person (Grosjean, 1992). Furthermore, bilingualism in the deaf community is "a form of minority language bilingualism in which the members of the Deaf community acquire and use both the minority language (sign language) and the majority language in its written form and sometimes in its spoken or even signed form . . . most deaf people who sign and who use the majority language in their everyday lives are indeed bilingual" (Grosjean, 1992, p. 311).

Grosjean points out that deaf bilinguals share many similarities with hearing bilinguals. For example, they are very diverse. They have developed competencies in their languages to varying degrees. Most deaf bilinguals do not look upon themselves as being bilingual. In their everyday lives, deaf bilinguals move along the language mode continuum to various degrees. Deaf bilinguals are characterized by certain specifics which differ from those of hearing bilinguals. There has been little recognition of deaf people's bilingual status. Deaf bilinguals, because of their hearing loss, will remain bilingual throughout their lives and from generation to generation. Certain language skills from the majority language (speaking above all) may never be aquired fully by deaf bilinguals. Deaf bilinguals rarely find themselves at the end of the monolingual sign language spectrum. Linguistic competence and the use thereof appear to be somewhat different, and probably more complex, than in spoken language bilingualism. Bilingualism in the deaf community brings with it implications for education. It is necessary to study deaf bilingualism and to relay relevant information to parents and educators. It is important that deaf people realize that they are indeed bilingual, that they accept this fact and feel a sense of pride in their identities. It is essential that deaf children are brought up as bilinguals (i.e., with sign language as their primary language and with the majority language as a second language) (Grosjean, 1992). Skutnabb-Kangas' (1994) definition of bilingualism in relation to deaf people is: (a) that the language of the bilingually deaf person has been learned from the beginning in the family, and both languages have been in use as a means of communication; (b) that the bilingually deaf person identifies herself/himself and is identified by others as bilingual; (c) that the bilingually deaf person has complete, equal mastery and control over the two languages, and has grammatical knowledge and ability to produce complete meaningful sentences in the other (second) language; and (d) that the bilingually deaf person in most cases can use either language to suit the situation or in response to external demands. We often take it for granted that children can be educated through the medium of their own language, but this is a myth. Skutnabb-Kangas points out that throughout the last 200 years of the European history it has been demonstrated that linguistic minorities are not going to attain linguistic equality. Natural multilingualism has often been regarded as divisive, undesirable, dangerous, uneconomical, avoidable, abnormal, and negative. However, Skutnabb-Kangas underscores that myths of this kind indeed are dangerous even in respect to world peace. Unless those representing the "majority language" start seeing the benefits of multilingualism themselves, they will not grant "minorities" linguistic equality.

☐ Biculturalism and Deafness

The bicultural person is a person who lives in two or more cultures, who adapts to each and who blends aspects of both. There is little doubt that many deaf people are indeed bicultural. Much less is known about biculturalism as compared to bilingualism among the deaf. Bilingualism and biculturalism are not necessarily the same. Many people are bilingual without being bicultural and, similarly, some people are bicultural without being bilingual. Bicultural people are characterized by at least three traits: (a) they live in two or more cultures; (b) they adapt, at least in part, to these cultures; and (c) they blend various aspects of the different cultures. There is probably little doubt that many deaf people meet these three criteria. The balanced bicultural individual who is as much part of one culture as of another is rare. Most bicultural people have stronger ties with one culture than with another, but it is nevertheless true that most deaf people are not only bilingual but also bicultural (Grosjean, 1992). "Biculturalism refers to dual modes of social behavior that are appropriately employed in different situations" (La Fromboise & Rowe, 1983). Many deaf adults feel that they are outsiders in the hearing world (Higgins, 1979). The debate over whether or not deaf people constitute a true "cultural" group is continuing on, in media as well as within the deaf communities (Padden, 1996). Padden points out some interesting facts regarding the deaf community: (a) although deaf people are far more likely to marry other deaf people, only a small number of such unions will produce deaf children; (b) at the same time, deaf people are different from other disabled groups in terms of transmission—inherited deafness is more frequent than inherited blindness, for example; (c) the relative frequency of deafness over generations has resulted in a fairly stable history organized in schools, local clubs, national organizations, religious groups. Furthermore, "Deaf people have always had to coexist with hearing people . . . that coexistence has changed . . . The new vocabulary of 'cultural' and 'bicultural,' I would argue, consists of modern ways to recognize the boundaries between Deaf and hearing people, and to imagine what these boundaries should be" (Padden, 1996, p. 82). Padden maintains that the school, and not the family, becomes a major socializing agent for deaf children. The long-term separation of deaf children from their families and neighborhoods created the basis for deaf school communities in the U.S.A. The school created the community boundaries. In the beginning of the 1970s, there was a social trend toward deinstitutionalization and deaf children began to attend other schools. This trend had an impact on the deaf community's sense of boundaries. Similar trends reported by Padden have also been observed in the Deaf community in Sweden. The deaf culture is unusual in that, for the overwhelming majority of deaf people, it is not passed on from parents to children, but rather is learned from peers, traditionally in the residential schools for the deaf (Meadow, 1975; Padden, 1980).

Some characteristics of the deaf culture are: (a) Language. Language plays a central role in both ethnic and cultural identification, which is certainly true in the case of the deaf (Reagan, 1988). ASL has historically been a language of group solidarity (Erting, 1978) and remains essential for membership in the American deaf community (Erting, 1978; Markowicz & Woodward, 1978; Padden & Markowicz, 1976); (b) Group identification refers to the view held by members of the deaf community that they are a culturally distinct group and "that entails a positive affective commitment to cultural deafness" (Reagan, 1988, p. 2). Deafness is not a medical pathology, but rather is understood in sociocultural terms (see Reagan, 1988; Parasnis, 1996). The actual degree of hearing loss is not generally seen as significant within the deaf community (Padden, 1980); (c) Deaf people seem to marry other deaf people (Padden, 1980); (d) Until quite recently, the history of the deaf has been unwritten, but now an historical awareness in the deaf community is beginning to increase (Padden, 1980); (e) Social behaviors in the deaf community differ from those in the hearing community in a variety of ways (e.g., eye contact patterns, physical contact and touching, use of facial expressions, gesturing). These differences may cause misunderstandings in the interaction between deaf and hearing people (Padden & Markowicz, 1976); and (f) An extensive network of organizations exists to meet the needs of the deaf community. Some examples of this in Sweden would be, for example, Sveriges Dövas Riksförbund (SDR—the Swedish National Association of the Deaf, mentioned earlier), dövföreningarna (the deaf associations), Dövas Hus (the House of the Deaf), "Tyst Teater" (theater of the deaf) and various social clubs and sport clubs. Organizations like this are essential in maintaining the deaf community (Padden, 1980), and a great variety may exist within the deaf subculture. There is reason to believe that the deaf community may be bicultural externally and multicultural internally (Reagan, 1988).

The communication barriers experienced by deaf people in the hearing society may prevent them from pursuing continued contact with other deaf people: ". . . the persistent experience of rejection and difficult interactions with hearing people, combined with more accepting and fluid interactions among deaf persons, may contribute to the development of separate communities and, some might argue, separate cultures" (Foster, 1996, p. 133). The Deaf community has a culture of its own (Schein, 1989), and serves as a quasi-adopted second family for many (see Dolby, 1992). According to the data gathered in Dolby's investigation (Dolby, 1992), group identification is established mainly on the basis of language, culture, and ethnicity.

Minority groups are often stigmatized. However, in most minority groups, new members are born into the culture. This is seldom a fact for new members of the deaf community. Most deaf children, having hearing parents, tend to enter the deaf community through the educational system. Attempts to "normalize" deaf people, for example via mainstreaming, have not been confined to advocates of the deaf community. Deaf people in the United States today resemble traditional immigrants becoming acculturated and assimilated into a larger society. The deaf community is a diverse group with varied interests. Deaf people are, on the one hand, proud of their social heritage and, on the other hand, developing their interests as individuals in a larger society (Emerton, 1996). Emerton suggests that "biculturalism" and "marginality" are to be used interchangeably.

"Marginality is perceived by many to be a negative term used to describe someone who is not accepted and resides on the fringe of the group" (Emerton, 1996, p. 137). "A person who is bicultural is often said to have the best of two or more social environments—the ability to participate in two cultures and the freedom to choose the best combination . . . Social mobile people are frequently marginal and such individuals may be rejected by the group to which they aspire and no longer accepted by the group from which they came. They may become individualistic and have a dual orientation to the social reality of any given social situation" (Emerton, 1996, p. 137).

The term "biculturalism" has only recently been introduced in the deaf community. The term refers "to negotiate tension between competing and profoundly contradictory beliefs, lives, and activities, those that are embedded in the lives of the hearing people on one hand and those of Deaf people on the other hand (and) is being used to describe a way of conceiving boundaries between Deaf and hearing people in a world where the residential schools and the Deaf clubs of the past no longer exist" (Padden, 1996, pp. 87–88). Furthermore, "To talk of the 'bicultural' is not to talk about an additive state, to be of two cultures, but more about states of tension. Deaf people coexist, indeed at work, with hearing people in different ways today than they did thirty or forty years ago. Their changing working lives have given rise to a new vocabulary that define more carefully than before, differences in languages and cultures . . . the middle-class professional Deaf people began to imagine new ways of representing themselves, largely in the form of calls for cultural ways of living and bicultural schools and workplaces" (Padden, 1996, pp. 95–96).

☐ A Swedish Survey on Deaf Culture

In a Swedish investigation, a questionnaire was given to subjects (n = 30) participating in a conference on deafness in Stockholm. The subjects, who had a special interest in the Deaf community, represented, besides the Stockholm-area, small cities and medium-sized cities. Data collected included: sex, affiliation in the deaf community, professional sectors of employment in the area of deafness, and years of employment. Two open-ended questions were administrated as well: What is meant by "deaf culture?" and "How can a person acquire know-how in that culture?" All together, 21 women (70%) and 9 men (30%) participated in the investigation. The results are presented in the following table. As demonstrated in Table 1, there was a distribution of affiliation in the Deaf community between those who reported membership in the Deaf community; those with no affiliation (but an interest to work in and get to know the Deaf community); those who had deaf family members (e.g., deaf parents or grandparents, a deaf son/daughter, a deaf spouse or a deaf sibling); and those with an identity as hearing impaired. Women reported to a higher degree than did men that they lacked affiliation in the deaf community and that they were affiliated to the Deaf community by another deaf family member.

As shown in Table 2, the most common professional sectors of the investigation group were those employed in the associations of the deaf (e.g., the deaf clubs), the educational sector, clerical work, and research.

Table 1. The investigation group's affiliation in the deaf community (n = 30)

	Women	Men	Total percentage (%)
Deaf Identity	20.0	13.0	33.0
Hearing Impaired Identity	6.5	6.5	13.0
Deaf Family Member	17.0	7.0	24.0
No Affiliation	27.0	3.0	30.0
			100%

Table 2. Professional sectors of employment in the area of deafness (n = 30)

	Women	Men	Total percentage (%)
Deaf Associations	13	17	30
Educational Sector	16	4	23
Clergical Work	11	3	14
Research	6	7	10
Social Work	7	—	7
Interpretation	7	—	7
Psychiatry	3	—	3
Psychology	3	—	3
Labor Market	3	—	3
			100%

Table 3. Years of employment in the area of deafness (n = 30)

	Women	Men	Total percentage (%)
0.5–5 Years	13	10	23
6–12 Years	17	—	17
12–20 Years	26	7	33
20–30 Years	10	7	17
30+ Years	3	7	10
			100%

Except for deaf associations, there was a higher degree of women occupying these areas. No men reported employment in areas like social work, interpretation, psychiatry, psychology, or the labor market.

In Table 3, it is demonstrated that the majority of the participants in the investigation held stable employment for quite a few years (between 12–20 years) in the area of deafness.

For the majority of the respondents (25 out of 30, 83%) deaf culture is linked with sign language: "Deaf culture means to me sign language in the Deaf community, our ways to socialize with one another, and the cohesiveness in the Deaf community. As deaf members we value our sign language highly and this affects our life and environment." "Deaf culture is for me also associated with sign language which, in itself, needs to be looked upon and cherished as a cultural heritage. The opposite is unfortunately too common these days!" "Deaf people's sign language is an instrument by which the deaf culture is transmitted" "... Through sign language they feel cohesiveness and a sense of belonging. They understand and accept each other across the boundaries. Their language also contributes to cultural differences between deaf and hearing people ..."

But deaf culture is also linked with: (a) the associations of the deaf: "The deaf club is my second home"; (b) the education for the deaf: "The schools for the deaf, the church, and the deaf clubs are essential components in the development of the deaf culture up til today. The deaf culture will die if the roots are cut off, and we need our history to be able to live in the future"; (c) the deaf people's special humor (e.g., deaf jokes); (d) deaf people's theatre; (e) deaf people's traditions: "Deaf people's way of thinking and living their lives ..."; "... a tradition, for example, meeting in the deaf clubs, gatherings in the school of the deaf ... a shared tradition for deaf people having stayed in boarding schools ... ; (f) deaf people's history: "All deaf people's own history of life and development is deaf culture for me. To live with the disability and how they have learned to cope with their daily lives. Out of this human being's life story, the deaf culture appears, demonstrating how people find ways to help each other." Furthermore, deaf culture is: a culture in which "everybody knows everybody," eye contact, body awareness and body language, being able to identity with the Deaf community, deaf awareness, cohesiveness across the generations, cohesiveness with deaf people in other countries, deaf priests, strong cohesiveness with the risk of being rejected from the group, the oppression of a minority group, alienation in the hearing society, hearing parents, early separation from family, the residential living for deaf people, ways of relating to the hearing society, the need for culture and sign language to merge, loneliness.

That deaf culture really is complex is described by someone as follows: "Deaf culture for me, is about the complexity of deafness. Life as a deaf person, life stories, and destinies. Deaf culture for me is not theatre, art and so on per se. These ways of expression are not particular for deaf people. However, the content in these different ways of expression can illustrate the Deaf culture, deaf people's lives. For example, the American artist Harry Williams, now deceased. He was painting violins without chords, separated violins, like two worlds. This example is a clear expression of the Deaf culture, not art per se but the content in art. The particular traits that deaf people in comparison to hearing people in society, for example the language, music, the pictures and so on, are typical deaf cultural expression ...well, o dear it is so difficult to describe this in words but easy to experience." In addition to the above, two respondents define culture as the following: "You don't really become aware about your own culture until you encounter a different culture: When you discover that the 'self-evident' can be done and be valued in other ways." "I believe there are great similarities between Swedish deaf culture and Swedish hearing culture."

Another question posed in this investigation was: "How does one acquire knowledge of and in the deaf culture?" Half of the investigation group declared 'learning sign language' as being important and the other half of the subjects emphasized 'going to the deaf clubs.' Some responses include: "Through further communication and broader areas of contact with deaf people"; "Having contacts with deaf people and becoming acqainted with the realities of the deaf existence"; "Taking advantage of different situations and communicating in sign language. Socializing with deaf people in private, not only professionally"; "Socializing as the only hearing person with deaf people"; "Initiating contact and interacting with deaf people."

In addition, the following examples were given as facilitators of gaining access to the deaf culture: living together with members of the Deaf community, working with deaf people ("Not working for but with deaf people"), studying and taking part in research, studying deaf people's history ("increasing the awareness of the differences between hearing and deaf cultures"), listening to and learning from deaf people ("... having an open and relaxed attitude towards deaf people ..."; "Becoming deaf ... "), watching video-programs about deaf people, dialoging with other deaf professionals, taking part in deaf people's activities—both daily activities and activities on the national level, sharing experiences of grown-up children of deaf parents, getting to know other cultures and hence understanding more about the one's own culture, understanding by empathizing. Also: "You cannot be competent in the deaf culture without having grown up with deaf people around you, for example being a hearing child of deaf parents. You can learn to understand, but you don't have the right feeling for it."

"Through socializing with deaf people on an equal basis, preferably having deaf friends sharing your own interests ... Listening and learning, not only observing and studying." "We need, first of all, extensive research in the area regarding the structures and descriptions of culture. First then you are able to study the phenomena. But so far we don't have this research and therefore you have to live together with deaf people in order to become competent in what the deaf culture entails."

☐ Bicultural/Multicultural Interaction in Working Life: Deaf versus Hearing

Human existence is inseparable from the cultural context. When deaf and hearing people work together, two cultures meet. A common language is the key to communication, whether in working life or in the private sphere. Lack of a common language may make cooperation and social relations in working life more taxing, and less smooth and less rewarding.

Researchers have provided guidelines for managing workforce diversity (Bartz, Hillman, Lehrer, & Mayhugh, 1990) or biculturalism at the workplace (Van Den Bergh, 1990). Swedish research describes the working conditions for hearing impaired people in the labor market (Backenroth, 1996d) and demonstrated the opportunities and the difficulties in bicultural working groups (i.e., working groups in which deaf and hearing people work together) (Backenroth, 1996a; 1996b; 1996c; 1997b), suggesting guidelines for management and employers (Backenroth, 1997a). Communication barriers between deaf and hearing people are often associated with differences in languages (Foster, 1996). Difficulties with communication reduce opportunities for developing friendships with hearing people. Information dissemination in a bicultural work group poses difficulties: "Even when supervisors make efforts to keep deaf employees up to date on information disseminated through meetings, there are limitations. Written or verbal summaries do not convey the more subtle messages transmitted through the tone of participants; the richness of the dialogue is lost to deaf workers, as are the banter and side conversations through which much of the information presented at meetings is filtered and interpreted" (Foster, 1996, p. 125). The communication barriers have implications for deaf people in working life: (a) deaf people may be left out of social and professional networks, informal gatherings, and conversations; (b) deaf people may miss information about the informal rules and organizational culture often transmitted through various networks (e.g., being the last one to know); (c) deaf people may miss opportunities of informal on-the-job training which may occur through conversation among co-workers; (d) deaf people may miss opportunities to develop relationships with co-workers due to an inability to access informal communication; (e) deaf people's lack of career development may restrict their opportunities in being promoted to managerial positions, and the process may be influenced by existing communication barriers; and (f) deaf people's sense of communication barriers may restrict the promotion of deaf employees to managerial positions (Foster, 1996). "While interpreters and notetakers are helpful in providing deaf people direct or formal instruction, they are much less helpful in facilitating access to incidental or informal learning experiences" (Foster, 1996, p. 130). In order for cultural identity to be fully integrated into society at large, it is imperative that bicultural staff

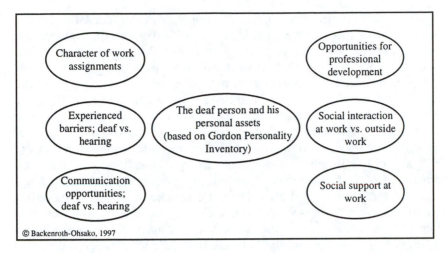

FIGURE 1. Multicultural interaction in signing work groups between the deaf person (n = 32) and his/her workplace (i.e., opportunities and barriers between the deaf and the hearing).

are employed (see Pinderhughes, 1989). A number of workplaces in Sweden have proposed "bilingual–bicultural" work groups in which the work groups aims to foster collaboration in two languages, SLL and Swedish, and two cultures (the Deaf minority culture and the majority Swedish culture). Since communication is made up of signs, written Swedish, lipreading, and non-verbal cues, the interaction taking place at work could be characterized as multicultural (see Figure 1).

In the following section, several case studies will illustrate the multicultural interaction in signing at bicultural work places.

Criteria for selection of the case studies has been twofold: (a) that the deaf person had scored fairly high/very high ratings (stanine 6–9) on the Gordon Personality Inventory on any variable demonstrating significant differences between deaf and hearing people (e.g., responsibility, emotional stability, and personal relations); (b) that the deaf person—in varying degrees—reported the work group did him/her justice.

Case Study 1: Peter

Peter is a 43-year-old divorced man, deaf from childhood, with a university education, holding a permanent teaching position at a school for the deaf. His work involves social contacts. Furthermore his tasks also require an independent nature, a high level of responsibility, and creativity. Peter has great opportunities to influence his work tasks. For teachers of the deaf, relations with hearing work associates can be psychologically stressful: "It is a strain to sign with people who don't master the language. I also notice hearing people being stressed due to the fact that they cannot keep up with the pace or because they don't understand." Peter likes his work very much but wants to develop further: "I want to develop being able to cooperate with my associates at my place of work. I want to have the feeling that I can be creative together with colleagues." Peter doesn't experience any barriers between deaf and hearing people: "I feel I am involved in hearing people's culture and understand why they say and do what they say and do." Communication does not always run smoothly: "Hearing people don't always understand me. They take advantage of deaf colleagues' knowledge in Swedish in order to communicate. I don't always understand hearing associates, although the signing competence has increased. There is a certain amount of insecurity connected to hearing people's motivation to communicate or not, and this influences my understanding." In spite of deficiencies in communication at work, Peter feels that he is able to do a good job and he has developed professionally to a high degree. Regarding the social contacts at work, Peter is both satisfied and dissatisfied: "A lot could be improved through structural planning. There is often a lack of time resulting in qualitatively poorer social contacts." In his spare time, when he is off work, Peter seldom visits the deaf club: "There is nothing there which attracts me or motivates me to be affiliated as a member there." He interacts with hearing work associates outside work: "We go out and relax together. We are a group of people arranging different activities, for example having tea at different places." The significant others at work are the work associates: "They give me a sense of security. Feedback in my work. Support. We have fun together. There are deaf colleagues who themselves are not so skilled in Swedish—they have difficulties in understanding. Deaf people continuously have to adapt to varying degrees of sign language. Hearing people do not have the ability nor the skill in sign language in order to be successful in signing and communicating through sign language." Social support in the work group is often experienced and manager's support is experienced fairly often: "But a lot could be improved, in particular decision-making."

On the Gordon Personality Inventory, Peter was rated rather high on emotional stability (stanine 6), as well as on ascendency, and high (stanine 7) on original thinking.

Case Study 2: Susan

Susan is a 43-year-old single university educated woman, deaf since childhood, holding a temporary job, also at a school for the deaf. Her job as a teacher involves a high degree of social contacts, independence, responsibility, developmental possibilities, and possibilities to influence her work. Susan finds her work fairly stressful: "There is no time to sit down and relax during breaks. The students take up most of your time and attention." However, she likes her work very much but would like to develop further: "I want to share more of my experiences with other colleagues. I travel abroad occassionally and am greatly enriched by it. I share experiences with colleagues in other countries and feel enriched by this opportunity." Susan experiences barriers between the deaf and the hearing culture: "The hearing culture is based on sounds." Communication obviously seems to work to a very high degree for Susan. She feels she understands and is understood by hearing work associates. Susan feels that she does a good job and to an equally high degree has developed professionally in the work group. She is satisfied with her social contacts at work. Outside work she seldom goes to the deaf club: "I try to go there once a week, providing there is an interesting lecture or a theater to go to." Outside work, she socializes with hearing associates who manage to communicate in signs. Her work associates and her manager are important significant people at the workplace. She often experiences social support in the work group, whereas support from the manager is felt to be average.

On the Gordon Personality Inventory, Susan was rated high (stanine 5) on responsibility, as well as on personal relations and vigor, and high (stanine 7) on both emotional stability and original thinking.

Case Study 3: Catherine

Catherine is a 30-year-old married woman, deaf from childhood, with a high-school diploma, holding a permanent position in a company as a producer. Her work requires sociability, independence, a high level of responsibility, creativity and—on occasion—is rather stressful, but she has fairly good opportunities to influence her work tasks. She likes her work very much but has developmental needs, such as to have more deaf work associates: "The level of sign language must be increased in the work group. Only then would I benefit more from my work." Regarding possible attitudinal barriers, Catherine feels they exist since she constantly has to ask what others are talking about. "Hearing people are irritated when deaf people roll their eyes, or use certain body language. Hearing people interrupt one another. Hearing people are also influenced by the interpreter's behavior. Hearing people and deaf people have different means of communication, different turn taking rules in a discussion. Hearing people are disturbed by sounds. Hearing people look down—I want more eye-contact when I sign. Hearing people listen more to each other. Deaf people are more prejudiced regarding the 'status' of the person who talks: they never let deaf people who finally pluck up the courage to speak to say anything." She understands hearing people though: "Thanks to the fact that I was brought up as a hearing-impaired person, and used to friends from different groups. But the level of sign language must be increased and the manager should urge, rather than offer, everyone to participate in a sign language course. The general attitude and approach here is essential . . . More hearing people try to sign during meetings. Hearing people partly understand me. But it feels like a wall between us at times. They may understand what I say but they don't understand me as a deaf person. They react a lot when I get angry. I adapt and use my voice often in order for the work to run smoothly." Sometimes Catherine feels she is done justice. She has developed professionally quite a lot in her work group. Catherine is partly satisfied with her social contacts at work. Outside work, she reports that she seldom visits the deaf club: "I am content with the contacts with my deaf associates at work. If I visit the deaf club, there will only be discussions about my work. Unfortunately, deaf people think that we who work professionally are conceited, so I feel a need to go to the deaf club just to prove it's not so. Often there aren't many young people there. Mostly retired people, I'm afraid." There are no significant people at the workplace for Catherine. However, the work group offers fairly regular social support, Catherine reports. Regarding managers, she rates them as being average with regard to support.

On the Gordon Personality Inventory, Catherine was rated high (stanine 7) on emotional stability, as well as on original thinking, and high (stanine 6) on vigor.

Case Study 4: John

John is a 50-year-old single man with a high-school degree holding a permanent position as a graphic designer. He became deaf in his adult years. His work can be characterized as follows: fairly social, highly independent, fairly responsible, highly developing with a high degree of being able to influence his work tasks, and with a fairly small degree of stress involved. John likes his work a lot and feels content with things as they are for the moment. John doesn't experience any barriers with hearing people at work: "I don't reason like that. If you can get along all right and cooperate, it doesn't matter whether you're hearing or deaf." Providing the communication situation is favorable, John understands hearing associates, particularly on one-to-one encounters. In groups, however, difficulties present themselves: "The situation is a bit different for me, as I acquired my deafness as an adult and cannot master sign language completely yet.

My hearing associates understand me though." John doesn't feel that he can fully develop at work but he reports that he has developed quite a lot professionally. He feels he does his work satisfactorily but reports he has professionally developed to a high degree. He is satisfied with the social interaction at work. He seldom visits the deaf club outside work: "My interests link me to my home and there is no community for adult deaf people. I also feel limited in sign language communication." John doesn't socialize with hearing associates outside work: "I don't share their interests . . . Many of them have families so we have different values of life." Work associates and the managers constitute significant persons at work. In addition, regarding an associate who was employed to work side-by-side to John: "He is important in many different ways. He is the manager who doesn't dominate but instead focuses on collaboration. He delegates responsibilities sometimes. He gives feedback. I have the advantage of having three people to turn to." Fairly often the work group is experienced as a social support but the manager constitutes a social support to a very high degree.

On the Gordon Personality Inventory, John was rated high (stanine 7) on personal relations, as well as on original thinking, and fairly high (stanine 5) on emotional stability.

☐ Conclusion

Today deaf people are demanding to be recognized as a cultural and linguistic minority group. Deaf people constitute a unique subculture in society. The Deaf community has had a more difficult time overcoming inferiority stereotyping by the majority culture than have other minority groups, since deaf people have been viewed as a disability group (Reagan, 1985). Members of the Deaf community are nowadays defining themselves as a cultural and linguistic minority group, not a disability group (Glickman, 1986; Nash, 1987; Hafer & Richmond, 1988; Gregory, 1992). Thus there has been a shift from a clinical-pathological view of deafness to a cultural view of deafness, and the deaf have been: ". . . seen as a cultural and linguistic minority group within a multicultural society" (Gregory, 1992, p. 184).

". . . deaf culture has been recognized as a minority culture with its own history, customs, values, and social patterns . . . (deaf people) share a language that differs from that of the dominant culture . . . traditions, beliefs, rules of behavior, stories, and jokes. These are transmitted through everyday social interaction and through participation in special schools, church groups, social and sports clubs, and other organizations. The Deaf community includes deaf, hearing impaired, and hearing individuals (usually spouses or the children of deaf parents" (Hafer & Richmond, 1988, p. 3).

There has been a small revolutionary shift in perspective among educators, linguists, and researchers involved in the education of deaf people
from the medical model, that states that deaf people are individuals with
an audiological disability, to a sociocultural model, emphasizing deaf people as a minority group with its own language and culture (Parasnis, 1996).
Although individual members of the Deaf community have varying degrees of linguistic competence, they are nevertheless bilingual (Reagan,
1988; Grosjean, 1992; 1996). Furthermore, "a more flexible definition of
bilingualism is adopted which recognizes that children who operate in two
languages can be called bilingual, regardless of the mode of languages used
or the level of competence" (Gregory, 1992, p. 193).

Oralism, a method of teaching, still remains influential today, as it is supported by the advocates of cochlear implants. "While cochlear implants are
portrayed in the media as providing a cure for deafness, in reality their
effect is much more limited, both in terms of the results of the operation
itself, which while providing a sensation of sound, does not restore hearing, and because they are only suitable for a very limited member of deaf
people" (Gregory, 1992, p. 191).

Today the perspective of hearing loss is enriched by not only medical aspects, but also psychological aspects and sociocultural aspects (Andersson,
1995). Bo Andersson, being himself a writer and a playwright, acquired his
deafness in adult years. He warns us not to be over-hasty in retrospectively
interpreting documents (Andersson, 1995): "How you perceive your own
history as disabled depends to a great deal on your interest for society
in general. The person focusing all the attention on the disabled through
history, can easily come to the conclusion that there exists a sense of abandonment and which is not really self-evident—a dismal situation which
today is encountered by increasing doubts from both researchers and disabled people themselves. Brutal and difficult times in history have not
necessarily involved that disabled have been treated particularly badly"
(p. 65). The best way to enhance interaction between deaf people and
hearing people is to adopt a natural attitude: "Many people seem quite
without reason, to have guilt feelings in relations to people with hearing
impairments or other disabilities as if they needed to apologize for the
fact that they can hear and we can't. This is detrimental for our relations
and can only restrain a natural interaction between hearing impaired and
normal people" (Andersson, 1995, p. 101).

Some examples of the characteristics of multiculturalism have been suggested (Highlen, 1996): (a) pluralism; (b) the reframing of "self" as "self-
in-relation," such as family, community, culture(s); and (c) acknowledging
clients' resources from their multiple backgrounds, and the resources they
have, assessing both facilitators and barriers incorporated in the person.
A multicultural program for the deaf would help in liberating them from

the hearing society's impact, and could, for example, deal with studies of the dominant culture, studies of the deaf culture, studies of other oppressed ethnic, cultural and linguistic groups, studies of subcultural groups within the deaf community, and studies of deaf people in other countries. At the same time it would be reasonable for hearing people to increase their knowledge about and be exposed to deaf people and deaf culture in their curricula. Hence, Deaf culture could be included as an area of study in multicultural and cross-cultural education programs and courses (Reagan, 1988).

The cultural deficit model, stating that norms and cultural patterns of minority groups varying from the majority group mostly were deviant and destructive, has been replaced by a bicultural model: "The bicultural model postulates that the minority individual learns two distinct behavioral repertoires for utilization in the minority and majority societies" (de Anda, 1984, p. 102). The success of different individuals within an ethnic minority is not based the on the degree of assimilation, but on the degree of the following six factors: (a) overlap or commonality between the two cultures with regard to attitudes, norms, and values; (b) availability of cultural translators, mediators, or models; (c) amount and type of feedback provided by each culture; (d) conceptual style and problem-solving approach; (e) degree of bilingualism; and (f) degree of dissimilarity in physical appearance (de Anda, 1984).

LaFromboise, Coleman, & Gerton (1993) view cultural competence within a multilevel continuum of social skill and personality development, suggesting that cultural competence requires: (a) a strong personal identity; (b) knowledge of cultural beliefs and values; (c) sensitivity to the affective processes of the culture; (d) clear communication in the language of the given cultural group; (e) performance of socially sanctioned behavior; (f) maintenance of active social relations; and (g) negotiation of the institutional structures of that culture.

The associations of the deaf constitute a valuable historical cultural heritage in the Swedish associations. But how do today's young people in Sweden perceive the deaf culture? Many deaf youngsters of today do not recognize their roots in history and they choose activities other than the associations of the deaf. Will the young generation continue to hold a historical inheritance in trust from their parents and grandparents, or will they pave new historical paths in the future? The deaf culture is essential to preserve since it enhances the cohesiveness and the identity in the Deaf community, which is important in the joint struggle for improvements of the conditions for the Deaf community in relation to the hearing society. The Deaf community has become increasingly pluralistic, suggesting that it gradually will give room for more individualism and gradually less collectivism. Furthermore, the Deaf community has increasingly developed away from the melting pot model where oralism reigned in society, colouring education; and in deaf people's relation to the professional establishment, dealing with questions pertaining to the Deaf community. The multicultural mosaic model can best be applied to today's society since interaction between deaf and hearing people is facilitated by deaf mediating individuals, or "culture-brokers," having cultural competence in both the Deaf community and the hearing-dominant society. These mediating bicultural people—or multicultural people—attempt to bridge the gap between deaf and hearing people, as illustrated by the case studies. According to Bochner (1981), and Furnham and Bochner (1986), the mediating individual acts as a link between different cultural systems and is characterized by the capacity to select, combine, and synthesize appropriate aspects of both cultures without loosing his or her cultural "core." The present study's deaf mediating individuals can be regarded as links between the deaf culture, to which they belong, and the hearing society in which they are working. They could also be said to represent two cultures in a bicultural working group. Some examples of mediating deaf individuals are, for example, deaf people working for deaf consumers in the associations of the deaf or deaf people having made achievements in higher education and working in areas where they mediate between deaf people and the hearing society. It may thus not be a random choice that these deaf mediating persons are working in bicultural working groups and in professions requiring social contacts. The deaf community is gradually becoming multicultural, as deaf professionals are working on European and International levels, and in various capacities are dealing with questions of interest for the Deaf community, in developing countries and in the United Nations, where they enrich existing knowledge and interact and mediate between deaf and hearing people.*

☐ References

Andersson, B. (1995). *Hörselskadade i historia och nutid.* [Hearing impaired today and yesterday]. Stockholm: Hörselskadades Riksförbund.

Andersson, Y. (1994). Deaf people as a linguistic minority. In I. Ahlgren and K. Hyltenstam (Eds.), *Bilingualism in deaf education, International studies on sign language and communication of the deaf, 27* (pp. 9–13). Hamburg, Germany: Signum.

Ahlgren, I. (1994). Sign language as the first language. In I. Ahlgren and K. Hyltenstam, *Bilingualism in deaf education, International studies on sign language and communication of the deaf, 27* (pp. 55–60). Hamburg, Germany: Signum.

*This study was financed by the Swedish Council for Work Life Research, Rådet för Arbetslivsforskning (RALF).

Arnets, B. (1983). *Psychosocial effects of understimulation in old age.* Stockholm: Karolinska Institute.

Backenroth, G. (1983). *Group counseling for parents of deaf and hearing impaired children.* Doctoral dissertation. Stockholm: University of Stockholm, Department of Psychology. Stockholm: Minab/Gotab.

Backenroth, G. (1984). Counselling in families with a deaf or hearing impaired child. *International Journal for the Advancement of Counselling, 7,* 267–274.

Backenroth, G. (1986). Counselling with the psycho-socially isolated deaf. *International Journal for the Advancement of Counselling, 9,* 125–131.

Backenroth, G. (1987). Group support for parents of deaf and hearing impaired children. *International Journal of Rehabilitation Research, 10,* 324–327.

Backenroth, G. (1989). Necessary prerequisites for deaf's self actualization in a hearing society. In R. C. King and J. K. Collins (Eds), *Social applications and issues in psychology* (pp. 251–260). Proceedings of the XXIV International Congress of Psychology, Sydney, Australia. Selected/revised papers, 8. Amsterdam: North-Holland.

Backenroth, G. (1991). *Möjligheter och svårigheter att arbeta med det sociala nätverket hos döva som söker psykologiskt stöd.* [Opportunities and difficulties working with the social network of deaf people seeking psychological support]. Stockholm: Stockholm University, Department of Stockholm, *61.*

Backenroth, G. (1992a). Resources and shortcomings in deaf clients' social networks. *International Journal of Rehabilitation Research, 15,* 355–359.

Backenroth, G. (1992b). Counselling persons with deafness and their social networks. In S. E. Robertson and R. I. Brown (Eds.), *Rehabilitation counselling: Approaches in the field of disability* (pp. 245–273). Rehabilitation Education Series, 5. London: Chapman & Hall.

Backenroth, G. (1993). Loneliness in the deaf community—a personal choice or an enforced choice? *International Journal of Rehabilitation Research, 16,* 331–336.

Backenroth, G. (1995). Deaf people's perception of social interaction in working life. *International Journal of Rehabilitation Research, 18,* 76–81.

Backenroth, G. (1996a). Disability. In B. Järvholm (Ed.), *Working life and health: A Swedish survey* (pp. 83–86). Stockholm: National Board of Occupational Safety and Health, National Institute for Working Life, & Swedish Council for Work Life Research.

Backenroth, G. (1996b, September 18–20). *Employment options and adult learning needs of adults with functional impairments.* Paper presented at the EU-workshop organized by Swedish EU Programme Office for Education, Training and Competence Development in cooperation with Cedefop and Swedish Ministry of Education and Science; Continuing vocational training and the European skill gap—a workshop on information technologies, labor market development and lifelong learning. Saltsjöbaden, Sweden.

Backenroth, G. (1996c). Disabilities in working life—a review of Swedish research and some theoretical considerations. *European Psychologist, 4,* 278–292.

Backenroth, G. (1996d). *Hörselskadades anpassning och rehabilitering på arbetsplatsen.* Stockholms universitet: Psykologiska institutionen, *89.*

Backenroth, G. (1997a). *Counselling management and employers with hearing and deaf employees.* Stockholm University: Reports from the Department of Psychology, No. 829.

Backenroth, G. (1997b). Social Interaction in deaf/hearing bicultural working groups. *International Journal of Rehabilitation Research, 20,* 85–90.

Backenroth, G., & Ahlner, B. (1997). *Hearing loss in working life: Psychosocial aspects.* Stockholm University: Reports from the Department of Psychology No. 837.

Baker, C., & Padden, C. (1978). Focusing on the non-manual components of ASL (American Sign Language). In P. Siple (Ed.), *Understanding language through sign language research.* New York: Academic Press.

Bartz, D. E., Hillman, L. W., Lehrer, S., & Mayhugh, G. M. (1990). A model for managing workforce diversity. *Management Education and Development, 21,* 321–326.

Berg, B., & Ekelund, R. (1997). *De normer och attityder bland döva som påverkar relationen till hörande—En kvalitativ studie ur döva ledares perspektiv.* [Norms and attitudes among deaf people influencing their relations to hearing—A qualitative study from the perspective of deaf leaders]. Psykologexamensuppsats. Stockholms universitet: Psykologiska institutionen.

Bergman, B. (1994). Signed laguages. In I . Ahlgren & K. Hyltenstam (Eds.), *Bilingualism in deaf education. International studies on sign language and communication of the deaf, 27* (pp. 15–30). Hamburg, Germany: Signum.

Berry, J. W. (1991). Understanding and managing multiculturalism: Some possible implications of research in Canada. *Psychology & Developing Societies, 3,* 17–49.

Bochner, S. (Ed.). (1981). *The mediating person: Bridges between cultures.* Cambridge, MA: Schenkman.

Bochner, S. (1986). Coping with unfamiliar cultures: Adjustment of culture learning? *Australian Journal of Psychology, 38,* 347–358.

Bochner, S., & Ohsako, T. (1977). Ethnic role salience in racially homogeneous and heterogeneous societies. *Journal of Cross-Cultural Psychology, 8,* 477–492.

Bott, E. (1955). Urban families: Conjugal roles and social networks. *Human Relations, 8,* 345–383.

de Anda, D. (1984). Bicultural socialization: Factors affecting the minority experience. *Social Work, 29,* 101–107.

Dolby, K. (1992). An investigation of the sign language community of the deaf: Can anyone join? *ACEHI/ACEDA- Journal, 18,* 80–92.

Emerton, R. G. (1996). Marginality, biculturalism, and social identity of deaf people. In I. Parasnis (Ed.), *Cultural and language diversity and the deaf experience* (pp. 136–145). New York: Cambridge University Press.

Erikson, E. (1968). *Identity, youth and crisis.* New York: Norton & Company.

Eriksson, P. (1994). *Dövas historia—daubhaR-daufr-döver-döv. En faktasamling* [The history of deaf people. A sourcebook]. *Del. 1.* Örebro: SIH-läromedel.

Erting, C. (1978). Language policy and deaf ethnicity in the United States. *Sign Language Studies, 19,* 139–152.

Foster, S. (1996). Communication experiences of deaf people: An ethnographic account. In I. Parasnis (Ed.), *Cultural and language diversity and the deaf experience* (pp. 117–135). New York: Cambridge University Press.

Freeman, R., Carbin, C., & Boese, R. (1981). *Can't your child hear?* Baltimore: University Press.

Furnham, A., & Bochner, S. (1986). *Culture shock: Psychological reactions to unfamiliar environments.* London: Routledge.

Furth, H. G. (1977). *Tänkande utan språk* [Thinking without language]. Stockholm: Wahlström & Widstrand.

Glickman, N. (1986). Cultural identity, deafness, and mental health. *Journal of Rehabilitation of the Deaf, 20,* 1–10.

Gregory, S. (1992). The language and culture of deaf people: Implications for education. *Language and Education, 6,* 183–197.

Grosjean, F. (1992). The bilingual and the bicultural person in the hearing and in the deaf world. *Sign Language Studies, 77,* 307–320.

Grosjean, F. (1996). Living with two languages and two cultures. In I. Parasnis (Ed.), *Cultural and language diversity and the deaf experience* (pp. 20–37). New York: Cambridge University Press.

Hafer, J. C., & Richmond, E. D. (1988). What hearing parents should learn about deaf culture. *Perspectives for Teachers of the Hearing Impaired, 7,* 2–5.

Hakuta, K. (1986). *Mirror of language: The debate of bilingualism.* New York: Basic Books.

Hanson, G. (1982). *Den heliga oralismen. Sveriges Dövas Riksförbund 60 år, 1922–1982* [The holy oralism. The Swedish National Association throughout 60 years, 1922–1982]. Leksand: Sveriges Dövas Riksförbund.

Herskovits, M. J. (1948). *Man and his works: The science of cultural anthropology*, New York: Knopf.

Higgins, P. (1979). Outsiders in a hearing world. *Urban Life, 8,* 3–22.

Highlen, P. (1996). MCT theory and implications for organizations/systems. In D. W. Sue, A. E. Ivey, and P. B. Pedersen (Eds.), *A theory of multicultural counseling and therapy.* Pacific Grove, CA: Brooks/Cole Publishing Company.

Hofstede, G. (1980). *Culture's consequences.* Beverly Hills, CA: Sage Publications.

Hofstede, G. (1991). *Organisationer och kulturer—om interkulturell förståelse* [Organizations and cultures—about intercultural understanding]. Lund: Studentlitteratur.

Horney, K. (1937). *The neurotic personality of our time.* New York: W. W. Norton.

Hyltenstam, K. (1994). Factors influencing the social role and status of minority languages. In I. Ahlgren and K. Hyltenstam (Eds.), *Bilingualism in deaf education, International studies on sign language and communication of the deaf, 27* (pp. 297–310). Hamburg: Signum.

Jacobs, L. (1974). *A deaf adult speaks out.* Washington, DC: Gallaudet University.

Kruth, L. (1996). *En tyst värld—full av liv* [A silent world—full of life]. Örebro: SIH-läromedel.

Kyle, J. G. (1985). Deaf people: Assessing the community or the handicap? *Bulletin of The British Psychological Society, 38,* 137–141.

Kyle, J. G. (1990, March). *The deaf community: Culture, custom and tradition.* University of Bristol: Centre for Deaf Studies. Paper presented at the International Conference on Sign Language in Hamburg.

Kyle, J. G., Jones, L. G., & Wood, P. L. (1985). Adjustment to acquired hearing loss: A working model. In H. Orlans (Ed.), *Adjustment to hearing loss* (pp. 119–138). Gallaudet Research Institute and U.S. Commission of Civil Rights. San Diego, CAL: College-Hill Press.

Kyle, J. G., & Woll, B. (1985). *Sign language.* Cambridge, England: Cambridge University Press.

LaFromboise, T. D., Coleman, H. L. K., & Gerton, J. (1993). Psychological impact of biculturalism: Evidence and theory. *Psychological Bulletin, 114,* 395–412.

LaFromboise, T. D., & Rowe, W. (1983). Skills training for bicultural competence: Rationale and application. *Journal of Counseling Psychology, 30,* 589–595.

Lane, H. (1988). Is there a 'Psychology of the Deaf'? *Exceptional Children, 55,* 7–19.

Leong, F. T. L., & Kim, H. H. W. (1991). Going beyond cultural sensitivity on the road to multiculturalism: Using the intercultural sensitizer as a counselor training tool. *Journal of Counseling & Development, 70,* 112–118.

Mahler, M. S., Pine, F., & Bergman, A. (1975). *The psychological birth of the human infant: Symbiosis and individuation.* London: Hutchinson & Co, Ltd.

Markowicz, H., & Woodward, J. (1978). Language and the maintenance of ethnic boundaries in the deaf community. *Communication and Cognition, 11,* 29–37.

Marshall, C. (1996). Culture, diversity, and disability. In P. B. Pedersen and D. C. Locke (Eds.), *Cultural and diversity issues in counseling* (pp. 77–81). Greensboro, NC: University of North Carolina.

Mead, M. (1963). Socialization and enculturation. *Current Anthropology, 4,* 184–188.

Meadow, K. (1975). The deaf subculture. *Hearing and Speech Action, 43,* 16–18.

Nash, J. (1987). Who signs to whom?: The American sign language community. In P. Higgins and J. Nash (Eds), *Understanding deafness socially* (pp. 81–100). Springfield, IL: Charles C. Thomas.

Nash, J., & Nash, A. (1981). *Deafness in society.* Lexington, MA: Lexington Books.

Padden, C. A. (1980). The deaf community and the culture of deaf people. In C. Baker and R. Battison (Eds.), *Sign language and the deaf community* (pp. 89–103). Silver Spring, MD: National Association of the Deaf.

Padden, C. A. (1996). From the cultural to the bicultural: The modern deaf community. In I. Parasnis (Ed.), *Cultural and language diversity and the deaf experience* (pp. 79–98). New York: Cambridge University Press.

Padden, C. A., & Humphries, T. (1988). *Deaf in America: Voices from a culture*. London: Harvard Press.

Padden, C. A., & Markowicz, H. (1976). Cultural conflicts between hearing and deaf communities. In *Proceedings of the Seventh World Conference of the World Federation of the Deaf* (pp. 407–411). Silver Spring, MD: National Association of the Deaf.

Parasnis, I. (1996). On interpreting the deaf experience within the context of cultural and language diversity. In I. Parasnis (Ed.), *Cultural and language diversity and the deaf experience* (pp. 3–19). New York: Cambridge University Press.

Pedersen, P. (1991). Multiculturalism as a generic approach to counseling. *Journal of Counseling and Development, 70*, 6–12.

Pinderhughes, E. (1989). *Understanding race, ethnicity and power: The key to efficacy in clinical practice*. New York: The Free Press.

Quigley, S., & Kretschmer, R. (1982). *The education of deaf children*. London: Arnold.

Reagan, T. (1985). The deaf as a linguistic minority: Educational considerations. *Harvard Educational Review, 55*, 265–277.

Reagan, T. (1988). Multiculturalism and the deaf: An educational manifesto. *Journal of Research and Development in Education, 22*, 1–6.

Ries, P. W. (1982). The demography of hearing loss. In H. Orlans (Ed.), *Adjustment to hearing loss* (pp. 3–21). Gallaudet Research Institute and U.S. Commission of Civil Rights. San Diego, CA: College-Hill Press.

Sachs, O. (1990). *Att se röster* [Seeing voices]. Stockholm: Prisma.

Schein, J. D. (1989). *At home among strangers*. Washington, DC: Gallaudet University Press.

Skutnabb-Kangas, T. (1994). Linguistic human rights—a prerequisite for bilingualism. In I. Ahlgren and K. Hyltenstam (Eds.), *Bilingualism in deaf education, International studies on sign language and communication of the deaf, 27* (pp. 139–159). Hamburg, Germany: Signum.

Stokoe, W. (1970). Sign language diglossia. *Studies in Linguistics, 21*, 27–41.

Stone, L. J., & Church, J. (1973). *Childhood and adolescence: A psychology of the growing person.* (3rd ed). New York: Random House.

Sue, D. W. (1992). The challenge of multiculturalism: The road less travelled. *American Counselor, 1*, 6–14.

Sue, D. W., Ivey, A. E., & Pedersen, P. B. (1996). *A theory of multicultural counseling and therapy*. Pacific Grove, CA: Brooks/Cole Publishing Company.

Sussman, M. B. (1965). Sociological theory and deafness: Problems and prospects. In The United States Department of Health, Education, and Welfare (Ed.), *Research on behavioral aspects of deafness*. Washington, DC: The United States Department of Health, Education, and Welfare.

Taft, R. (1977). Coping with unfamiliar cultures. In N. Warren (Ed.), *Studies in cross-cultural psychology, 1*. New York: Academic Press.

Triandis, H. C. (1995). *Individualism and collectivism*. Boulder, CO: Westview Press, Inc.

Triandis, H. C., McCusker, C., & Hui, C. H. (1990). Multimethod probes of individualism and collectivism. *Journal of Personality and Social Psychology, 59*, 1006–1020.

Tseng, W-S., & McDermott, J. F. (1981). *Culture, mind and therapy: An introduction to cultural psychiatry.* New York: Brunner/Mazel.

Van Den Bergh, N. (1990). Managing biculturalism at the workplace: a group approach. *Social Work with Groups, 13*, 71–84.

CHAPTER

Jessica Ball

Identity Formation in Confucian Heritage Societies: Implications for Theory, Research, and Practice

Theoretical frameworks and research procedures used to study identity formation have been predicated on Western assumptions of the primacy of the individual and have focused on youth growing up in Western sociocultural contexts. Investigators and practitioners need to understand similarities and differences in the ways in which young people experience the tasks of psychosocial development across varying sociocultural, political, and historical conditions. The cultural mediation of identity formation is discussed with reference to youth growing up in Confucian heritage societies. Indications of important differences in developmental tasks and goals for Chinese youth in Asia are found in the author's exploratory research on identity formation, risk-taking behaviors, and counseling in Singapore and Malaysia.

Pardon him, Theodotus: he is a barbarian, and thinks that the customs of his tribe and island are the laws of nature.

— G. B. Shaw, Caesar and Cleopatra

Identity is grounded in developmental changes that occur over the lifespan and in the culture in which an individual grows up. Therefore, identity formation must be understood with reference to the sociocultural, historical,

---

This chapter is based on a paper presented at the XXVI International Congress of Psychology, 15–21 August, Montreal, Canada.

147

and political conditioning of individual development in specific geographic settings. To date, theoretical frameworks and research procedures used to study identity formation have been predicated on Western assumptions of the primacy of the individual and have focused predominantly on socioeconomically privileged youth of Western European descent growing up in North America (e.g., Erikson, 1968; Havighurst, 1972; Marcia, 1980).

This chapter is based on the theoretical stance that given the embeddedness of processes of identity formation and other core aspects of development in specific cultural contexts, the elaboration of multiculturalism as a "fourth dimension" (and not only as a set of methods) is essential for advancing our understanding of human behavior and of the reproduction and recreation of culture through individuals articulating their identities in social interactions. In this chapter, multiculturalism is viewed as an orientation, and the psychosocial construction of identity as an axis of subjectivity. "Culture" and organized patterns of individual behavior and experience define one another through continuous processes of reproduction and change. Multiculturalism is a fourth force in psychology because this inextricable, mutually causal relationship between culture and individual behaviors pervades theoretical boundaries.

This chapter grows out of a decade of the author's work as a researcher, counselor, and educator in Malaysia, Singapore, and elsewhere in Southeast Asia. The work described briefly here draws upon the concept of self in the tradition of symbolic interactionism (Mead, 1934). The work was stimulated by the author's general goal of understanding how culturally-constructed systems of meanings and intentions and how normatively-specified patterns of socialization and family interaction affect the development of identity and, therefore, the elaboration during adolescence of distinctive ways of relating oneself to an interpreted world. Drawing upon indicators found in the author's research and counseling practice, the substantive focus of this chapter discusses some normative processes, challenges, and aims of development among Chinese youth growing up in "Confucian heritage" societies in East and Southeast Asia.

Asia is heterogeneous on psychosocial, spiritual, economic and many other dimensions. Nevertheless, there are important commonalities among "Confucian heritage" societies, including Singapore, China, Taiwan, Hong Kong, Japan, and Korea. Among other things, the predominant cultural groups in these countries share certain beliefs, values, and practices in their approaches to family life and the socialization of children (Bond, 1996; Ho, 1986). In my research, I found several indicators of important differences, as well as similarities, in developmental tasks and goals for Chinese youth in Asia compared to youth growing up in Euro-American settings.* It is hoped that the examples in this chapter will serve as one point of departure in elaborating multiculturalism as a fourth dimension in psychology, extending its scope and broader utility.

Although over one-fifth of humanity is Chinese, their experiences as individuals have yet to be extensively described, compared, or understood in psychology. With reference to identity formation among Asians, the cultural construction of identity or the embodiment of culture within the self has not been a focus of serious investigation in psychology. Little research evidence or accumulated clinical lore are available to tell us about normal developmental processes among Chinese youth or the distinctive psychological challenges that Chinese youth may encounter as they negotiate the transition from childhood to adulthood. Similarly, regarding Asian populations, the cultural construction of identity or the embodiment of culture within the self has not been a focus of serious investigation in psychology. However, comparative cultural studies have clearly portrayed the radically different conceptualizations of the Self and of life from Eastern and Western perspectives. Thus, we might expect that, compared to Euro-American youth, Chinese youth in Asia encounter quite different psychosocial challenges during their formative adolescent years (e.g., Ogbu, 1988; Roll, 1980).

Questions of identity formation are integral to a consideration of "multicultural education," "multicultural counseling," and "multicultural health policy and program development" and other areas of applied research and practice. Given the lack of attention in psychology to the development of identity in Asian populations, it follows that the implications of culturally diverse developmental processes and goals with reference to Confucian heritage societies remain largely unexplored—or ignored—in several areas of activity. Some of these include: (a) research measuring self-concept and identity formation, where masculine, individualistic assumptions which have formed the bedrock of Western psychological tradition have prevailed; (b) international consultation practices, wherein Western perspectives and social policies have often been imposed on the problems of youth in Asia; (c) the export of tertiary education and other education from the United States of America (herein, U.S.A.) and Canada to developing countries, which is akin to the exercise of trying to fit square pegs into round holes; and (d) approaches to training counselors and clinical psychologists

---

*The terms Western or Euro-American are used for lack of a better term, recognizing the substantial variability within Western societies (e.g., Triandis, 1995). Cross-national research (e.g., Schwartz, 1994) has elucidated the ways in which East and West are not dichotomous and how mainstream American culture, in particular, is as different from Western European cultures as it is from Chinese cultures.

to work with Asian youth and their families, where the universal validity and efficacy of Eurocentric goals and interventions has been widely pre-supposed. As a result, the way that psychology in Asia and other parts of the Third World is evolving often has the appearance of an impoverished mimesis of the discipline in the old imperialist centers. Fanon (1986), Frosh (1989), Ponterotto and Casas (1991), Seve (1978) and others have shown how the practices and motives of colonialist psychology, in its attempts to discipline the psychology of the colonized, are often quite transparent.

☐ Relationship-centeredness/ Individual-centeredness

Cultural comparisons have emphasized the individual-centeredness of Western cultures and the collectivism and situation-centeredness of East-ern cultures (Bond, 1996; Johnson,1985; Kagitcibasi & Berry,1989; Roland, 1989; Tu, 1985). Triandis (1995) has emphasized (more strongly than Hofstede, 1980) the idea that individualism entails giving priority to per-sonal goals over the goals of the in-group, whereas collectivism entails giving priority to in-group goals over personal goals. In Chinese societies in Asia, heavy demands are usually placed upon young people to display behaviors that reflect Confucian values, including filial piety, thrift, and maintenance of patriarchal social structures (Bond, 1986; Hsu, F. L. K., 1985). All studies of Confucian heritage societies agree on the primacy of the family and the obligation of younger family members to meet the ex-pectations of their elders (Hsu, J., 1985; Yang, 1988; Wu & Tseng, 1985). Assertions of personal opinions, feelings, and desires for separation from others are, in themselves, strongly discouraged (Cua, 1989; King & Bond, 1985).

In Euro-American societies, freedom of expression and achieving a sense of personal uniqueness and autonomy are paramount, and the embedded-ness of the individual in social contexts is downplayed (Bellah, Madsen, Sullivan, Swidler & Tipton, 1985; Lasch, 1984; Slater, 1970). Findings of mainstream social science research enable us to conclude that—at least among socioeconomically privileged individuals of Western European de-scent in North America—the manner in which one chooses to form con-nections with, or remain aloof from, societal institutions, such as family, education, work, and religion, is mostly a matter of one's own preferences, ingenuity, and initiatives.

Consolidation of personal identity or sense of self may be assumed to be a universal developmental challenge. For Chinese young people, the difficulty of forming a deeply felt, cohesive sense of personal identity and authenticity involves coming to terms, through internal adjustments, with

the expected subjugation of self to collective needs and the expected alter-
ation of self presentation depending upon situational demands. My clinical
experience in Singapore suggests that Chinese young people also experience special challenges to establishing self-esteem as a result of their lack
of personal control over many of the events shaping their lives. For example, several of my young adult clients felt that their accomplishments
reflected the wise decisions or effective guidance of their teachers, parents, or group members. They often complained of limited opportunities
for experimentation with various forms of self-expression, because of the
high degree of structure and surveillance imposed by adults. They felt that
they rarely had the "luxury" of following through on a personally chosen
and elaborated project about which they may have felt quite passionate
(e.g., pursuing a particular art form, course of study, romantic interest, or
sexual orientation). In contrast, Western youth, especially those who are
Caucasian and socioeconomically privileged, enjoy for a time at least the
illusion of more personal control.

Many Euro-Americans hold a view of Chinese young people as deferen-
tial and passive, especially in response to perceived authorities. However,
my observations as a teacher, counselor, and investigator of Chinese youth
in Singapore and Malaysia did not support this view. Rather, Chinese
young people push at the shell of personal identity and distinction as
much as Anglo-American or Canadian youth, who have been the subject of much of our research on identity formation. In discussions about
their experiences of coming to know and express their identities, they see
themselves as oriented very much toward developing a meaningful and
fulfilling sense of self and set of life projects that can become vehicles for
consolidating and expressing their identities.

The ways in which many Chinese youth in Asia differ importantly from
many of their Western counterparts are related to traditional Chinese socialization practices that are intended to teach the young person to think
holistically and longitudinally. In Singapore, for example, while some values may be taking on an increasingly Western cast, patience, filial piety,
and appreciation of the interdependence of all things remain Chinese
virtues (Bond, 1996). Thus, in striking contrast to the American mythic
ideal of the "self-made man," most Chinese young adults are encouraged
to believe that everything is conjoined by mystery and fate, and to recognize that whether one achieves personal distinctiveness or goals does not
depend solely on what one does as an individual.

It is easy for Western researchers to misperceive the Chinese acceptance
of provided roles as indicating passivity, and foreclosing a search for personal meaning and a uniquely created sense of self. This is not so. We are
helped out of our ignorance here by the neo-Confucian scholar Tu Wei-
Ming (1985). He has argued cogently against the misguided impression

that traditional Chinese society, steeped in Confucianism, has been based on the imposition of unquestioned authority of parents upon generation after generation of submissive offspring who are compelled to accept provided identities. Clearly, there would be little potential for healthy psychosocial development if all young people were socialized to follow only the dictates of a gerontocratic dogmatism without any appeal to a superordinate goal or transcendent framework of intention. These attenuated conditions for personal growth are not what one encounters in Confucian heritage societies such as Singapore, Hong Kong, or Taiwan. Interviews with Chinese young people in Singapore revealed their ideological support for the system of rules and obligations that govern most aspects of their lives and their personal appreciation of the social support they recevied from relatives and public institutions in achieving their best in the areas towards which they were directed and socially rewarded. As Tu (1985) and others have pointed out, socialization and self development in Confucian heritage societies are built on a foundation of willing participation on the part of the young person him/herself. With the exception of young people seen in therapy, the expressed allegiance of Chinese youth in Singapore to the sociocultural and political system of which they were a part far overrode their frustrations and regrets about the lack of individual freedoms with regard to self-expression and experimentation. These they tended to regard as less fundamental for ensuring personal and social well-being than taking up one's prescribed roles, responsibilities, and privileges as part of the collective.

The misimpression of a dogged obedience to authoritarian prescriptions for the sake of security and conformity alone is predicated on the false assumption that, since there are clear limits to the choices available to young people in Confucian heritage societies, there is no opportunity for them to exhibit any voluntarism on matters considered important in Western individualism, such as forms of interactions with elders (Tu, 1985). On the contrary, the subjugation of the individual in a Confucian approach to socialization involves a complex process of psychological adjustment, acceptance of limitations, and harmonization of oneself with one's surroundings. Their motivation is strengthened and reinforced by strenuous education in areas of moral, civic, and cultural education both in and out of school, tutelage by extended family members, and government sanctions.

☐ Interpersonal Reciprocity in Identity Formation

In Confucian heritage societies, there is a deep conviction that one can never fully realize oneself in isolation from others. In fact, it is interesting to note, though perhaps not essential to the primary purpose of this chapter, that the Confucian conceptualization of human nature and social processes has much in common with symbolic interaction theory, which views the self as created in the context of communication and the sharing of interactive symbolic processes (Mead, 1934). In Confucian thought, in order to develop fully, the participation of the "other" is not only desirable, but absolutely essential (Tu, 1985). The route to "heaven" in the sense of identity achievement and self-actualization is through courageously facing up to the challenge of one's immediate social relationships. A central premise, then, is that one can only come to know who one is in a holistic sense through one's existence as a center of relationships: "For as centers of relationships, we do not travel alone to our final destiny; we are always in the company of family and friends, be they remembered, imagined, or physically present" (Tu, 1985, p. 247). More concretely, in Singapore for example, Chinese young people are often presented with decisions made by the government, their parents or other relatives about their studies both in and out of school, careers, jobs, places of residence, and for some, their social activities and their marriage. Most young Chinese in Singapore are bound to their parents as pre-adolescents, adolescents, and adults, through obligations of filial piety. It is common for them to remain in their parents' home until they marry in their mid- to late twenties, and even then they may not leave the family home.

A basic principle governing identity formation in Confucian thought is reciprocity (Yang, 1986). Children are seen as requiring the structuring, guiding, supporting relationship of the parent or other mentor/companion. If the other person is kind and sets a positive example, the child is likely to internalize the goals of that caregiver. In turn, the child is likely to be filial towards him or her. In this connection, not only through the parent-child relationship, but also through the teacher-student relationship, the husband-wife relationship, and certain other types of relationships, one deepens and broadens one's selfhood (Tu, 1985). This picture of a kind of communal self-awareness and reciprocity hardly gives the impression of youth being cowed or threatened into submission by an unyielding authority. No doubt, of course, many traditional Chinese parents fall short of Confucian ideals just as parents do in Judeo-Christian-based societies. Indeed, with reference to the widely accepted constructs of individualism and collectivism as points of reference for much cross-cultural research, there is a need to recognize the multidimensionality, complexity, and variability within cultural groups, as recent reviews of theoretical and methodological developments during the past two decades since Hofstede's work about these constructs have underscored (Triandis, 1995; Schwartz, 1992).

Time Perspective

Not only does Confucian tradition embody a different sense of cause and effect in identity formation compared to mainstream Western ideas, but also there is a different time perspective. Referring again to the longitudinal perspective on self-actualization, Confucian thought holds that the development of a clear and true sense of self takes much time and mental clarity and experience of suffering and challenges in the world. Indeed, the challenge of identity formation may be too great to expect this achievement in one lifetime. As achievement-oriented as many Chinese are, a basic Confucian notion is that achieving an authentic, chosen identity may occur over many lifetimes.

Confronting Limitations

In the West, there is a widespread popular belief that conforming and the acceptance of provided social constraints and role obligations somehow prevent or damage the construction of a meaningful identity. Western youth are encouraged early to seek their own way and to believe that in accomplishing things alone, they can consolidate the desired separateness of their egos. Seen through psychological research, Western youth are very bound by their egos. As many proponents of critical psychology have shown (e.g., Fanon, 1986; Frosh, 1989; Seve, 1978) and others (e.g., Sampson, 1987) have shown, the language of individualism and the atomistic models of cognitive-behaviorism help to obscure the social relations in which the self is constituted, recasting the individual as a rational and detached unit using social resources as instruments in the pursuit of self-centered goals.

In Confucian heritage societies, social structures and role obligations are seen as potential resources for personal growth through a kind of communal self-awareness and developmentally appropriate challenges to assume increasing social responsibilities. The confrontation of limitations may be viewed as a vehicle for learning more about oneself and stretching one's capabilities in ways that are beneficial to the elaboration and strengthening of personal identity and, at the same time, beneficial to the collective (Marcel, 1964). One common expression of this is the tendency of many Chinese young people to see things more pragmatically than do many Western youth and to evaluate alternatives in terms of potential implications for one's family, community group, or country, as well as for oneself (Bond, 1996).

On an individualism-collectivism dimension, the aims of socialization in Confucian heritage societies can be seen as *both*, rather than *either-or*. Marcel (1964) has elucidated the mutually self- and other-enhancing interdependence which he terms "creative fidelity" in Confucian socialization. The ardent individualism of many Western societies, especially Anglo-American society, is subsumed in a superordinate collectivism that derives from Confucian conceptions of order and stability; in return for obedience and loyalty to the collective, especially one's family, the individual accumulates "face" and security. Once one's duties to the collective have been performed, one is encouraged to pursue his (and sometimes her) own interests (Ho & Chiu, 1994). Individual gratification and variation are accepted ideas in Confucian thought, though they are not emphasized as much as ideas about subserving individuals to the good of the collective.

☐ Areas of Special Methodological Interest

Selected Methodological and Clinical Issues

The foregoing commentary is sufficient to support the hypothesis that the Confucian construction of processes of identity achievement is not the same as in Euro-American cultures and cannot be represented using Eurocentric and individualistic models or gauged using the same tools. Conceptually, the language and perspective of individualism may help us to understand the psychosocial development of certain North Americans, especially socioeconomically enfranchised males of Western European descent. However, this worldview does not help us to understand the experiences of youth in other cultures whose identity achievement may be differently constituted (Hoare, 1991; Kakar, 1991). Indeed, Geertz (1984, p. 126) noted that the Western notion of the self as "bounded" and "unique" with ego identity as self-central is a "peculiar" concept from many non-Western cultural perspectives, and not just from a Confucian perspective. Western investigators must be aware of the extent to which they have presumed an ethnocentric, masculine concept of identity.

Surveys of value priorities of American adults have shown an increasing preoccupation with the needs of the autonomous self (Rokeach & Ball-Rokeach, 1989). Similarly, as recent critiques have underscored (Hoare, 1991; Sampson, 1989), American psychology's current theories of the Self and the Person have become increasingly predicated on the necessity or the ideal of insular individualism. Some studies have found that people who are closely aligned with the dominant culture in the U.S.A. (e.g., Anglos and immigrants who score high on acculturation measures devised by American investigators) score higher on measures of self-actualization than minorities and less assimilated immigrants (Leong & Tata, 1990; Wong-Rieger & Quintana, 1987). One suspects that investigators have devised a conceptualization of acculturation and measures of self-actualization that reflect their own ethnocentric criteria.

In research by American psychologists, girls generally score significantly lower in studies of self-realization and higher on those measuring altruism compared to boys (Leong & Tata, 1990; Gilligan, 1982; 1988). Some recent feminist theorists have contended that a stable, mature identity is rooted in an ethic of relational connectedness and caring (e.g., Gilligan, 1988; Sampson, 1985; 1989). This view resembles the view in Confucian heritage societies that the identity-achieved individual is able to accept and include the needs and prescriptions of others in a connected, reciprocally constituted self-system (Cua, 1989; Tu, 1985).

Methodologically, some cross-cultural psychologists have been particularly errant in forging ahead with research in cultures foreign to themselves, supplied with translated questionnaires and interview schedules without initially assessing the cultural context and establishing what constructs and procedures resonate with the research participants (see a critical review by Kagitcibasi, 1992a). It is not expected that an investigator can fully transcend the bias of his or her own worldview (e.g., Pedersen, 1987; Shweder, 1991). Instead, investigators must seek the help of cultural informants, participatory research methods, and other research strategies (e.g., Greenfield, 1994; Kindermann & Valsiner, 1989; Much, 1995). Research that relies on intercultural dialogue as a springboard for defining core constructs and innovating culturally inclusive procedures can transcend the narrow parochialism that has characterized much identity research (Kagitcibasi, 1992b). More generally, psychologists must accept that we cannot approach a meaningful interpretation of individual self-reports and observed behaviors without knowing their cultural conditioning and their significance from within a particular sociocultural system. Multiculturalism offers a fourth force or perspective for furthering this endeavour.

Youth Risk Behaviors

A large scale study of risk behaviors among a representative sample of youth in Singapore (Ball & Moselle, 1995) showed that the vast majority of Singaporean youth either abstain completely or engage in low levels of risk behaviors. These behaviors include engaging in low levels of alcohol, tobacco, and other substance use, physical violence, sexual intercourse, and suicidal gestures. Compared to youth in the U.S.A. (Centers for Disease Control, 1993) and Canada (McCreary Centre Society, 1993), our research showed Singaporean youth as having much more health-protective, "wholesome" lifestyles than their North American counterparts. Preliminary findings from our studies of youth in Malaysia show similarly low levels of risk behaviors.

Several distinctive features of life in Singapore and other Southeast and East Asian countries undoubtedly figure centrally in shaping the healthy lifestyles of most youth. Reflecting upon dimensions that have been shown in Western-based research as important to risk behaviors among youth (e.g., Baumrind & Moselle, 1984; Jessor, 1992; Donovan, Jessor, & Costa, 1991; Elliott, Huizinga, & Menard, 1989; Flay & Petraitis, 1994), factors that may account for our research findings include: (1) the prevalence of intact nuclear families and of extended family ties in Confucian heritage societies; (2) strong bonds to conventional social institutions such as one's family, school, uniformed youth group, or religious group; (3) high academic expectations and goals; (4) low levels of risk behaviors among adult role models; (5) government and community-level sanctions; and (5) prevention programs.

A plethora of Western-based studies of developmental challenges during adolescence have interpreted the propensity of youth to engage in risky behaviors as an almost inevitable expression of the process of seeking autonomy and individuality. The assumption seems to be that youth must act out or "externalize" their approach-avoidance conflicts and choices by experimenting with alternative behaviors and ways of evaluating things. This is the "sturm" and "drang" of the "moratorium" stage of identity development that Marcia (1980) and others have posited as a necessary step in the work toward identity achievement. Through this process of trying on identities and experimenting with behaviors, the individual may creatively produce a point of view and lifestyle that has the distinctive stamp of personal choice on it.

In contrast, in Confucian heritage societies (and perhaps other societies), risk-taking behaviors are perceived by many young people as distracting one from the task of establishing a sense of identity through achievement, productivity in the work force, and performance of role responsibilities in one's family. For example, nearly all young adults in Singapore whom I interviewed in a preliminary study of identity formation told me emphatically that young people in their country are not likely to achieve an individual identity, even among their peers, through unconventional acting out behaviors such as wearing unusual clothing, distinctive hairstyles, body piercing, substance abuse, sexual activities, or vandalism. Rather, they described how they achieved a positive sense of who they are through the demonstration of skills that entitle and empower them to take on increasingly valued roles within the social structures of their communities. In facing the challenge of adapting oneself for fulfilling filial obligations and advancing the well-being of one's family and larger collectivity, one's self development is enhanced and one comes to know one's "true nature."

Counseling and Clinical Psychology

As mentioned previously, questions of identity formation are integral to a consideration of multiculturalism in counseling and clinical psychology. Psychotherapy emerged in Europe and North America as a response to personal problems and aims important within a narrow band of socioeco⁻nomically privileged Westerners. Applications of psychotherapy are now being considered beyond the sociocultural contexts to which this approach is indigenous. In this enterprise, concepts of psychological adjustment and maladjustment are often etically conceived, and formulaic. As Sue and Sue (1990) argue, models of primary and secondary prevention, as well as models of brief therapy interventions developed in the West, are often assumed to be universally applicable. Trainers and providers of counseling and therapy must be aware of the historically and culturally situated na-ture of goals and expectations for psychosocial development and change through intervention (Pedersen, Draguns, Lonner, & Trimble, 1989).

Many Western psychotherapists working with youth assume that an important goal of intervention is to help the client consolidate and ex-press a unique and positive sense of individual identity. Counselors often aim to help young people to respond to problems in ways that are con-gruent with the client's special sense of who he or she is, apart from the intrusive expectations of others. From the perspective of the Confucian tradition, these goals may seem to reflect a kind of narcissistic object fasci-nation which trivializes the process of coming to know oneself, harmoniz-ing oneself with one's surrounding, and furthering one's spiritual growth through service and through confrontation with limitations. Further, from the perspective of many Asians, Western counseling techniques seem to encourage aggressive and destructive social behavior in the service of self-ish goals that abdicate responsibilities to the collective. It is not difficult to appreciate how unreflected efforts to extend the reach of psychological "help" to populations in Asia can be viewed by many Asians as posing a potential threat to the very fabric of which their cultures and identities are constituted (see Ponterotto & Casas, 1991).

In many Asian cultures, the self does not live in a narrowly construed life- and time-bound matrix (e.g., Kakar, 1991). The self is not amenable to introspective analyses of the meaning of one's personal identity, the symbolism of one's experiences, or identification of psychological needs considered apart from the needs of others (Hoare, 1991). Thus, at the very least, therapists and counselors working with individuals from Confucian heritage societies need to recognize the limits of construing the self-as-object and move toward a perspective of self-as-center of relationships, translating this holistic perspective into working with clients. In a similar vein, Hobfoll, Monnier, and Wells (1996) have suggested that adopting a communal coping perspective in coping research, we can better understand the adaptive approaches of non-Eurocentric groups.

Assuming that there are situations for which counseling or psychotherapy would seem to be useful, given the presenting problems and intentions of a prospective client, what can we expect when working with youth from Confucian heritage societies in terms of the kinds of issues that are likely to be salient? Beginning with a view of some conditions which give rise to problems among some Euro-American youth, an important challenge for young people in the West is to construct a sense of self-worth through personal achievements, and to determine their own set of values, spiritual beliefs, sense of belonging, and direction in life (Johnson, 1985). Many of the difficulties that young people experience, and that may bring them to counseling, therapy, or into the juvenile forensic system, often stem from their overwhelming sense of latitude and interpersonal isolation. This can often be exacerbated by a lack of readily discernible external structures, purpose, and spiritual meaning in life. In contrast, clinical experience and conceptual considerations suggest that the psychological problems experienced by young people in Confucian heritage societies are more likely to stem from an overwhelming sense of personal constraint and obligations to social institutions including the family, education, work, and national goals and organizations (Lau, Lew, Hau, Cheung, & Berndt, 1990).

A growing number of therapists have found success in using psychotherapy with some of their Chinese clients (e.g., Ball, 1994; Tien, 1989; Tung, 1991). However, since Western psychotherapy and counseling modalities are not indigenous to Confucian heritage cultures, psychologists working as therapists, counselors, trainers, or training consultants need to guard against presuming the meaning of the client's perspective, goals, and social circumstances. In the wake of poststructuralism, the humanistic enterprise in the social sciences has, in theory, been seriously challenged. In practice, however, the literature with which the Euro-American enclave of psychotherapy represents itself continues to demonstrate a willingness to arrogate to itself the humanistic role of determining what is to be valued and desirable aims of psychological intervention; namely, identity achievement, individuation, self-assertion, self-fulfilment, self-actualization, and similar goals. On the contrary, a central assertion of this chapter is that psychological interventions that do not take account of the embeddedness of the individual as part of a particular cultural context must be viewed as fundamentally flawed (Pedersen, 1990). We have much to learn by clearing out of the way, as counselors, therapists, and researchers, and becoming active listeners, supporters, and collaborators. In adopting the perspective of multiculturalism in the investigation and practice of counseling and clinical psychology, we are motivated to develop more local and situated, particularistic, dialogically-validated approaches to prevention, assessment, and intervention.

Working as a therapist in a culturally responsible, potentially useful way with Chinese youth in Asia requires an appreciation of the Confucian approach to socialization. In particular, the therapist must understand the growth-enhancing potential of apparent obstacles to self-fulfilment. In a Confucian heritage society, the many moral duties and socially prescribed roles presented to young people do indeed obstruct the single-minded pursuit of personal interests or desires by setting limits on what goals can be pursued. However, in a well-ordered Confucian heritage society, instead of merely constraining conduct, social duties and moral prescriptions also facilitate or provide supportive conditions for attainment of personal goals (Cua, 1989; Tu, 1985).

A distinctive feature of Confucian ethics and traditional Chinese culture that is widely discussed among scholars is the function of duties and prescriptions in facilitating self-actualizing qualities of the individual (Cua, 1989). This "enabling" aspect of traditional Chinese culture is complex and well beyond the scope of this chapter. The general idea, however, is that social duties and moral prescriptions are not merely a matter of fitting into a social and political structure and conforming to prescribed rules of conduct. Rather, the function is to harness basic motivation (feeling, desires) toward the pursuit of higher-order, transformative, culturally valued goals. That is, through the exercise of creative ability, involving imagination and reflective choice, the original nature of our desires can be transformed into something beautiful and noble. This path is available to everyone.

Within this framework, Cua (1989) has likened the individual's creative activity within the limiting conditions of duties, moral prescriptions, and circumstances to that of a potter who makes a vessel out of clay or a carpenter who makes a utensil out of wood. Thus, self-actualization is not only possible but is in fact intended as part of the imposition of social duties and moral prescriptions in traditional Chinese socialization practices. One might say that it is not the material one has to work with but rather what one intends and what one does with it that matters.

An understanding of this framework was very much implicit in the worldview that my Chinese young adult clients in Singapore brought to therapy. They nearly always came with the assumption that certain aspects of their lives were fixed and were therefore not subject to discussion. Certain conditions were perceived as immutable, such as their socioeconomic status, or specific choices that had been made for them by elders or by the government, such as their major course of study in university, their housing, their marriage partner, or their occupation. Occasionally they vented some frustrations about these unalterable aspects of their lives. However, their starting point for psychotherapeutic work was not at how to go about changing these, as might be expected from a Western young adult. Rather, their agenda was to work on making the necessary internal adjustments in order to harmonize themselves with these conditions, and how to use the opportunities for self-fulfillment that they were convinced were inherent in these conditions, however obscure these opportunities might have seemed at the moment.

Over a decade of bearing witness to the booming business of "parachute consulting" wherein Westerners purporting to be "experts" arrive from big city airports in Southeast Asia with bag in hand to "deliver" mental health-related training programs, I found that most were culturally uninformed at best. Three interlocking steps that Western consultants need to take are to: (1) assess the cultural context before deciding on a course of action; (2) guard against starting from an initial position about the goals or approaches that are most appropriate or "right" after hearing about the presenting problems or circumstances; and (3) take steps to define the goals, structure, and ways of evaluating an intervention collaboratively, and routinely engage in participatory review of these with clients, trainees, and others vested in or affected by the activity. There are many additional actions and attitudes associated with a multicultural approach to interventions (e.g., Pedersen, 1990; Sue & Sue, 1990). However, these three steps are suggested as starting points for helping to ensure that culturally diverse clients and training recipients are "informed consumers" of and active participants in the construction and evaluation of interventions and training.

☐ Conclusions

The case of youth in Confucian heritage societies offers an example of how multiculturalism is useful as a fourth force in psychology for integrating into our research, theories, and practices the ecology of culture and self as ongoing, mutually-defining processes. This chapter outlines some major domains of theory, research, and practice within which a movement toward more culturally inclusive and multiculturally responsible study of identity processes needs to occur. This will entail: (1) the acceptance in mainstream psychology of participatory, non-hegemonic, culturally-inclusive research methodologies; (2) research that begins with an assessment of the cultural context and sociohistorical conditioning of individual experience; (3) use of knowledge of the cultural historical foundations upon which local constructs of identity and how to achieve it are predicated; (4) a shift from construing culture as a category of determining variables in a linear cause–effect formulation, to recognizing the centrality for psychology of understanding the mutually-defining processes of cultural construction and identity formation; and (5) accepting that people may act out of culturally grounded subject positions that may vary not only from one person to another but within individuals across a multiplicity of fractal identities (e.g., Gilroy, 1990/1991).

Different perspectives and multiple methods are needed to enrich our understanding of processes of constructing identity and the content of identity as it is expressed in interactive behaviors in various contexts (Kaur & Saraswathi, 1992; Triandis, McCusker, & Hui, 1990). I hope that the discussion and examples in this chapter provide an impetus to those in social sciences, human services, and educational communities to respond positively to the challenges, as well as the potential, of an evolving multiculturalism in theory, research, and practice. Cultural and cross-cultural studies of human development across the lifespan using methods that are themselves culturally resonant and inclusive promise to yield insights into both similarities and differences in identity formation, health behaviors, and service needs in various cultural settings. Beyond the focus of this chapter on youth in Confucian heritage societies, a shift in conceptualizing culture and identity as mutually-defining, constructive processes, rather than as linear and static elements, will be helpful for understanding the increasingly diverse demographic, sociocultural, and ideological landscape that characterizes most societies and countries today.

☐ References

Ball, J. (1994, November). Processes and aims of identity development East and West: Implications for psychotherapy for Chinese young people. In L. Y. Cheng, H. Baxter, and F. Cheung (Eds.), *Psychotherapy for the Chinese—II.* Selected Papers from the Second International Conference, 20–23 November, Department of Psychiatry, Chinese University of Hong Kong.

Ball, J., & Moselle, K. (1995). Health risk behaviors of adolescents in Singapore. *Asian Journal of Psychology, 1*(2), 54–62.

Baumrind, D., & Moselle, K. (1984). A developmental perspective on adolescent drug abuse. *Advances in Alcohol and Substance Abuse, 4,* 41–67.

Bellah, R., Madsen, R., Sullivan, W., Swidler, A., & Tipton, S. (1985). *Habits of the heart.* Berkeley, CA: University of California Press.

Bond, H. H. (Ed.). (1996). *Handbook of Chinese psychology.* New York: Oxford University Press.

Bond, M. H. (Ed.). (1986). *The psychology of the Chinese people.* New York: Oxford University Press.

Centers for Disease Control, National Center for Chronic Disease Prevention and Health Promotion (1993). Measuring the health behavior of adolescents: The Youth Risk

Behavior Surveillance System and recent reports on high-risk adolescents. *Journal of the U.S. Public Health Service, 108,* Supplement 1.

Cua, A. S. (1989). The concept of Li in Confucian Moral Theory. In R. E. Allinson (Ed.), *Understanding the Chinese mind: Philosophical roots* (pp. 209–235). Hong Kong: Oxford University Press.

Donovan, J. E., Jessor, R., & Costa, F. M. (1991). Adolescent health behavior and conventionality-unconventionality. An extension of problem-behavior theory. *Health Psychology, 10,* 52–61.

Elliott, D. S., Huizinga, D., & Menard, S. (1989). *Multiple problem youth: Delinquency, substance use, and mental health problems.* New York: Springer-Verlag.

Erikson, E. H. (1968). *Identity: Youth and crisis.* New York: W.W. Norton.

Fanon, F. (1952/1986). *Black skin, White masks.* London: Pluto Press.

Flay, B. R., & Petraitis, J. (1994). The theory of triadic influence: A new theory of health behavior with implications for preventive interventions. In G. Albrecht (Ed.), *Advances in medical sociology: Vol. 4. A reconsideration of health behavior change models* (pp. 19–44). Greenwich, CT: JAI Press.

Frosh, S. (1989). *Between psychology and psychoanalysis: Minding the gap.* London: Macmillan.

Geertz, C. (1984). From the native's point of view. In R. Shweder R. LeVine (Eds.), *Culture theory* (pp. 123–136). Cambridge, England: Cambridge University Press.

Gilligan, C. (1982). *In a different voice.* Cambridge, MA: Harvard University Press.

Gilligan, C. (1988). Remapping the moral domain: New images of self in relationship. In C. Gilligan, J. V. Ward, and J. M. Taylor (Eds.), *Mapping the moral domain* (pp. 3–19). Cambridge, MA: Harvard University Press.

Gilroy, P. (1990/1991). "It ain't where you're from, it's where you're at": The dialectics of diasporic identification. *Third Text, 13* (Winter), 3–16.

Greenfield, P. M. (1994). Independence and interdependence as developmental scripts: Implications for theory, research, and practice. In P. M. Greenfield and R. R. Cocking (Eds.), *Cross-cultural roots of minority child development* (pp. 1–39). Hillsdale, NJ: Lawrence Erlbaum.

Havighurst, R. J. (1972). *Developmental tasks and education.* (3d ed.). New York: David McKay Co.

Ho, D. Y. F. (1986). *Chinese patterns of socialization in Confucian heritage cultures.* Paper presented to Workshop on Continuities and Discontinuities in the Cognitive Socialization of Minority Children. United States Department of Health and Human Services, Washington, DC, 29 June–2 July.

Ho, D. Y. F., & Chiu, C. Y. F. (1994). Component ideas on individualism, collectivism, and social organization. In U. Kim, H. C. Triandis, C. Kagitcibasi, S. C. Choi, and G. Yoon (Eds.), *Individualism and collectivism: Theory, method, and applications* (pp. 137–158). Thousand Oaks, CA: Sage Publications.

Hoare, C. H. (1991). Psychosocial identity development of self and cultural others. *Journal of Counseling and Development, 70,* 45–53.

Hobfoll, S. E., Monnier, J., & Wells, J. (1996). Collectivist coping: Removing gender and cultural bias from coping research. *International Journal of Psychology, 31*(3/4), 104.

Hofstede, G. (1980). *Culture's consequences: International differences in work-related values.* London and Beverly Hills, CA: Sage Publications.

Hsu, F. L. K. (1985). The self in cross-cultural perspective. In A. Marsella, G. DeVos, F. Hsu (Eds.), *Culture and self* (pp. 24–55). New York: Tavistock Publications.

Hsu, J. (1985). The Chinese family: Relations, problems, and therapy. In W-S. Teng, & D. Y. H. Wu (Eds.), *Chinese culture and mental health.* London: Academic Press.

Jessor, R. (1992). Risk behavior in adolescence: A psychosocial framework for understanding and action. *Developmental Review, 12,* 374–390.

Johnson, F. (1985). The Western concept of self. In A. Marsella, G. DeVos, and F. Hsu (Eds.), *Culture and self* (pp. 91–138). New York: Tavistock Publications.

Kagitcibasi, C. (1992a). Research on parenting and child development in cross-cultural perspective. In M. Rosenzweig (Ed.), *International psychological science* (pp. 137–160). Washington, DC: APA.

Kagitcibasi, C. (1992b). Linking the indigenous and universalist orientations. In S. Iwawaki, Y. Kashima, and K. Leung (Eds.), *Innovations in cross-cultural psychology* (pp. 29–37). Lisse, Netherlands: Swets & Zeitlinger.

Kagitcibasi, C., & Berry, J. W. (1989). Cross-cultural psychology: Current research and trends. *Annual Review of Psychology, 40,* 493–531.

Kakar, S. (1989). *Intimate relations.* Chicago: The University of Chicago Press.

Kaur, B. & Saraswathi, T. S. (1992). New directions in human development and family studies: Research, policy, and programme interfaces. *International Journal of Psychology, 27,* 333–349.

Kindermann, T., & Valsiner, J. (1989). Research strategies in culture-inclusive developmental psychology. In J. Valsiner (Ed.), *Child development in cultural context* (pp. 13–50). Toronto, Ontario: Hogrefe.

King, A.Y.C., & Bond, M. H. (1985). The Confucian paradigm of man: A sociological view. In W-S Tseng and D. Y. H. Wu (Eds.), *Chinese culture and mental health.* London: Academic Press.

Lasch, C. (1984). *The minimal self: Psychic survival in troubled times.* New York: W. W. Norton.

Lau, S., Lew, W. J. F., Hau, K. T., Cheung, P. C., & Berndt, T. J. (1990). Relations among perceived parental control, warmth, indulgence, and family harmony of Chinese in Mainland China. *Developmental Psychology, 26,* 674–677.

Leong, F. T. L., & Tata, S. P. (1990). Sex and acculturation differences in occupational values among Chinese American children. *Journal of Counseling Psychology, 37,* 208–212.

Marcel, G. (1964).*Creative fidelity.* Trans. R. Rosthal. New York: Farrar, Strauss & Giroux.

Marcia, J. E. (1980). Identity in adolescence. In J. Adelson (Ed.), *Handbook of adolescent psychology* (pp. 159–187). New York: John Wiley & Sons.

McCreary Centre Society (1993). *Adolescent health survey. Province of British Columbia.* Vancouver, BC: McCreary Centre Society.

Mead, G. H. (1934). *Mind, self, and society.* Chicago: University of Chicago Press.

Much, N. (1995). Cultural psychology. In J. A. Smith, R. Harre, and L. Van Langenhove (Eds.), *Rethinking psychology* (pp. 97–121). London: Sage Publications.

Ogbu, J. (1988). Cultural diversity and human development. *New Directions for Child Development, 42,* 11–28.

Pedersen, P. (Ed.). (1987). *Handbook of cross-cultural counseling and therapy.* New York: Praeger.

Pedersen, P. (1990). The multicultural perspective as a fourth force in counseling. *Journal of Mental Health Counseling, 12,* 93–95.

Pedersen, P., Draguns, J., Lonner, J., & Trimble, J. (1989). *Counseling across cultures* (3rd ed.). Honolulu, HI: University of Hawaii Press.

Ponterotto, J. G., & Casas, J. M. (1991). *Handbook of racial/ethnic minority counseling research.* Springfield, IL: Charles C. Thomas.

Rokeach, M., & Ball-Rokeach, S. J. (1989). Stability and change in American value priorities, 1969–1981. *American Psychologist, 44*(5), 775–784.

Roland, A. (1989). *In search of self in India and Japan.* Princeton, NJ: Princeton University Press.

Roll, E. J. (1980). Psychologists' conflicts about the inevitability of conflict during adolescence: An attempt at reconciliation. *Adolescence, 15,* 661–670.

Sampson, E. E. (1985). The decentralization of identity. *American Psychologist, 40*(11), 1203–1211.

Sampson, E. E. (1987). Individuation and domination: Undermining the social bond. In

C. Kagitcibasi (Ed.), *Growth and progress in cross-cultural psychology* (pp. 84–93). Lisse, Netherlands: Swets & Zeitlinger.

Sampson, E. E. (1989). The challenge of social change for psychology. *American Psychologist, 44*(6), 914–921.

Schwartz, S. H. (1992). Universals in the content and structure of values: Theoretical advances and empirical tests in 20 countries. In M. Zanna (Ed.), *Advances in experimental social psychology*, Vol. 25, (pp. 1–65). Orlando, FL: Academic Press.

Schwartz, S. H. (1994). Beyond individualism/collectivism: New cultural dimensions of values. In U. Kim, H. C. Triandis, C. Kagitcibasi, S-C. Choi, and G. Yoon (Eds.). *Individualism and collectivism: Theory, method and applications* (pp. 85–119). London: Sage Publications.

Seve, L. (1974/1978). *Man in Marxist theory, and the psychology of personality.* Sussex, England: Harvester Press.

Shweder, R. A. (1991). *Thinking through cultures.* Cambridge, MA: Harvard University Press.

Slater, P. (1970). *The pursuit of loneliness.* Boston: Beacon Press.

Sue, D. W., & Sue, D. (1990). *Counseling the culturally different: Theory and practice.* New York: John Wiley & Sons.

Tien, S. S. (1989). The phases of renewal: Steps to integration of the self in psychotherapy. *Journal of Contemporary Psychotherapy, 19*(3), 171–181.

Triandis, H. C. (1995). *Individualism and collectivism.* Boulder, CO: Westview.

Triandis, H. C., McCusker, C., & Hui, C. H. (1990). Multimethod probes of individualism and collectivism. *Journal of Personality and Social Psychology, 59,* 1006–1020.

Tu, W-M. (1985). Selfhood and otherness in Confucian thought. In A. Marsella, G. DeVos, and F. Hsu (Eds.), *Culture and self* (pp. 231–251). New York: Tavistock Publications.

Tung, M. (1991). Insight-oriented psychotherapy and the Chinese patient. *American Journal of Orthopsychiatry, 6*(2), 186–194.

Wong-Rieger, D., & Quintana, D. (1987). Comparative acculturations of Southeast Asian and Hispanic immigrants and sojourners. *Journal of Cross-Cultural Psychology, 18*(3), 345–362.

Wu, D. Y. H., & Tseng, W-S. (1985). The characteristics of Chinese culture. In W-S. Tseng and D. Y. H. Wu (1985). *Chinese culture and mental health* (pp. 3–13). New York: Academic Press.

Yang, C. F. (1988). Familism and development: An examination of the role of family in contemporary Mainland China, Hong Kong, and Taiwan. In D. Sinha and H. S. R. Kao (Eds.), *Social values and development: Asian perspectives* (pp. 93–123). London: Sage Publications.

Yang, K-S. (1986). Chinese personality and its change. In M. H. Bond (Ed.), *The psychology of the Chinese people* (pp. 106–170). Hong Kong: Oxford University Press.

Barry H. Schneider
Michael J. Karcher
Wayne Schlapkohl

Relationship Counseling Across Cultures: Cultural Sensitivity and Beyond

*Most techniques currently used by psychologists to enhance the interpersonal rela-
tionships of children and adults are grounded in Western beliefs about psychological
health, about individual autonomy in relationships, and about the helping process.
In this chapter, we outline some of the different assumptions about relationships that
may be brought to the counseling arena by clients who are not members of the majority North American culture. We argue that psychologists who are members of the
majority culture can be effective in relationship counseling with clients of different
cultural origins if they are sensitive to cultural differences in the ways individuals understand their obligations to significant others. Some modalities of counseling
may provide opportunities for enhanced understanding between individuals from
different cultures, which may be of therapeutic value in its own right. This is illustrated by a case study of two American adolescents in pair therapy. In conclusion,
we argue that multiculturalism can serve as a lens that increases the utility of psychodynamic, behavioral, and cognitive perspectives in a multicultural society and
world.*

Since the beliefs of clients and therapists about interpersonal relationships,
are, to a considerable extent, culturally determined (Dion & Dion, 1996;
Hsu, 1981; Hendrick & Hendrick, 1986), it is not surprising that the effects
of culture influence every stage of interventions designed to enhance interpersonal relationships. When psychologists of the majority culture work
with clients who are immigrants or members of minority groups, and

167

when psychologists contemplate the implementation of interventions in cultures that are unlike those where the techniques were developed, they are probably considering the use of a procedure developed in a Western, individualistic culture with clients whose cultures are more collectivistic. This is because most immigration brings people from more collectivistic societies to more individualistic ones (Peters & Larkin, 1989), and because it is the English-speaking countries that have invested most heavily in the development and evaluation of psychological interventions.

The central argument presented in this chapter is that most existing psychological interventions aimed at enhancing relationships are grounded in the values of the North American majority culture. This value orientation places a high priority on individual autonomy within relationships and on the attainment of individual goals. Such values often conflict with those of minority or immigrant clients. Therefore, the uncritical application of many traditional techniques of relationship counseling in a multicultural society amounts to a perhaps unintentional imposition of the beliefs of the "mainstream" culture on many cultural minorities. This imposition may alienate this needy group of potential service users. It also may produce counseling that achieves the aims of the counselor but estranges clients from their cultural heritage.

Similar intrusions on the beliefs and values of the client population can occur wholesale when methods of relationship counseling developed in North America are used indiscriminately in other societies. Although most of the examples provided in the following pages pertain to interventions implemented in the multicultural Western societies that have emerged after decades of immigration, many of our arguments apply by analogy to the multiculturalism of the profession of psychology worldwide. We use the rubric of "relationship counseling" quite broadly to encompass both preventive and therapeutic interventions with children, adolescents, and adults. Accordingly, relationship counseling as discussed in this chapter might be conducted by a teacher with an entire class, by a school counselor or school psychologist with children or adolescents experiencing adjustment problems, or by a clinical psychologist who receives referrals for individual or group therapy.

We write from a Canadian multicultural perspective, though we also consider literature from the United States. Whereas Canada is known for the English and French cultures that have been recognized officially since its confederation, contemporary Canadian society is, in reality, much more diverse. In Toronto, the home city of two of the authors, 38% of the inhabitants are immigrants (Statistics Canada, 1992b). Almost a quarter (23%) of Toronto's inhabitants speak neither official language at home, with Chinese and Italian both being the most common alternatives to English and French (Statistics Canada, 1992a). Optional Saturday-morning

public-school classes designed to educate immigrant children in the languages of their cultural heritage are conducted in 36 languages; the information hot-line for public transportation functions in 84 languages.

Canada's policy of multiculturalism emphasizes the maintenance of its
many cultural heritages, though not all individuals and political parties
subscribe fully to this point of view. In the daily work of psychologists in
Toronto, we regularly get to know clients from literally dozens of cultures,
including many of mixed cultural heritage. Hence, when Canadians think
of the cultural composition of their country, a relatively large number
of ethnicities come to mind. Nevertheless, it has been observed that there
are more similarities than differences in Canadian and U.S. thinking about
multiculturalism (Das & Niemi, 1992).

A shared concern among psychologists and counselors in Canada and
the United States of America (herein, U.S.A.) is the disparity between the
beliefs and expectations majority-group professionals and their minority-
group clients bring to the therapeutic relationship. Cultural minorities in
North America are not profiting to the extent they might from mental
health services, according to surveys by True (1990) with the Chinese-
American community, by Karno and Edgerton (1969) with Mexican-
American communities, by Kitano (1969) with Japanese Americans, and
by Lee and Mixon (1995) with Asian Americans. Both African Americans
and Native North Americans are often reluctant to seek counseling and
frequently terminate therapy after the first session (French, 1989; Terrell
& Terrell, 1984; Thompson & Cimbolic, 1978).

☐ The Pursuit of Individual Goals in Relationships

The conflict between the White Western emphasis on individualism and
the more predominant collectivist world view has probably received more
attention in the literature on cross-cultural counseling than any other issue. Thus counseling is one of the "astonishingly wide array of domains"
(Kagitcibasi, 1994, p. 52) that has captured the attention of researchers
interested in the dichotomy between individualism and collectivism. This
is because the preservation of individual autonomy is an implicit foundation of the Western conception of psychological health for persons and
for relationships (Dion & Dion, 1996; Landrine, 1995). Such thinking is
particularly characteristic of majority-culture North Americans. Recent research indicates that in the value hierarchies of Western Europeans, who
are often grouped together with North Americans in classifications of cultures, the priority placed on individual autonomy is tempered by concern for egalitarianism and harmony (Bellah, Madsen, Sullivan, Swidler,
& Tipton, 1985; Schwarz & Ros, 1995).

North American psychologists often assume that a psychologically healthy individual is self-aware, self-determined, and self-interested (Richardson & Christopher, 1993), even when engaged in a relationship with a significant other. To not view oneself as a distinct, separate individual is often seen as a sign of psychopathology (Landrine, 1995). Relying too much on others may lead to being diagnosed as having a "dependent personality disorder" (American Psychiatric Association, *Diagnostic and Statistical Manual of Mental Disorders* (4th ed.), 1994). The failure to maintain the distinction between one's own needs and those of one's family or society, and failure to give priority to one's own needs is seen as a sign of ego-boundary difficultly. Accordingly, the viability of an interpersonal relationship is seen as resting on each member's perception that the benefits of the relationship exceed its costs (e.g., Nisbett & Ross, 1980).

In many other cultures, there may not be as clear a distinction between the personal and the social (e.g., Markus & Kitayama, 1991). In many Native North American (Garrett & Garrett, 1994) and Asian (Fernandez, 1988) cultures, the fulfilment of one's personal, individual needs and desires regardless of the effect this has on family or societal harmony might be considered not a sign of healthy ego boundaries, but a sign of selfishness, isolation, and dysfunctionality. Lin and Rusbult (1995) observed that members of collectivistic societies do not regard their relationships as entirely their own concern. Before deciding whom to befriend or marry, they may consider first and foremost the expectations of their family and community. Such values may lead to conflict between clients from a collectivist culture and psychologists who may try to help them calibrate their estimates of personal gain in relationships.

The more collectivist alternative is to conceptualize one's identity in terms of one's social position and social interactions. Gaines (1982) calls this social sense of self the *indexical self*, because the self is perceived or indexed by contextual features of social interactions. One *is* a sister, a member of a clan, or a citizen of a village. One's being is defined through being part of the group. Therefore, rather than desiring to be taught how to express individual desires, non-Western clients may desire a therapist's help in reaching their family's or community's goals, in achieving or promoting harmony in the group, or in dealing with rejection from the group. Landrine (1995), speaking of the distress that non-Western clients experience over not meeting these role expectations, states that if Western clinicians attempt to assist such clients in finding their individualistically defined "true selves," their efforts may have iatrogenic effects. Similarly, she states, clients distraught over separation from the family or community are not necessarily histrionic or overreacting; within their own cultural frames of reference, what may be at stake is their very sense of who they are.

☐ Cultural Perspectives on the Decision that Relationships Need Repair

Clients in many individualistic societies may find it more acceptable to seek professional help in order to change and improve their relationships and relationship skills than their counterparts in many collectivistic societies. For instance, many clients from Asian cultures may be concerned that presenting a personal problem to a psychologist will lead to their family losing face. Chen, Leong, and Geist (1993) reported that, when seeking counseling, Asian college students are less likely than Caucasians to *present* emotional and interpersonal problems and more likely to present career and academic issues, even though, according to their responses to the Brief Symptom Inventory, the Asians reported actually *experiencing* more difficulties than the Caucasians in non-academic areas, including interpersonal sensitivity.

Features of different cultures may also determine in part whether the client and members of his or her family and community regard the professional psychologist as a credible source of advice regarding interpersonal relationships. Most collectivistic societies are characterized by close attachments to members of one's extended family (Harrison, Wilson, Pine, Chan, & Buriel, 1995; Markus & Kitayama, 1991). In situations where majority-culture Western children or adults might turn to professionals, more collectively minded individuals typically turn to their families (e.g., in Costa Rica [DiRosier & Kupersmidt, 1991] and in Italy [Manetti & Schneider, 1996]). Munakata (1986) observed that Japanese families are expected to care for members who experience psychological distress; mental disturbance is considered a private (*"uchiwa"*) family affair in which outsiders, including professionals, should not intervene. In this context, the psychologist may not be perceived as an appropriate consultant on interpersonal relationships.

Some of the reluctance to seek professional help may relate to the fact that, in many collectivistic societies, the rules on how one is to act in social relations are more explicit than elsewhere (Fernandez, 1988; Gudykunst & Ting-Toomey, 1988). For example, in traditional Chinese culture, there are precise rules of culture that guide social situations. A guest must refuse a host's offer (of tea, dinner, etc.) at least once before accepting. It is very acceptable to initiate conversations with a familiar individual, but not with strangers (Gao, Ting-Toomey, & Gudykunst, 1996). If the rules for relationships are that explicit, clients may understand relationship problems as reflecting, in an unambiguous way, their own failure to respect them. They may see little need to consult a psychologist, since they may have little need for a professional opinion regarding the meaning of their behavior. If there is any ambiguity regarding what they are expected to do in a social situation, the appropriate consultant is an authoritative representative of the culture who is well versed in its rules. Thus, this group of clients may experience difficulties in their interpersonal relationships, but may not see psychological intervention as a sound way of resolving them.

Because of cultural differences in values and norms, clients and therapists may not agree that a particular social behavior warrants concern and intervention. The majority North American culture places considerable emphasis on the peer relations of both children and adults. Because of this, there are many social skills programs in schools designed to prevent or alleviate problems in peer relations. Newcomers from some other cultures may not share this priority. Young and Ferguson (1981) found many parents in Calabria, Italy, who believed that excessive socializing by their children would hinder the academic and vocational success they needed to escape the poverty that characterized the region. Many of the parents in that study, as well as a sizeable minority of their sons, expressed indifference about being isolated socially. Accordingly, the many Calabrians who have immigrated to Canada and other countries might not embrace the majority's emphasis on interpersonal relations. A similar priority for academic prowess is frequently expressed by the parents of Canadian children of East Asian origin (Sigel, 1988). Parents with more academic or familial priorities may question the schools' spending time in promoting their children's social competence, and may not perceive the need for children to practice social skills outside of school.

Systematic cross-cultural comparisons in the literature confirm that Western parents and teachers are in general more concerned about children's atypical social behavior than are parents and teachers from other cultures. For instance, Weisz, Suwanlert, Chaiyasit, Weiss, and Jackson (1991) presented Thai and American parents and teachers with the same vignettes of children behaving in either undercontrolled (e.g., fighting or disobeying) or overcontrolled (e.g., shyness or fearfulness) ways. Adults in Thailand rated both types of child behavior as less serious, less worrisome, less likely to reflect personality traits, and more likely to improve with time than did the Americans. Using a similar research design, Lambert et al. (1992) found that, in general, Jamaican parents and teachers rated vignettes of children's undercontrolled and overcontrolled behavior as less unusual than did American parents and teachers. Jamaican parents were also more likely to think that both behaviors would improve given time. English-speaking North Americans may be quicker to intervene or seek interventions for their children's peer-directed aggression or withdrawal than Europeans, according to Schneider, Attili, Vermigli, and Younger's (1997) comparison of the thinking of mothers in Rome, Italy, and Ottawa, Canada. Cultural differences in delineating normal and abnormal behavior must receive particular consideration when counselors hold the institutionally and politically sanctioned power to attribute pathology to the social behavior of children from different cultural backgrounds.

The specific child behaviors that concern adults differ from culture to culture, and these may well be related to the relative importance of individual autonomy and group belongingness in the value hierarchy. Quietness, lack of competitiveness, and lack of eye contact may be perceived as troublesome in societies where the right to achieve individual goals is more highly valued. However, these same behaviors may be perceived as exemplary behavior in a Hopi child (Landrine, 1995), where individual competitiveness is frowned upon, or in China, where children are expected to be modest and polite (e.g., Chen & Rubin, 1994). Chinese adults regard the overt expression of aggression by children as troublesome, probably because it is a severe threat to the harmony of the group, a very fundamental concern in this culture (Chen & Rubin, 1994).

The cultural context is also important in understanding the presenting problems of adults referred because of peer-relations problems. For example, many Western clinicians would have little to offer a person from Japan suffering from a syndrome called *taijin kyofusho* (Kasahara, 1986). This syndrome is the fear of offending others, or that one's body displeases or is offensive to others. According to Kasahara, Japanese mental health professionals see such cases every day. Both Japanese and Western mental health professionals would traditionally be trained to see the symptoms as problematic (Kasahara, 1986). However, it is unlikely that sensitive treatment of this syndrome could occur without the counselor's recognition that it is a reflection of the deeply-ingrained Japanese concern for public appearance and reputation (Lanham, 1986) carried to excess. Like personality disorders in the DSM-IV, this syndrome reflects a problematic manifestation of a culturally-defined and valued personality trait.

In summary, the cultural context determines in part individuals' assumptions about the choices people have in their relationships, their willingness to seek help for relationship problems, their thresholds for regarding interpersonal behaviors as problematic, and the particular behaviors they perceive to be dysfunctional. Because of this, the dominant-culture psychologist and the minority or immigrant client may have very different understandings of the nature and severity of the presenting "problem."

☐ The Process of Relationship Counseling Across Cultures

Most Western schools of thought about relationship counseling assign a central role to the therapeutic alliance between the therapist and the client. This relationship is one that can be explored safely, allowing clients to better understand their own styles of relating and then transfer these new understandings to their other relationships. According to several accounts, clients from other cultures often approach relationship counseling with very different expectations and find it strange that the therapist wants to develop a personal relationship with them. Lambert and Lambert (1984) go as far as developing a role-induction program for immigrants referred for psychotherapy in Hawaii. Such programs may be seen either as educating the client or as cultural indoctrination.

Clients from minority and non-Western cultures may be confused by what they may see as the passive stance taken by many Western therapists whose initial aim may be, essentially, to establish a sound relationship with them. These psychologists might be non-directive with clients of any cultural background; but might believe more specifically that it is best to assume a non-directive style with culturally-different clients in order to avoid imposing their own values. This is one of the few areas in cross-cultural counseling where some quantitative research has been conducted. The data indicate, perhaps counter-intuitively, that many non-Western clients expect and desire a directive counseling style. Firstly, directive interventions are more similar to the counseling that exists in many of their cultures of origin, cultures where figures of authority are assigned prodigious respect. This is especially true of Asian cultures. Counseling in India has been described as very directive and includes extensive advice giving (Scorzelli & Reinke-Scorzelli, 1994). Failure to conform to this style might lead to the impression that the therapist has nothing to offer. This belief may stem from the client seeing the therapist as a form of doctor, whose effectiveness is determined by his/her use of tools, techniques, and methods believed to have healing power (Frank & Frank, 1991).

Secondly, many immigrants' lives are filled with practical issues in adjusting to the economic and social worlds of their host countries. Non-directive styles of counseling emphasizing self-exploration may not help clients meet these practical needs or lead them to feel that therapy is worth the investment of time. However, it is important that psychologists not assume that all clients from societies where authority figures are revered and where therapists are directive will necessarily want directive counseling. People may rebel against the authoritarian norms of their home cultures. In the former communist countries, educational, and other authorities were highly directive in their personal advice to parents and children (Bronfenbrenner, 1970). Clients from these countries could either expect such directiveness or resent it.

In one systematic study of this issue, Waxer (1989) asked Canadian university students of Cantonese and Anglo-European origin to read transcripts of Carl Rogers and Albert Ellis counseling "Gloria" from the film

"Three Approaches to Psychotherapy." In this film, Albert Ellis was very directive; Carl Rogers was very non-directive. Although students in both cultural groups rated Ellis as less sensitive than Rogers, Chinese-Canadian students found Ellis more sensitive and polite to the client than did the Anglo-European raters. Similarly, the Chinese-Canadian students rated Rogers as much less sensitive and polite than did Canadian students of majority cultural background. More importantly, Chinese-Canadian subjects reported that they would be more willing to see Ellis than Rogers, whereas the Canadian students of the majority culture were much more willing to see Rogers than Ellis.

Based only on their clinical experience, Canino and Spurlock (1994) conclude that Hispanic-Americans also prefer a directive approach to counseling. Berman (1979) studied the responses of potential counselors to video-tapes of client vignettes. The actors who portrayed the clients were from various cultures. These tapes were viewed by African-American and White American counselor trainees who were asked how they would respond to the clients. African-American trainees stated that they would use more influencing skills than did White American trainees, providing more practical advice and introjecting their own values and opinions. There is less consensus regarding the degree of directiveness preferred by Native North American clients. Some authors have argued strongly that non-directive styles are most congruent with Native values of harmony and non-interference (e.g., Garrett & Garrett, 1994; Herring, 1992), though others have maintained that Native North Americans find non-directive counseling ineffective (e.g., LaFromboise, Trimble, & Mohatt, 1990; Thomason, 1991).

There also may be a communication style that is optimal for working with culturally diverse children in schools. Delpit (1995) documented many striking differences between the direct, frank language used by inner-city American schoolchildren and the more indirect modes of expression preferred by their middle-class teachers. She detailed how these and other differences in communication style aggravated interpersonal relationships within the school and in the community.

Cultural differences in norms for self-disclosure in interpersonal communication may also frustrate therapists seeking to establish what they see as a therapeutic relationship with their culturally-different clients. There are important cultural differences in determining the stages of a relationship at which it is appropriate to use familiar forms of language and to disclose private feelings (Argyle, 1986). North American clients are some of the quickest to self-disclose. Thus, therapists may believe that they do not have a satisfactory working relationship with their clients who do not "open up," when in fact these clients may only be following their own cultural norms for politeness and for withholding self-disclosure. Canino and Spurlock (1994) observed that Chinese Americans may have learned to be more restrained, and Native North Americans may be more observant and quiet than Caucasian Westerners. For their culture, Chinese Americans may not be emotionally flat or inhibited, although a therapist of majority North American culture might perceive them as such.

☐ Alternatives to Individual Therapy

Systems theorists question the underpinnings of individual therapy for all clients regardless of cultural origin. They do so based on the observation that most clients come to therapy because of problems that involve other people or institutions, rather than problems confined to their own mental space. As noted above, most clients seeing therapists of different cultural origin are likely to be members of societies in which the attainment of one's individual goals is considered less primordial a value than it is in North America. In recognition of this, some sources advocate a systemic approach to therapy, which may be more consistent with the collectivistic world-view, when working with Native North Americans (e.g., Garrett & Garrett, 1994; French, 1989; McWhirter & Ryan, 1991), Hispanic Americans (Canino & Spurlock, 1994), Asian Americans (Fernandez, 1988), and African Americans (Canino & Spurlock, 1994). This may take the form of family therapy, group therapy, or consultation with parents and teachers.

In consulting with parents of children who are aggressive with their peers, psychologists often provide directive training in disciplinary techniques. Parents are taught to be systematic, consistent, and, for the most part, positive. There is ample data that demonstrate the long-term effectiveness of these interventions in reducing aggressiveness and the peer rejection that accompanies it. In working with families in this way, psychologists are making the assumption that the parents feel free to change their parenting. Mead (1971) observed that North Americans believe that each set of parents is free to determine their own way of raising children. Families from other cultures may not see themselves as having this prerogative. In many cultures, parents rely on advice from members of their extended families and on well-ingrained cultural prescriptions in deciding how to raise their children.

It is also erroneous to assume that similar parenting behaviors have similar effects in all cultures (Baumrind, 1972; Hoffman & Saltzstein, 1967). According to Baumrind (1972; 1995), North American children, in general, respond best to authoritative parental discipline that involves verbal reasoning, and in which punishment and rewards are used rarely and only when necessary. Nevertheless, many of the most assertive, mature, and independent African-American girls in her sample came from the authoritarian rather than authoritative African American families. Like other members of economically disadvantaged communities, these parents may be trying to raise their children to conform to rules so that they might adjust successfully to the world of work and be able to advance economically. Delpit (1995) suggests that the more directive parenting style predominates in African-American families because, living in a racist society and in economically stressed communities, African-American parents have had to be direct and explicit in instructing their children's conduct if they were to ensure the children's safety. Thus, it may not always be appropriate to proselytize parents who do not feel free to depart from culturally-ingrained patterns of child-rearing.

In summary, traditional Western assumptions about the process of relationship counseling may be even more unfamiliar to clients of minority cultural origin than to other potential service users. Some potential service users might find the prospect of forming a personal relationship with the therapist quite curious. Some might expect direct, authoritative advice. However, the psychologist may be competing with other sources of advice that the clients see as credible, such as older members of their extended families. Systems work may be more consistent than individual therapy with the value orientations of people from many non-North American cultures. Certain types of value-laden changes suggested by counselors, such as in parenting style, may neither be welcome nor effective.

☐ The Content of Relationship Counseling Across Cultures

In this section, we have selected several of the major approaches to relationship counseling that have achieved acceptance in Western psychology and that have been proven effective. We consider each of these as a product to some extent of the North American priority on the promotion of individual interests and goals.

Problem-solving ability is the objective of many North American counseling programs for adults, families, and children (e.g., Cowen et al., 1996; Kendall, 1991). These clients are encouraged to articulate their own goals for social situations and to direct their thinking ("means-end thinking" in Spivack and Shure's [1974] terminology) and behavior toward ways of achieving them. These interventions emphasize a rational process in which individuals first contemplate their alternatives in responding to a troublesome situation. Having enumerated all their options, they then evaluate the advantages and disadvantages of each in terms of its consequences (Spivack & Shure, 1974; Elias & Clabby, 1992). The optimal consequence is the attainment of one's goals in an effective manner that minimizes negative consequences. Obviously, this is consistent with a culture that emphasizes autonomy and promotion of one's own interests in relationships. This type of counseling may not be as suitable for clients from cultures that place higher emphasis on cooperation. It also may be somewhat alien to cultures in which there are very high expectations for children (or adults) to be obedient, since it encourages questioning, illuminates "self-centered" options, and validates the client's own goals in interpersonal situations as the primary determinant of behavior. In addition, not all cultural contexts place the same premium on logical, rational, linear thinking as underlies social problem-solving programs. Western thinking about social situations and problems has been described as "linear." It is based on a scientific method in which deductive reasoning is used to determine causal relations between events and to organize events sequentially. Non-Western thinking may be characterized as "simultaneous"; it may involve the perception of the simultaneous occurrence of events without attempting to organize them in a causal order (e.g., Lee & Armstrong, 1995). As noted by Nelson (1986, p. 445), "the ultimate function of the mind is not necessarily to be logical, but ... to find ways to get along in the social world to which each person must adapt in order to survive." The social worlds of many members of cultural minority groups may not feature the many alternatives that the designers of social problem-solving programs train children to contemplate.

Quite obviously, assertiveness training epitomizes the promotion of one's own interests as a legitimate right in relationships. As should be clear from the preceding discussion, members of all cultures may not see this as their right to the same extent as North Americans of the majority culture would. Perhaps the most extreme example in the psychotherapy repertoire of the embodiment of the North American priority on individual autonomy is in rational-emotive psychotherapy, where what some may see as more-than-moderate concern about what others think about them is regarded as the underlying cause of much human misery. Scorzelli and Reinke-Scorzelli (1994), in a survey of graduate students in India, discovered that an astounding 87.1% of those surveyed considered Western cognitive approaches to therapy, such as those of Beck and Ellis, to conflict with their own values and beliefs. These cognitive techniques are based on the assumption that individuals are better off if they strive to make their behavior and emotions consistent with their own needs and goals.

In addition to their role in the counseling of relationships which are already in need of repair, individualistic concepts of psychological health permeate the content of many of the interventions Western psychologists design in order to prevent children from developing peer-relations difficulties. For example, the very popular Magic Circle program, which was designed to enhance the self-concepts of children in the early elementary-school grades, consists largely of exercises aimed at increasing children's awareness and expression of their feelings (Ball, 1974; Summerlin, Hammett, & Payne, 1983). At least implicitly, individual self-expression is seen as leading to psychological well-being by itself, divorced from the social interactions in which the feelings emerge and from the feelings of others. Although children might learn a bit about other children's perspectives as a result of their participation, the group is there, primarily, to listen.

In addition to the many prevention programs for children and adults of all ages that feature social problem-solving techniques as core content, others employ a structured social learning that includes live or filmed modelling of desired behaviors, followed by practice and feedback (Goldstein, 1995). The content of the modelling displays is, of course, laden with culturally ingrained values. These more directive social-skills training programs inevitably portray to participants what the program designer considers an optimal level of social participation and outgoingness. Even though we argue below for the advantages of children learning to function according to the rules of different cultures, it must be remembered that even in multicultural schools, a disproportion of children's social exchanges occur with members of their own cultural groups (e.g., Denscombe, 1983; Hallinan & Teixeira, 1987; Howes & Wu, 1990). Therefore, it is important to avoid efforts at teaching children to be either more timid or more bold than the norms of their cultures.

For example, as explained above, it might be counterproductive to try to convince a Chinese child that shyness is generally dysfunctional. In other cultures, there may be a danger in trying to make children too passive. For example, African-American children are often perceived to be "rough" by White-American standards (Foster, Martinez, & Kulberg, 1996). As related by the African-American participants in a social-skills training program led by Foster, Martinez and Kulberg (1996), a form of verbal duelling, called "basing," "dissing," or "playing the dozens," may not be intentionally hurtful. The trainees considered it a culturally normative form of wittiness that is common among African-American males. However, some African-American parents, and counselors working with adolescents of African-American heritage, regard this behavior as more hurtful than the children's accounts suggest (Karcher, 1993).

It should be apparent by this point that, in a multicultural context, caution is needed when using any of the many interventions developed by North American psychologists of the majority culture to assist people in becoming more assertive or more expressive in their interpersonal relationships, even though traditional social-skills training has been found to be effective in Japan (Yusa & Lieberman, 1993; Sato, Sato, & Takyama, 1993), and although problem-solving programs have been found to be beneficial with Asian Americans (Yu, 1993) and with African Americans (Elias & Clabby, 1992). Cultures vary widely in how the target behaviors are interpreted by relationship partners and peers. Similarly, some methods of relationship counseling may operate subtly to increase the separateness of individuals, by encouraging them to become less dependent on the influence of others or to consider a wide range of options for their behaviors in relationships. These strategies are most appropriate for societies in which individual autonomy is a core value.

In the preceding sections, we have argued that most relationship counseling is steeped in the North American value hierarchy that places priority on individuals' freedom to pursue their own interests. In doing so, we wish to point out that this is a culturally-based value priority that others might not share, but not one that is necessarily wrong. Nevertheless, psychologists who work with clients from cultures where this priority is not shared will be more effective if they both understand the alternative approaches available to them and are flexible in their willingness to use them (Ramirez, 1991). It is important for counselors who work with minority clients to help their clients develop social problem-solving skills that empower their clients to function more effectively in the majority community, where they can function as "cultural ambassadors" (Ramirez, 1991).

Professionals may also serve these clients by providing a therapeutic context in which cultural differences in social attitudes and behaviors may be discussed and validated through genuine social interactions. This may be especially poignant in the presence of a majority-culture peer. In the following section, we suggest ways in which counselors might become adept at incorporating multiple cultural viewpoints, and then we illustrate a therapeutic modality that is structured to help children develop cross-cultural competence through the building of multicultural relationships.

☐ An Alternative to Relationship Counseling Based on Individual Goals

We maintain that the encounter between the cultures of the psychologist and client provides many opportunities for them to exchange and assess culturally-based assumptions about interpersonal relationships, what constitutes the problems that emerge in them, and how best they should be resolved. This exchange may be beneficial by itself in enhancing interpersonal relationships because many of the difficulties people from a non-dominant culture experience arise from the conflict of relationship norms between cultures. Furthermore, there may be a richness of alternatives developed in cross-cultural counseling that is rarely found in counseling only with culturally similar clients. One of the core functions of counseling is to teach clients new ways of responding to the world, allowing for greater flexibility or more options (Ivey & Simek-Downing, 1980). With members of two cultures working together, the client and therapist can generate and consider more and more diverse ways of responding to others (Tyler, Sussewell, & Williams-McCoy, 1995). We believe that for many pairings of clients and psychologists who are of different cultures, the juxtaposition of culturally-driven beliefs may improve the client's interpersonal relationships by illuminating multiple ways of understanding them and transforming them. But for such cross-cultural encounters to be health-promoting, as opposed to manipulative or damaging, counselors must uncover an awareness of their own cultural values, beliefs, and biases. Pedersen and Ivey (1993) suggest concrete steps counselors can take, both during counseling and on their own, to develop their own cultural awareness and sensitivity.

It also may be useful to implement what Portes (1990) calls "calibration of cultural meanings." Here, time is spent learning about the client's culture and talking about the psychologist's own expectations. This might include the psychologist discussing his or her values and views of counseling and interpersonal relationships. Portes may regard this calibration as a preliminary that facilitates the relationship between psychologist and client. However, many clients in multicultural centers experience conflict because the different cultures in which they must function are characterized by different assumptions about relationships. Therefore, we can see such calibration of cultural meanings as an important component of the therapeutic process. This is based on the assumption that learning to relate both to members of the majority and minority cultures is seen as a desired outcome, as has been argued, for example, by French (1989) and by Garrett and Garrett (1994), who maintained that Native North Americans must learn to be at least somewhat bicultural if they are to avoid serious adjustment problems.

Thus, the exploration of cultural differences in the expectations for social behavior in relationships could, by itself, be considered very meaningful core content for counseling with culturally-diverse clients. There is no reason to believe that many, if not most, clients are not at least somewhat willing to work with culturally different psychologists in achieving this understanding (see Atkinson's [1983] review of research on the perceived importance of counselor-client ethnic similarity).

Exchange of Cultural Information in Pair Therapy

Pair therapy provides an example of how one intervention may support the use of several psychological strategies in developing children's cultural competence, social connectedness, and emotional health (Selman &

Schultz, 1990). This therapy is based on the premise that in learning to resolve conflicts, children are confronted with the fact that there are differing perspectives that must be talked about and negotiated if they are to get along with their peers. These different perspectives may have their roots in different culturally determined belief systems. Therefore, children are placed in situations in which their different perspectives are brought out in the open and used to help them resolve problems. In pair therapy, two children meet with an adult who provides a forum for negotiation and assists them in reflecting on their ideas and strategies. Through repeated experience in negotiating their differing perspectives, the children are given the opportunity to develop new skills and insights (Lyman & Selman, 1985). It is hoped that the experience leads to the sharing of intimacy, and, if that is what the children want, to friendship. Pair therapy is conducted in schools, clinics, and residential treatment centers, and is sometimes combined with family and/or individual intervention. In a number of recent trials, pair therapy has been conducted with members of different cultures. This affords an opportunity for learning about the different cultures and overcoming cultural barriers in relating to an age-mate.

A Case Study of Cross-cultural Pair Therapy and the Power of Relationships

In the case that follows, we illustrate how pair therapy facilitates a systems focus on the multiple demands of the child's school, home, and community cultures. We show the importance of opportunities for real interactions and social skills development when culturally influenced problems are presented.

Jeff and Orlando were two seventh graders in a U.S. urban school who differed in terms of their ethnic backgrounds and who were referred for counseling for similar reasons. Their teachers believed both that the two children enlisted immature or awkward social skills and that ethnic prejudices seemed to be adversely affecting their school behavior. They were not friends prior to entering into pair counseling, but through the development of a friendship in "pairs" for one hour a week during their seventh grade year, they found a place where they could discuss not only the problems that resulted from their cultural differences, but also those intrapsychic concerns they shared in common.

Initially the two boys appeared, to each other and to the counselor, as quite different. Jeff was an Anglo, second-generation Irish Catholic. He was short, with red hair and a fiery temper. Orlando was a first generation American of Puerto Rican decent with strong Catholic leanings. He was taller than Jeff, but heavy, passive, and quiet. Orlando appeared anxious at school each day because of the many other students in his school who claimed allegiance to Latino gangs that were defined by country of origin. Being uninterested in gang membership, he had to fend off predatory advances by several groups and received no support from the Puerto Rican gang. During the sixth grade, he became depressed and withdrew from his peers. Jeff, on the other hand, was one of eight Anglo students in a grade of three hundred. Daily he had to contend with racist jokes made by students of color. He typically responded with his own racial epithets which invited numerous fights. To discourage these fights, Jeff aligned himself with some older African-American students. They also teased him and tricked him incessantly, but warded off the attacks of many Latinos who feared offending Jeff's patrons. For Jeff and Orlando, school was a dizzying, frightening place, in part, because of their ethnicities.

It was not until they began their relationship together in pairs that it became clear to their counselor, himself a middle-class Anglo from the South, that ethnic conflict was not the concern that weighed most heavily on the boys' minds. Repeatedly, during the early sessions, the counselor interjected questions about ethnic relations at school in general and about the boys' experiences in particular, all of which seemed to fall on deaf ears. The boys would play board games and talk, but never about ethnic issues. There was uncharacteristically little conflict or negotiation of power between them. Instead, through their play and discussions they began to see that they had a great deal in common. They first discovered that they were both religious. Off and on they would spontaneously discuss what Nakkula (1993), and Way, Stauber, Nakkula, and London (1994) found out about the high school both boys planned to attend two years later: that in this community, religion serves as a protective factor against risk-taking behaviors and the assaults of prejudice. This was the first similarity that brought down walls between the boys. But the most critical similarity, in terms of their behavior problems at school, was their common source of anger.

Both boys simultaneously loved their fathers and felt great anger towards them. Their extended reflections on and discussion in pairs about this shared experience seemed to ameliorate the stress and isolation they experienced in school. Their social interaction patterns, which many of the adults assumed were the result of stressors related to ethnic membership, appeared to be rooted in anger towards their fathers. Jeff was angry at his father for dying the year before in a construction accident. Orlando was angry at his father for leaving his mother and bringing him to the United States, but also because he wanted to spend more time with his father, who worked two jobs.

Their discussions about this shared experience seemed to relieve their most conspicuous difference: their different, but equally extreme interpersonal negotiation strategies in school. Jeff had been extremely passive and deferent with the African-American students whom he hung around and who teased him, yet he was very aggressive and impulsive with his peers and teachers. Orlando had been very quiet and withdrawn. As they played together, these same patterns of relating reappeared and were identified and addressed with the counselor's assistance. The boys slowly learned to negotiate more successfully. They began to engage in more direct and respectful discussions of their interests. After several months, and in the safety of the relationship the boys developed, they were first able to express their feelings about their fathers and about their relationship with each other. As they began to talk with each other about their anger during sessions, and as their friendship developed, both began to function more adaptively in school with their peers and teachers. Jeff became less impulsive and annoying to his peers and teachers, and thus he was picked on less and began to develop new friendships. Not only did Orlando become more socially assertive in school, but with Jeff's encouragement Orlando became more honest with his father.

Remarkably, the benefits of their relationship extended beyond both the changes in the quality of their relationships at home and at school. After coming to see each other as similar, they began to talk about the experiences at school as members of different ethnic groups. Out of what appeared to be a genuine concern for each other, the boys worked to help each other deal with their ethnically-centered problems in school. What stood out most to the counselor was that fact that through the development of a relationship based on shared experiences, the boys began to discuss the cultural conflicts they had earlier dismissed. They were also able to provide perspectives on their problems, borne out of cultural and personal experience, that were more effective than what the counselor could provide. Whereas none of the counselor's discussions of race or class seemed to move the boys, their relationship together provided the boys an experience that lessened the sting of alienation they experienced in school. We believe that the pair-therapy format facilitated these changes by permitting the boys to articulate their social goals, to relate to each other on their own terms, to learn, try out, and master the skills that would make them more culturally competent at school.

This case illustrates the importance of steady attention to cultural issues but also of remaining open to concerns that may best be explained by the psychodynamic, humanistic, behavioral, or cognitive schools of psychology. In Jeff and Orlando's case, much of the counselor's clinical attention and therapeutic structuring was focused on the boys' cognitions and social problem-solving skills. Attention to this dimension allowed Jeff to rein in his impulsiveness through thinking about the consequences of his behavior. Yet it also appeared that Jeff's acting out and Orlando's internalizing behaviors reflected emotional conflicts borne out of their family dynamics.

Had the therapist only attended to issues of culture, ethnic isolation, and discrimination, the boys might never have dealt with their emotional disturbances or social-skills deficits. Had the therapist not adopted a systems-oriented approach, the influence of the families, gangs, and peers might never have been understood. Thus, this case illustrates that multiculturalism might not be considered a school, theory, or force in its own right, but as a lens the use of which enhances the value of the existing schools of thought in a multicultural society.

☐ Multiculturalism: A Fourth Force in Relationship Counseling?

Maslow (1968, pp. iii–iv) held that psychology is ready for a "fourth force" that would go beyond what is rational and assign less of a premium to the promotion of individual interests and the delineation of individual needs. Multicultural approaches to relationship counseling share much of this spirit. Moving from an ethnocentric to a multicultural perspective may be one harbinger of such a fourth force because this would entail, in most cases, more of a focus on the interconnectedness of individuals rather than on their separateness. Both the transpersonal psychologists (Walsh & Vaughan, 1993), who first called for a fourth force, and the proponents of multiculturalism who have followed suit (see Pedersen's interview in Sandhu, 1995) would endorse a de-emphasis on individual desire in relationship counseling.

Multiculturalism does not require wholesale abandonment of our concepts of pathology, social competence, and psychosocial adjustment, but greater attention to the role of culture in their formulation. It does entail some re-examination of our assumptions about what constitutes social competence and what we consider a "social skill," with greater attention to the social context—or, more accurately, the multiple social contexts—that surround the specific relationships in which the social skills are to be applied. Psychologists must re-think their basic assumptions regarding what it means to be a professional psychologist active in relationship counseling, and question the premium many place on individual "talk therapy."

For multiculturalism to reflect a fourth force in psychological intervention may require that it facilitate the harmonious integration of the best of each psychological community. It need not compete with other forces and theories nor pit its techniques against other established interventions. Multiculturalism can best be seen as a meta-theory that provides a new dimension to relationship counseling. It can serve as a lens that permits effective use of cognitive, dynamic, and humanistic approaches with culturally different clients in a multicultural contextualization.

Multiculturalism implies a culturally sensitive context for therapeutic techniques, though it does not dictate technique.

This is not to say that new techniques for relationship counseling in a multicultural context should not emerge. These techniques will surely be based on a recognition of the different assumptions about relationships that are held by members of different cultures. Counseling can provide an opportunity for comparing and reflecting upon these differences. It is imperative that whatever techniques emerge from a multicultural perspective, or that are re-interpreted in its wake, be evaluated far more extensively than they have been. We present the information in this chapter with some caution because there is only limited research on cross-cultural relationship counseling. The speculations we have offered based on theory and clinical experience may exaggerate cultural differences in optimal counseling practice. There is a critical need for research to inform practice in this area, and there are increasing opportunities for action-oriented researchers to confirm the effectiveness of interventions that seem more consistent with theoretical models of cultural difference than do more conventional ways of conducting relationship counseling.

More needed than alternative approaches is a space where theories and cultures can interact effectively and cooperatively. Our review of Western approaches to relationship counseling when applied to individuals from collectivistic societies has several important implications for theory and practice. Minority clients may benefit from a balance between the traditional emotion- and self-focused therapies and the development of relationship skills that are useful not only in dealing with individualistic cultures, but also in bridging two cultures. One key to effective relationship counseling in a multicultural society will be the balance of emphases on achieving autonomy, cultural connectedness, and intimacy in relationships. A competent multicultural relationship counselor must understand the basic cultural differences, investigate their influence on cognitive, psychodynamic, and humanistic processes, and must ensure that the context of intervention supports the full expression of cultural diversity.

☐ References

American Psychological Association. (1994). *Diagnostic and statistical manual of mental disorders* (4th ed.). Washington, DC: Author.

Argyle, M. (1986). Rules for social relationships in four cultures. *Australian Journal of Psychology, 38,* 309–318.

Atkinson, D. (1983). Ethnic similarity in counseling psychology: A review of the research. *The Counseling Psychologist, 11,* 79–92.

Ball, G. (1974). *Magic Circle: An overview of the human development program.* LaMesa, CA: Human Development Training Institute.

Baumrind, D. (1972). An exploratory study of socialization effects on Black children: Some Black-White comparisons. *Child Development, 43,* 261–267.

Baumrind, D. (1995). *Child maltreatment and optimal caregiving in social contexts.* New York: Garland.

Bellah, R. N., Madsen, R., Sullivan, W. M., Swindler, A., & Tipton, S. M. (1985). *Habits of the heart: Individualism and commitment in American life.* Berkeley: University of California Press.

Berman, J. (1979). Counseling skills used by Black and White male and female counsellors. *Journal of Counseling Psychology, 26,* 81–84.

Bronfenbrenner, U. (1970). *Two worlds of childhood: U.S. and U.S.S.R.* New York: Russell Sage Foundation.

Canino, I., & Spurlock, J. (1994). *Culturally diverse children and adolescents: Assessment, diagnosis, and treatment.* New York: Guilford.

Chen, D., Leong, F., & Geist, R. (1993). Cultural differences in psychological distress between Asian and Caucasian American college students. *Journal of Multicultural Counselling and Development, 21,* 182–190.

Chen, X., & Rubin, K. H. (1994). Family conditions, peer acceptance and social competence and aggression in Chinese children. *Social Development, 3,* 269–290.

Cowen, E. L., Hightower, A. D., Pedro-Carrol, J. L., Work, W. C., Wyman, P. A., & Haffey, W. G. (1996). *School-based prevention for children at risk: The Primary Mental Health Project.* Washington, DC: American Psychological Association.

Das, S., & Niemi, R. (1992). Democratic attitudes in multicultural settings: A cross-national assessment of political socialization. *Youth and Society, 23,* 313–334.

Delpit, L. (1995). *Other people's children: Cultural conflict in the classroom.* New York: New Press.

Denscombe, M. (1983). Ethnic group and friendship choice in British primary schools. *Educational Research, 25,* 184–190.

DeRosier, M., & Kupersmidt, J. (1991). Costa Rican children's perceptions of their social networks. *Developmental Psychology, 27,* 656–662.

Dion, K. L., & Dion, K. K. (1996). Cultural perspectives in romantic love. *Personal Relationships, 3,* 5–17.

Elias, M., & Clabby, J. (1992). *Building social problem-solving skills: Guidelines from a school-based program.* San Francisco: Jossey-Bass.

Fernandez, M. (1988). Issues in counselling Southeast Asian students. *Journal of Multicultural Counselling and Development, 16,* 157–166.

Foster, S., Martinez, C., & Kulberg, A. (1996). Race, ethnicity, and children's peer relations. In T. Ollendick and R. Prinz (Eds.), *Advances in clinical child psychology: Volume 18* (pp. 133–172). New York: Plenum.

Frank, J. D., & Frank, J. B. (1991). *Persuasion and healing.* Baltimore: Johns Hopkins University Press.

French, L. (1989). Native American alcoholism: A transcultural counselling perspective. *Counselling Psychology Quarterly, 2,* 153–166.

Gaines, A. (1982). Cultural definitions, behaviour, and the person in American psychiatry. In A. J. Marsella and G. M. White (Eds.), *Cultural conceptions of mental health and therapy* (pp. 167–192). London: Redel.

Gao, G., Ting-Toomey, S., & Gudykunst, W. (1996). Chinese communication process. In M. H. Bond (Ed.), *The handbook of Chinese psychology* (pp. 280–293). New York: Oxford.

Garrett, J., & Garrett, M. (1994). The path of good medicine: Understanding and counselling Native American Indians. *Journal of Multicultural Counselling and Development, 22,* 134–144.

Goldstein, A. (1995). Coordinated multi-target skills training: The problem of generalization enhancement. In W. O'Donohue and L. Krasnor (Eds.), *Handbook of psychological skills training: Clinical techniques and applications* (pp. 383–399). Boston: Allyn & Bacon.

Gudykunst, W., & Ting-Toomey, S. (1988). *Culture and interpersonal communication.* London: Sage Publications.

Hallinan, M. T., & Teixeira, R. A. (1987). Opportunities and constraints: Black-white differences in the formation of interracial friendships. *Child Development, 58,* 1358–1371.

Harrison, A., Wilson, M., Pine, C., Chan, S., & Buriel, R. (1995). Family ecologies of ethnic minority children. In N. Goldberger and J. Veroff (Eds.), *The culture and psychology reader* (pp. 292–320). New York: New York University Press.

Hendrick, C., & Hendrick, S. (1986). A theory and method of love. *Journal of Personality and Social Psychology, 50,* 392–402.

Herring, R. (1992). Seeking a new paradigm: Counselling Native Americans. *Journal of Multicultural Counselling and Development, 20,* 35–43.

Hoffman, M., & Saltzstein, H. D. (1967). Parent discipline and the child's moral development. *Journal of Personality and Social Psychology, 5,* 45–57.

Howes, C., & Wu, F. (1990). Peer interactions and friendships in an ethnically diverse school setting. *Child Development, 61,* 537–541.

Hsu, F. L. (1981). *Americans and Chinese: Passage to difference.* Honolulu, HI: University of Hawaii Press.

Ivey, A., & Simek-Downing, L. (1980). *Counseling and psychotherapy: Skills, theories, and practice.* Englewood Cliffs, NJ: Prentice-Hall.

Kagitcibasi, C. (1994). A critical appraisal of individualism and collectivism: Toward a new formulation. In K. C. Kim, H. C. Triandis, C. Kagitcibasi, S. Choi, and G. Yoon (Eds.), *Individualism and collectivism* (pp. 52–65). London: Sage Publications.

Karcher, M. J. (1993). *Capping: Ethnographic analysis of forms of intimacy and autonomy among adolescents.* Unpublished manuscript. Harvard University.

Karno, M., & Edgerton, R. B. (1969). Perception of mental illness in a Mexican-American community. *Archives of General Psychiatry, 20,* 233–238.

Kasahara, Y. (1986). Fear of eye-to-eye confrontation among neurotic patients in Japan. In T. S. Lebra and W. P. Lebra (Eds.), *Japanese culture and behaviour* (pp. 379–387). Honolulu HI: University of Hawaii Press.

Kendall, P. C. (Ed.). (1991). *Child and adolescent therapy: Cognitive-behavioral procedures.* New York: Guilford.

Kitano, H. (1969). Japanese-American mental illness. In S. Plog and R. Edgerton (Eds.), *Changing perspectives on mental illness* (pp. 257–284). New York: Holt, Rinehart & Winston.

La Fromboise, T. D., Trimble, J. E., & Nohatt, G. V. (1990). Counseling intervention and American Indian tradition: An integrative approach. *Counseling Psychologist, 18,* 628–654.

Lambert, R., & Lambert, M. (1984). The effects of role preparation for psychotherapy on immigrant clients seeking mental health services in Hawaii. *Journal of Community Psychology, 12,* 263–275.

Lambert, M., Weisz, J., Knight, F., Desrosiers, M., Overly, K., & Thesiger, C. (1992). Jamaican and American adult perspectives on child psychopathology: Further exploration of the threshold model. *Journal of Consulting and Clinical Psychology, 60,* 146–149.

Lanham, B. (1986). Ethics and moral precepts taught in schools of Japan and the United States. In T. Lebra and W. Lebra (Eds.), *Japanese culture and behaviour* (pp. 280–296). Honolulu, HI: University of Hawaii Press.

Landrine, H. (1995). Clinical implication of cultural differences: The referential versus the indexical self. In N. Goldberger and J. Veroff (Eds.), *The culture and psychology reader* (pp. 744–766). New York: New York University Press.

Lee, C. C., & Armstrong, K. L. (1995). Indigenous models of mental health intervention: Lessons from traditional healers. In J. G. Ponterotto, J. M. Casas, L. A. Suzuki, and C. M. Alexander (Eds.), *Handbook of multicultural counseling* (pp. 441–456). Thousand Oaks, CA: Sage Publications.

Lee, W. M., & Mixon, R. J. (1995). Asian and Caucasian client perceptions of the effectiveness of counseling. *Journal of Multicultural Counseling and Development, 23,* 48–56.

Lin, Y., & Rusbult, C. (1995). Commitment to dating relationships and cross-sex friendships in America and China. *Journal of Social and Personal Relationships, 12,* 7–26.

Lyman, D., & Selman, R. (1985). Peer conflict in pair therapy: Clinical and developmental analyses. *New Directions for Child Development, 29,* 85–102.

Manetti, M., & Schneider, B. (1996). Stability and change in patterns of parental social support and their association with children's early school adjustment. *Journal of Applied Developmental Psychology, 17,* 101–115.

Markus, H. R., & Kitayama, S. (1991). Culture and the self: Implications for cognition, emotion, and motivation. *Psychological Review, 98,* 224–253.

Maslow, A. (1968). *Toward a psychology of being.* New York: Van Nostrand-Reinhold.

McWhirter, J., & Ryan, C. (1991). Counselling the Navajo: Cultural understanding. *Journal of Multicultural Counselling and Development, 19,* 74–82.

Mead, M. (Speaker). (1971). The American Family: Margaret Mead identifies the forces working to undermine the family (Cassette Recording). North Hollywood, CA: Centre for Cassette Studies.

Munakata, T. (1986). Japanese attitudes toward mental illness and mental health care. In T. S. Lebra and W. P. Lebra (Eds.), *Japanese culture and behaviour* (pp. 369–378). Honolulu, HI: University of Hawaii Press.

Nakkula, M. J. (1993). *Toward methodological dialogue in adolescent risk research.* Cambridge, MA: Harvard University.

Nelson, K. (1986). Event knowledge and cognitive development. In K. Nelson (Ed.), *Event knowledge: Structure and function in development* (pp. 439–457). Hillsdale, NJ: Lawrence Erlbaum.

Nisbett, R., & Ross, L. (1980). *Human influence: Strategies and short comings of social judgement.* Englewood Cliffs, NJ: Prentice-Hall.

Pedersen, P. B., & Ivey, A. (1993). *Culture-centered counseling and interviewing skills: A practical guide.* Westport, CT: Praeger.

Peters, G., & Larkin, R. (1989). *Population geography* (3rd ed.). Dubuque, IA: Kendall/Hunt.

Portes, P. (1990). Political upheaval, cultural assimilation and the origin of counselling needs. *International Journal for the Advancement of Counselling, 13,* 11–18.

Ramirez, M. (1991). *Psychotherapy and counseling with minorities: A cognitive approach to individual and cultural differences.* New York: Pergamon.

Richardson, F. C., & Christopher, J. C. (1993). Social theory as practice: Metatheoretical options for social inquiry. *Journal of Theoretical and Philosophical Psychology, 13,* 137–153.

Sandhu, D. S. (1995). Pioneers of multicultural counseling: An interview with Paul D. Pedersen. *Journal of Multicultural Counseling and Development, 23,* 198–211.

Sato, S., Sato, Y., & Takyama, I. (1993). Social skills training for socially withdrawn kindergarten children: The modification of socially isolated behaviour. *Japanese Journal of Behaviour Therapy, 19,* 1–12.

Schwarz, S., & Ros, M. (1995). Values in the West: A theoretical and empirical challenge to the individualism-collectivism dimension. *World Psychology, 1,* 91–122.

Schneider, B. H., Attili, G., Vermigli, P., & Younger, A. (1997). A comparison of middle-class English- Canadian and Italian mothers' beliefs about children's peer-directed aggression and social withdrawal. *International Journal of Behavioral Development, 20,* 211–226.

Scorzelli, J., & Reinke-Scorzelli, M. (1994). Cultural sensitivity and cognitive therapy in India. *The Counselling Psychologist, 22,* 603–610.

Selman, R. L. & Schultz, L. H. (1990). *Making a friend in youth: Developmental theory and pain therapy.* Chicago: University of Chicago Press.

Sigel, I. (1988). Commentary: Cross-cultural studies of parental influence on children's achievement. *Human Development, 31*, 384–390.

Spivack, G., & Shure, M. (1974). *Social adjustment of young children: A cognitive approach to solving real life problems*. San Francisco: Jossey-Bass.

Statistics Canada. (1992a). *Home Language and Mother Tongue*. 1991 Census of Canada. Catalogue number 93–317. Ottawa, Canada: Industry, Science and Technology Canada.

Statistics Canada. (1992b). *Immigration and Citizenship*. 1991 Census of Canada. Catalogue number 95–316. Ottawa: Supply And Services Canada.

Summerlin, M. L., Hammett, V. L., & Payne, M. L. (1983). The effect of magic circle participation on a child's self-concept. *School Counselor, 31*, 49–52.

Terrell, F., & Terrell, S. (1984). Race of counselor, client sex, cultural mistrust level, and premature termination from counseling among Black clients. *Journal of Counseling Psychology, 31*, 371–375.

Thomason, T. (1991). Counselling Native Americans: An introduction for non-Native American counsellors. *Journal of Counselling and Development, 69*, 321–327.

Thompson, R., & Cimbolic, R. (1978). Black students' counselor preference and attitudes toward counseling center use. *Journal of Counseling Psychology, 25*, 570–575.

True, R. H. (1990). Psychotherapeutic issues with Asian American women, *Sex Roles, 22*, 477–486.

Tyler, F., Sussewell, D., Williams-McCoy, J. (1995). Ethnic validity in psychotherapy, In N. Goldberger and J. Veroff (Eds.), *The culture and psychology reader* (pp. 789–807). New York: New York University Press.

Walsh, R., & Vaughan, F. (1993). The art of transcendence: An introduction to common elements of transpersonal practices. *Journal of Transpersonal Psychology, 25*, 1–9.

Waxer, P. (1989). Cantonese versus Canadian evaluation of directive and non-directive therapy. *Canadian Journal of Counselling, 23*, 263–272.

Way, N., Stauber, H. Y., Nakkula, M. J., & London, P. (1994). Depression and substance use in two divergent high school cultures: A quantitative and qualitative analysis. *Journal of Youth and Adolescence, 23*, 331–357.

Weisz, J., Suwanlert, S., Chaiyasit, W., Weiss, B., & Jackson, E. (1991). Adult attitudes toward over and undercontrolled child problems: Urban and rural parents and teachers from Thailand and the United States. *Journal of Child Psychology and Psychiatry and Allied Disciplines, 32*, 645–654.

Young, H., & Ferguson, L. (1981). *Puberty to manhood in Italy and America*. New York: Academic Press.

Yusa, Y., & Lieberman, H., (1993). Group social skills training in Japan and the United States. *International Journal of Mental Health, 22*, 65–72.

Yu, M. (1993). Divorce and culturally different older women: Issues of strategies and intervention. *Journal of Divorce and Remarriage, 21*, 41–54.

CHAPTER 10

Paul Pedersen

The Positive Consequences of a Culture-centered Perspective

Until recently, the field of psychology has been a monocultural science, even though it was born in Central Europe and has spread throughout much of both the Western and non-Western world. Gielen (1994) documents the trends suggesting that this monocultural emphasis in psychology is changing. "Following a brief review of global society, it is argued that (a) at present American psychology routinely neglects perspectives and findings developed in other countries; (b) this is true even if foreign contributions appear in English, (c) this state of affairs differs from the situation prevailing in the hard sciences; and (d) in response to the multicultural movement and global developments, mainstream psychology in the United States and elsewhere will become less ethnocentric in the near future" (p. 26).

There are contemporary global changes that are having increased influence in psychology, demonstrating the positive consequence of a culture-centered perspective. First, the ratio of non-American to American psychological researchers is gradually but steadily increasing (Rosensweig, 1992), suggesting that psychology is growing faster outside than inside the United States of America (herein, U.S.A.). Second, all fields are becoming more global in their focus as a result of technological innovations. Third, there is a multicultural movement, particularly in the social sciences, that has raised sensitivity to cultural variables. Fourth, the topic of cultural and multicultural issues is becoming more widely accepted in psychology. Fifth there is a re-examination of cultural bias in psychology, so that instead of assuming values and beliefs there is more emphasis on discovering each population's unique explanation of its behavior and meaning.

Thompson, Ellis, and Wildavsky (1990) described "cultural theory" as providing the basis for a new perspective, dimension or "force" in psychology: "Social science is steeped in dualism: culture and structure, change and stability, dynamics and statics, methodological individualism and collectivism, voluntarism and determinism, nature and nurture, macro and micro, materialism and idealism, facts and values, objectivity and subjectivity, rationality and irrationality, and so forth. Although sometimes useful as analytic distinctions, these dualisms often have the unfortunate result of obscuring extensive interdependencies between phenomena. Too often social scientists create needless controversies by seizing upon one side of a dualism and proclaiming it the more important. Cultural theory shows that there is no need to choose between, for instance, collectivism and individualism, values and social relations or change and stability. Indeed we argue there is a need not to" (p. 21). The chapters in this book have attempted to demonstrate these positive consequences of a multicultural or culture-centered perspective (Pedersen, 1997).

☐ A Review of the "Fourth Force" Position

The previous chapters in this book have described the need for multiculturalism in psychology, the difficulties in establishing multicultural perspectives, and what has to happen before multiculturalism can claim to be a fourth force in psychology. These chapters can be reviewed in terms of separating what is known from what is not yet known about the role of culture in psychology.

First, we know that fundamental changes are taking place in the social sciences and particularly psychology. Some sort of paradigm shift is occurring. We know that these patterns of change are more than a continuation of historical patterns and represent a significantly different set of rules or patterns. There is still a great deal of disagreement about the basis of these fundamental changes but there is increased attention to the metaphor of "culture" or "multiculturalism" as the basis for understanding these changing rules. We do not know what impact the notion of culture or multiculturalism will have on traditional psychological theories. These changes do not eliminate the importance of psychodynamic, behavioral, or humanistic perspectives, but rather allow them to become more relevant by making culture central rather than marginal.

Second, we know there is a necessary distinction between the processes of multicultural contact, including the behaviors, attitudes, perceptions, and feelings of participants, and the institutional structures which characterize, support, or hinder intercultural contact. We know that there is a multicultural process within particular culturally heterogeneous societies. We do not know whether multiculturalism can become a significantly global fourth force by also providing similar processes and structures across and among nations and societies. There is a danger in overstating the validity of multiculturalism as an international phenomenon, even though at the same time there is some hope and promise for multiculturalism to have a positive global impact in the future.

Third, we know that each society has had a different interpretation of "multiculturalism." In South Africa, cultural relativism justified oppression, de-emphasizing the importance of differences, in the promotion of apartheid practices as legitimate. Multiculturalism meant that different cultures had different mental health needs, and dislocation was seen as a problem of cultural adjustment to the dominant culture. As a consequence, the term "multicultural" in post-apartheid society is not ideologically neutral and must be re-defined and reframed to emphasize potential positive consequences of a multicultural perspective.

Fourth, we know that multiculturalism is not yet a dominant force in psychology (as reflected in contemporary text books), even though it may be playing an increasingly important role in research and theory building. There is a tendency to overstate the importance of multiculturalism as an established fact rather than an aspiration for the future. There are many barriers to establishing multiculturalism as a fourth force which continue to have a powerful influence. It will be important to better understand these barriers before they can be removed and multiculturalism can become more central to psychology as a reality.

Fifth, we know that the dominant culture in a monocultural perspective—at least for the U.S.A.—has been grounded in the values of the North American majority culture. This perspective has emphasized the importance of individual autonomy, the attainment of individual goals, and the minimizing of cultural perspectives of more collectivist minorities, immigrants, or others who place more emphasis on relationships. We do not know what the psychological implications will be for either individualism or collectivism as co-existing cultural perspectives.

Sixth, we know that culture and multiculturalism are broadly defined, acknowledging both within-group and between-group similarities and differences beyond nationality and ethnicity. We know that members of the deaf community define themselves as a cultural and linguistic minority group rather than as a disability group. We know that the cultural deficit model is as hurtful when applied to people who are deaf or who are labeled according to any other affiliation as when it is applied to ethnic or national minority groups. We have not, however, fully explored the consequences of defining multiculturalism broadly in a more inclusive perspective.

Seventh, we know that cultural similarity among youth may be more salient across cultures than other obvious national and ethnic differences. We know that youth from many if not most cultures share similar tasks of psychosocial development with one another across various sociocultural, political, and historical conditions that separate them from previous generations. We know that these youth–culture influences are having a profound impact on identity development. Theoretical frameworks for studying identity formation have typically been based on monocultural or dominant culture—typically Western—assumptions and that there is a need for an understanding of identity formation which is more sensitive to rapidly changing global social context.

Eighth, we know that multiculturalism will not only change the content of our thinking but the very process of thinking itself. The notion of social homogeneity which has been emphasized in the past is giving way to a perspective of cultural heterogeneity. Instead of self-homogenization, a multicultural perspective will advocate self-heterogenization; and instead of social homogeneity, the new perspective will advocate cross-cultural migration. This new way of thinking emphasizes both the complexity and the dynamism of multiculturalism as a fourth force.

Ninth, we know that a multicultural perspective enhances the meaningfulness of psychotherapy by providing a context in which to accurately assess, understand, and recommend change. We know that all counseling and therapy occurs in a multicultural context reflected in the biases of both the provider and the consumer of therapy. A multicultural systems perspective, as might typically be used in family therapy, seems to be the most promising approach to managing the complex and dynamic context in which therapy occurs, although we have much to learn about multiculturally-sensitive psychotherapy.

This summary of what we have learned from reading the previous chapters in this book describes the beginning of a process for describing and anticipating the many changes in psychology—and particularly counseling/clinical psychology—in an increasingly multicultural, global context. We will now move on to examine some of the changes occurring in psychology and the adequacy of multiculturalism as a metaphor to describe those changes.

☐ The Search for Global Universals in Psychology

Psychology has been an "imported discipline" for most of the world's cultures who have adopted and transferred Western psychology's theories and problems to a quite different cultural milieu. Kagitcibasi (1996) points out the limitations for psychology as an imported discipline:

"What is common in the ideographic, hermeneutic, emic, indigenous, relativist, cultural approaches is an emphasis on the uniqueness of concepts in each cultural context, because they derive their meanings from these contexts. There is also a stress on the variability and the uniqueness of the individual case (person, culture, etc.) that requires its study from within and in its own right, defying comparison. In contrast, the nomothetic, positivist, etic, universalist, cross-cultural approaches study the 'typical' not the unique, which can be compared using a common standard or measure. The emphasis is on the underlying similarities that render comparison possible. There appears to be a basic conflict between the emic and the etic if accepted as exclusive orientations, because being stuck in one would negate the other" (p. 11).

The importance of context is a continuing theme in much of contemporary psychological research, in part, because of the increased importance of cultural and cross-cultural psychology, and partly because of the life-span inclusive approach to understanding human development. Context is often conceptualized as 'culture as the organizer of meaning' in each context. First, psychologists are joining anthropologists in studying contextual issues. Second, there is more recognition of cultural bias and ethnocentric orientations in theory and research derived from Western cultural contexts. Third, collaboration between psychologists from Western and non-Western cultural contexts is increasing. Finally, there is increased emphasis on within-group variables across cultures in psychological research. Western psychology has promoted the "separated self" as the healthy prototype across cultures, making psychology part of the problem—through an emphasis on selfishness and lack of commitment—rather than part of the solution (Kagitcibasi, 1996).

Sinha (1997) described a similar perspective as "indigenizing" psychology to emphasize that (1) psychological knowledge is not to be externally imposed; (2) psychology needs to address every-day activities outside experimentally-contrived laboratories; (3) behavior is best understood from the local frame of reference; and (4) psychology must reflect the sociocultural reality of its social context. "The ultimate goal of indigenous psychology is the development of a universal psychology that incorporates all indigenous (including Western) psychologies . . . It only asserts that pan-human psychological principles and theories cannot be taken for granted or assumed merely because they are developed in the West" (p. 160). It is therefore not destructive to challenge mainstream theories and principles of psychology, but indigenization may be a step toward discovering true universals in psychology.

The search for a universal psychology has been a continuing theme in the literature. A unified perspective requires cross-cultural coherence, generalizing findings across cultural boundaries in the search for both cultural similarities and cultural differences. The importance of national cultures has been widely accepted as a barrier to the discovery of universals emphasizing "objective" rather than subjective data. "There are many reasons why psychology has failed to become a unified science, and I have tried to indicate what some of the major problems are that face us in our attempts to reach this goal. I have also tried to indicate how we can best proceed in our endeavors to reduce the fissionable nature of psychology. Greater resource to cross-cultural studies is certainly one of the most important ways of furthering this goal: science must be universal, and there cannot be a psychology for the United States, and another for India or Japan or Nigeria. We search for universal laws, and these must be tested in many different countries" (Eysenck, 1995, p. 11).

People are changing the environment even while being changed by it, in a continuous feedback loop. The human impact and the impact on humans can not be considered independently as we study global change, imposing a basic uncertainty principle to human predictability. Understanding global change requires a complex system. "In this regard, the notion of a complex system in the mathematical theory of general systems is relevant. The starting point is the notion of a *system as a relation among items or objects. A complex system is then defined as a relation among the systems.* Items which form a complex system through interaction (i.e., subsystems) have their own recognizable boundary and existence while their behavior (functioning) is conditioned by their being integrated in the overall system. The human body is an obvious example; its parts (i.e., organs) are recognizable as such but their functioning (and even existence) is conditioned by their being part of the total system, i.e., body" (Mesarovic, McGinnis, & West, 1995, p. 27).

Other approaches emphasize the importance of nonlinear processes, especially in applications of chaos and complexity theory. "The messages that this group of theories brings is that adaptation is a nonlinear process, and therefore so are most of the dynamics we find in nature. We too are part of nature, and it follows that we operate by similar intrinsic dynamics. Therefore change is a nonlinear, perhaps even a chaotic or complex process by which all life forms adapt . . . What does this group of theories offer social scientists? Nothing less than validation. It offers social scientists validation in their attempts to describe and define phenomena of a previously ineffable nature" (Bütz, 1997, p. xvii). The importance of linear, mechanistic, logical, positivist assumptions where therapists are sometimes considered the "police of mental life" are matched with a quite different holistic epistemology.

Bütz (1997) contrasts the more exclusive conventional psychological perspective with a new and much more inclusive approach to coping with development: long-lasting and meaningful change. This new framework will build on diversity as a positive vehicle for meaningful change. "This process may be painful and even feel chaotic, but on the other side of it is a new adaptation. How is it possible that society can foster this kind of process and connotation of adaptation? Through acceptance. Because the models that emphasize prediction and control, rational thought, and a linear worldview center on rejecting that which they cannot explain. Acceptance seems to be the key. Stated another way, acceptance is tolerance, tolerance of the difficult process life is and always will be ... What is it that must be tolerated? Others—for each other's own frailties, for the bifurcations, complexities, and chaotic experiences that must be endured to allow this evolution. If tolerance and acceptance are some of the watchwords for this new myth, then diversity becomes a core issue in allowing the pattern to form" (Bütz, 1997, p. 239).

Cross-cultural psychology has presumed general laws of human behavior, and the discovery of those laws is the goal of cross-cultural psychology. What is also clear is that cultural context has an essential role in the search for general laws. "In general, what we observe in our analysis, above all, is an invigorated attempt to reintroduce some form of contextualism in a psychology that has long ignored the importance of the environment, broadly defined, as a constitutive component of human behavior. It is not clear that most current cross-cultural approaches, which seem to assign secondary status to the role of culture in psychological explanation, will be successful in this quest, but it is very encouraging to see that after a slow start cross-cultural psychology has found a voice that is heard beyond the borders of its own provinces" (Lonner & Adamopoulos, 1997, p. 77).

Kuhn (1970) expressed the belief that a major paradigm shift will occur when scientific theories can not adequately account for ideas, concepts, or data and when some new competing perspective better accommodates these data. Elements of analytical reductionism in psychology seem to be giving way to a more holistic, culturally inclusive, and integrative approach which recognizes that people from all populations are both similar and different at the same time. In that regard, the dual emphasis on both the universal and the particular become complementary and necessarily joined in a combined explanation. Culture provides a metaphor for joining the universal and the particular at the same time. The culture models or schema are both public and private. "In this sense, cultural models are empirical analogues of culture understood as knowledge. As we shall see they are not analogues in any simple sense, since public models are not exactly the same thing as mental models. But approaching culture as a collection of models has the advantage of showing that making sense of culture as an aspect of mind requires that we both distinguish and relate these two notions of model"(Shore, 1996, p. 44).

Cultural boundaries are not static, but rather, dynamic reflections of accelerated change, and interact through contact in bidirectional ways where each party learns from the other. "The psychological conception of culture is not the culture external to the individual, but the cultural internalized as a result of enculturation within the individual. Introducing the concept of internalized culture opens the door to a new territory of thought. Interest is now focused on how culture is experienced and internalized by the individual. Thus the psychological conception gives full recognition to individual differences in cultural processes" (Ho, 1994, p. 13).

Increased attention in psychology is being given to the effect of contact among culturally different people or groups in multicultural settings. "This new emphasis on culture at the cross-national and cross-ethnic levels has resulted from (1) the search for culturally sensitive assessments in diagnosis and treatment of psychopathology; (2) world wide voluntary and non-voluntary migrations of individuals and groups; and (3) problems resulting from acculturation and adaptation" (Tanaka-Matsumi & Draguns, 1997, pp. 468–469). Culture has become more of a dynamic and constructed concept. "Psychology has finally realized that culture has a major role to play in the way psychology is shaped. That is so because we humans are all ethnocentric. This is a fundamental reality, reflecting that we all group up in a specific culture (even when it is cosmopolitan and a mixture of other cultures) and learn to believe that the standards, principles, perspectives and expectations that we acquire from our culture are the way to look at the world. Unexamined assumptions are one of the central aspects of culture. When we construct psychological theories, the more the subject matter deviates from biological and physiological phenomena, the more our culture intrudes in the shaping of the theories that we construct" (Triandis, 1997, p. ix).

☐ The Multicultural Alternative

Multiculturalism has been described in this book as a "fourth force" or fourth dimension but neither of these terms are completely adequate. The fourth force implies competition with humanism, behaviorism and psychodynamism, which is not the intent. By comparing the fourth dimension of multiculturalism to the fourth dimension of time giving meaning to three dimensional space, then complementarity is indicated but other problems arise. "The very term dimension itself indicates the inadequacy assigned to the human role. One would not characterize the role of natural phenomena in analogous terms, e.g., by talking about the ocean dimension or atmosphere dimension of global change" (Mesarovic, McGinnis, & West, 1995, p. 9). Cultures, like every other subsystem, are constituent parts of global systems. Multiculturalism is a means of coping with cultural and social diversity in society. "In less than three decades multiculturalism

has become a word immediately recognized by policy makers, social commentators, academics and the general public in Western industrial countries, if not elsewhere. The rapid adoption of the term multiculturalism
has occurred in a situation where there is increasing international concern
about the limitations of existing policies to address changing patterns of
inter-ethnic relations" (Inglis, 1995, p. 15). The term "multiculturalism,"
while popular, is used in a variety of ways. The demographic-descriptive
usage refers to ethnic or racial diversity in a population. The programatic-
political usage refers to programs and policy initiatives in response to diversity. The ideological-normative usage is a slogan for political action by
diverse groups in contemporary society.

Huntington (1993) pointed out the importance of multicultural and
multiethnic factors in understanding the national and international relationships and managing the potential conflict between those diverse
groups, as did Dana (1998): "A multicultural perspective insists that we
must not only be equal under the law, we must also be able to understand ourselves as the authors of the laws that bind us ... This issue is
central to mental health problems, research, diagnosis and services. Ultimately, each multicultural group must provide the idiosyncratic perspective and cultural/racial idiom in which all providers become fluent. This
is the meaning of culturally competent mental health services" (Dana,
1998, p. 13). In this way every experience can be seen as a multicultural
experience. Multiculturalism refers to all educational and training practices, research, administration or direct service where issues of nationality,
ethnicity, language, socioeconomic status, gender, lifestyle, age, religion,
ability, or any other of the almost endless list of formal and informal affiliations are addressed.

Sue et al. (1998) identify sources of resistance to the term "multiculturalism as a fourth force." First, some view multiculturalism as competing
with already established theories of psychological explanation in ways that
threaten the profession of psychology. Second, the terms "multiculturalism" and "diversity" are closely associated with affirmative action, quotas,
civil rights, discrimination, reverse discrimination, racism, sexism, political
correctness, and other emotionaly-laden terms. Third, to the extent that
multiculturalism is connected with postmodernism (as in multiple perspectives and belief systems), the arguments against postmodernism as a
valid theory would also apply to multiculturalism. Fourth, those favoring
a universalist perspective contend that the same practices of counseling
and therapy apply equally to all populations without regard to cultural
differences. Fifth, others contend that there are no accepted standards for
describing multiculturalism as a theory in practice, and that it is too loosely
defined to be taken seriously. Sixth, there are no measurable competencies for multicultural applications of psychology nor adequate standards

of practice. Seventh, some argue that multiculturalism is too complicated and it would be unrealistic to expect psychologists to attend to such a range of factors simultaneously. Eighth, it can be argued that more research is needed on multicultural competencies, standards, methods and approaches. Ninth, some assert that multicultural standards cannot be incorporated into the profession of psychology until all groups have been included. Tenth, others hold the view that multiculturalism represents reverse racism, support of quotas, and is anti-White. In discussing these sources of resistance, Sue and colleagues (1998) point out the tendency to misrepresent or misunderstand the notion of multiculturalism and the dangers of that misunderstanding.

Multiculturalism in the U.S. context has been misunderstood partly as an outcome of the controversy raised by D'Souza (1991), who equated multiculturalism with a "politically correct minority perspective" (pp. xii–xiv) which demanded intellectual conformity in the name of putative commitment to diversity. Given the gross oversimplification of issues in the arguments, both those who support and those who oppose the argument about "political correctness" are wrong.

Others have opposed multiculturalism in the fear that it would heighten ethnic conflict, divisions, and tensions, although there is no supporting evidence for those fears. "This is because when combined, as it is in the case studies, with a strong emphasis on policies of social justice, it removes much of the basis for resistance among ethnic minority groups. The focus on social justice also counters criticisms that multiculturalism simply serves to continue the exploited powerlessness of these minority groups" (Inglis, 1995, p. 66). However, in situations where there has been extended and violent conflict or a history of ethnic hostility, any reconciliation will be problematic. While the multicultural model's ability to turn around conflict is problematic, the lack of better alternatives leaves no other choice, as long as the potential for success is realistic and the difficulties are acknowledged.

☐ Ethnopolitical Applications

The volatility of multicultural issues has in large part replaced inter-state conflict between nations, with intra-state conflict between culturally-defined populations, and replaced soldiers with civilian combatants. In these multicultural conflicts there are no well defined battlefields, and so, multicultural communities turn inward in self-destruction. The problems of multicultural misunderstanding are amplified by problems of poverty and hunger, waves of refugees, and the impetus for revenge by victims that

destroy trust, promote violence, and eliminate support structures necessary for psychological health.

In covering the full range of biological to sociocultural concerns, psychology is uniquely suited to aid in prevention and rehabilitation regarding ethnopolitical conflict. However, psychology has historically been less
proactive than the other social sciences, except through interdisciplinary
activities. Psychological research and psychosocial interventions are in the
position to help prepare science-practitioners to coordinate the resources
of specialized paths and focus on this problem. To make a relevant impact on the problem of ethnopolitical conflict, psychology as a profession
must change. The nature of this change toward a "new" profession of psychology will include establishing multi-centered, multi-national institutes
which provide relevant training to discover what kinds of reconciliation
work, why conflict escalates, and how to better manage ethnopolitical
tensions to prevent destructive conflict.

At least five types of ethnopolitical conflicts are to be addressed in a
joint conference organized by the American Psychological Association and
the Canadian Psychological Association in the near future. First, there
is ethnic conflict resulting in all-out war, mass expulsions, or genocide.
Second, is when ethnic conflict leads to chronic violence and war, but
reconciliation remains possible. Third, is when ethnic conflict is producing
chronic instability, but there are relatively low levels of violence and high
potentials for reconciliation. Fourth, is when ethnic conflict produces high
levels of violence, but reconciliation has occurred or is occurring. Fifth, are
ethnic conflicts that died out before they became serious.

[1] *A Joint Presidential Initiative of the Presidents-elect of the American Psychological Association and the Canadian Psychological Association*

*With the end of the Cold War, a new, but it also seems, an ancient form of
warfare, is becoming more common around the world. A series of conflicts have
erupted that are rooted in ethnic fear and hatred, historic patterns of privileg-
ing, actual and perceived victimization, failed government, economic stress, and
ecological disasters. Although these armed conflicts are intensely political, they
do not follow the usual pattern of wars between states. Some major examples*

---

[1] American Psychological Association/Canadian Psychological (1998). *A joint presidential ini-
tiative of the Presidents-elect of the American Psychological Association and the Canadian Psychological
Association.* (Unpublished document, American Psychological Association, Washington D.C.)
Reprinted with permission.

are current or recent intra-state wars such as those in Israel/Palestine, Bosnia, Croatia, Northern Ireland, Kashmir, Sri Lanka, Tibet, Afghanistan, Tadjikistan, Burma, Indonesia (East Timor), Russia (Chechnya), Georgia (Abkhazia), Turkey (Kurdistan), Iraq (with Kurdish and Shi'a populations), Lebanon, Armenia and Azerbaijan, Sudan, Rwanda, Burundi, Angola, Ethiopia, and Guatemala. Not all of these are strictly new conflicts, but the end of the Cold War has spawned many of them, aggravated others, and exposed older ones as essentially ethnic, rather than between hostile political ideologies.

These wars are fought by rival ethnic groups with their own cultural identities. They come to believe that a rival group or a state controlled by a rival group threatens their very existence. Each group defines its own identity in part by opposition to the evil other and sees that other as less than human. These conflicts are charged with communal memories of victimization, and they create psychological processes that contribute to further violence and genocide.

The nature of the fighting has also changed. Ethnopolitical wars include atrocities such as mass rape and "ethnic cleansing," and they often occur within communities, with former neighbors committing personal violence against each other, sometimes in the name of "race," or "nation," or "religion," or linguistic identity, or some combination of these. In such recent wars, over 80% of casualties have been non-combatants, mostly women and children, who suffer shelling, displacement, land mines, poverty, community destruction, hunger, and disease. These armed conflicts destroy trust, and they create post-traumatic stress on a vast scale. They immerse youth in systems of violence, uproot populations, destroy community structures that had supported mental health, and leave ineradicable memories that invite new cycles of revenge.

We worry that this kind of war will become more widespread in the twenty-first century, and we deem it urgent that psychologists apply their knowledge and talents to these problems. Since the conflicts have strong psychological components, psychologists can assist in analyzing the causes of ethnopolitical conflict. In addition, psychologists have useful tools for the prevention of ethnopolitical warfare. Where violence has already occurred, intervention by psychologists can help reconstruct war-torn societies and aid the victims.

Mission Statement of the APA/CPA Initiative

The ACA/APA Initiative is described in a mission statement by the Presidents-elect of the APA and ACA which is included, with permission, in this chapter. The mission of the Joint Presidential Initiative is to apply the tools of psychology to ethnopolitical conflict. Its primary goals are (1) to stimulate scholarship on the causes of ethnopolitical war and on effective methods of intervention and prevention; and (2) to encourage the training of psychologists in prediction, intervention, conflict resolution, ending cycles of revenge, and violence-prevention as it applies to ethnopolitical warfare. The initiative also seeks to stimulate comparative analysis of all ethnopolitical conflicts throughout the world and to apply what has been learned about them.

Scholarship

Ethnopolitical war has many causes—political, cultural, economic, historical, and religious, among others. But the psychological causes have been neglected. Research on the origins of such wars is a multidisciplinary task in which psychology must be one of the key elements of a larger mosaic. Analysis is difficult since rival groups construct very different histories of the conflict, and all parties see themselves as victims whose story has not been told properly. Often the best scholarship is done by international teams having multiple perspectives and people with extensive field experience in the relevant cultures.

Our initiative aims to stimulate rigorous analysis of the psychological processes that fuel ethnopolitical conflict. The initiative will emphasize the psychological components of these situations, and will include scholarly, multidisciplinary conferences and publications to disseminate the results of the research done by major scholars in this area. These projects will also generate more original research. To avoid culturally limited perspectives, we will use international teams of leading scholars. The goal is not to take political positions but to analyze such violent conflicts in a careful, inclusive manner that brings forward diverse ideas, data, methodologies, interpretations, and conclusions.

Scholarly activities will also analyze which intervention and prevention efforts are most effective. In regard to areas already affected by war, there is need for scholarship on how various cultures respond to chronic multiple stresses; on the impact of war on families and communities; on ways of developing trust, empathy, and constructive communication between embittered enemies; and on ways of promoting civic reconciliation. Means of breaking cycles of violence and building peaceful relationships do exist and must be analyzed so that they can be used fruitfully. It is crucial that culturally relevant methods of addressing war-related stresses on a societal scale be found for each case to avoid past errors that have occurred when outsiders have applied inappropriate and sometimes even harmful methods for dealing with these problems.

In regard to violence prevention, there is need for scholarship on what psychosocial factors place communities at risk of armed conflict. What kinds of steps most effectively reduce hostility? What can be learned from cases in which multi-ethnic communities live together in peace for long periods of time? Much greater emphasis needs to be placed on prediction and prevention. To address these needs, the initiative will include international, action-oriented research able to identify the best practices in intervention, prediction, and prevention of violence. Approaches developed in local communities and by practitioners in many parts of the world can and should be combined with the findings of scientific research by more academic psychologists.

Training

Scholarship can point the way toward intervention, but it is no substitute for work on the ground that addresses human needs in local communities. Intervention efforts immediately encounter difficulties of scale, cost, cultural relevance, and sustainability. It is impossible for APA and CPA to aspire to the role of global therapist in war situations. Sending Western-trained relief teams into war zones around the world will not address psychological needs on the scale that is required. Approaches validated in North America or elsewhere in societies with highly developed professional psychological traditions may need tailoring to local cultures and circumstances. Furthermore, although the initiative seeks to encourage psychologists to conduct long-term work in war-affected countries, most North American psychologists who do so are unable to stay for the lengthy periods required to complete their work. But war-torn countries typically have very few trained psychologists. Our training priority, then, is to build local capacity through a training-of-trainers approach that prepares psychologists to train people from their own cultures who can then perform the first hand interventions and relief work locally.

Effective interventions must draw upon and be integrated into local institutions and processes. Local communities already include structures such as women's groups and traditional methods of healing and conflict resolution that may provide potentially valuable resources for intervention and prevention work. Local people and paraprofessionals often provide valuable advice on which methods are appropriate for their conditions. For all these reasons, training should be done in multi-national partnerships that enable mutual learning between psychologists and practitioners from various parts of the world. These trained cadres then will be able to carry out the project mission in a wide variety of situations. We envision the establishment of several institutes in which to train specialists who will be able to carry out such projects, and in which to carry out relevant applied research. The ultimate aim is to prepare communities to heal the wounds of war; to reduce trauma, discrimination, and prejudice; to build resilience; to advance nonviolent conflict resolution and tolerance; and to sensitize communities on key policy issues concerning psychosocial well-being.

This initiative welcomes collaboration with a wide range of organizations, national and ethnic groups, and disciplines, in the quest to end ethnopolitical wars and to foster peace.

Promotional Summary: The APA/CPA Initiative to Mobilize Psychology Toward Understanding and Ameliorating the Effects of Ethnopolitical Conflict

Ethnopolitical Conflict: A Growing Problem

With the end of the Cold War, the world has entered a new phase. Previously the dominant form of war was between nations and their armies, and most of the casualties were combatants. Over the past decade, however, the pattern of warfare has shifted from inter-state wars to intra-state, intercommunal wars fought by rival ethnic groups. Since the end of the Cold War, there have been approximately thirty such conflicts fought each year. Now, fighting occurs in and around communities, and over 80% of the casualties are noncombatants, mostly women and children.

In contemporary conflicts, civilian populations are primary targets of campaigns of terror marked by butchery, gender-specific violence, and human rights abuses on a massive scale. There are no well-defined battlefields, as fighting at the community level and the use of landmines turn agricultural communities into killing fields.

The destruction of communities and their infrastructures amplify ongoing problems of poverty and hunger, creating deadly cycles that are difficult to break. Intercommunal conflict creates waves of displaced people, and refugee problems often foment additional instability and violence. These conflicts take a terrible physical toll but they also take a heavy toll psychologically, as they create communal memories of victimization, destroy the bonds of social trust, immerse youth in systems of violence, forge images of an evil and inhuman enemy, and destroy community structures that had supported mental health.

Psychology in Relation to the Problem of Ethnopolitical Warfare

Psychology as a discipline is particularly relevant to ethnopolitical warfare because it covers the full range from biological to sociocultural perspectives that must be integrated in understanding the origins and effects of war. Psychology alone among the social sciences includes a treatment arm—clinical psychology—that can help in healing the aftereffects of stress and trauma for victims and combatants from ethnopolitical conflict, and aid in preventing such conflicts. Nevertheless, psychology has devoted less attention and fewer resources to the cause of ethnic conflict than have anthropology, political science, and sociology. Thus, even as it is centered in psychology, the APA/CPA initiative must be informed by the perspectives and contributions of other social sciences. Similarly, psychology's approach to ethnopolitical warfare must go beyond the contributions of scholars and clinicians to include the perspectives of survivors of ethnopolitical conflict and the experience of those who work with survivors in governmental and non-governmental agencies.

The problem of ethnopolitical warfare demands urgent attention by everyone committed to human well being. Psychology has much to contribute because the causes and consequences of ethnic conflict have important psychological components. Growing recognition of the importance of psychological issues is evident in the recently completed U.N. Study on the Impact of Armed Conflict on Children, which identifies the need to address psychosocial problems as an essential part of conflict prevention and post-conflict reconstruction. In addition, many non-governmental organizations (NGOs) have begun conducting psychosocial interventions as part of projects to improve health, nutrition, education, and family integrity in war-torn communities. Further, researchers studying ethnopolitical warfare have a growing awareness of the need for a multidisciplinary perspective that incorporates the emotional, cognitive, and social psychology of ethnopolitical conflict.

The challenge for psychology is to prepare a new generation of scientist-practitioners to participate in research and intervention in ethnopolitical warfare. At present, psychological training proceeds in rather specialized paths—in social, cognitive, and developmental as well as clinical psychology—that do not adequately equip psychologists for working in zones of ethnic conflict or for understanding the situational, historic, and cultural complexities of ethnic conflicts. In short, psychology cannot fulfill its responsibility to contribute to reducing the toll of ethnopolitical warfare through its current structure of training and professional practice. In essence, a new profession must be created. It was to meet this need, that the Presidents-Elect of two of the leading psychology organizations in the world—the APA and CPA—developed their joint initiative.

The Opening Conference

An international conference is planned to announce the APA/CPA initiative by bringing together the best known students of ethnopolitical conflict from the English-speaking world. The conference will examine different levels of ethnic tension, hostility, and conflict, and compare these systematically to each other in an attempt to draw tentative generalizations about what kinds of reconciliation efforts work, and what kinds do not, why conflict escalates in some cases but de-escalates in others. As mentioned earlier, five levels of conflict will be examined.

1. *Ethnic conflicts resulting in all-out war, mass expulsions, or genocide (e.g., Armenian genocide; Jews and other groups in the German Holocaust; Bosnia; Rwanda in 1994).*
2. *Ethnic conflicts producing chronic violence and war but where reconciliation remains possible (e.g., Northern Ireland; Burmese civil wars; Guatemala from the 1960s to the 1980s; Kurds in Iran, Turkey, and Iraq; Tamils/Sinhalese conflict in Sri Lanka).*
3. *Ethnic conflicts producing chronic instability but relatively low levels of violence and a high potential for reconciliation (e.g., Flemish/Walloon division in Belgium; French/English division in Canada; East Indian/Polynesian division in Fiji; Chinese/Malay division in Malaysia).*
4. *Ethnic conflicts that produced high levels of violence but in which reconciliation occurred or is occurring (e.g., South Africa; Nigeria; Indonesia after the civil wars of the 1950s and 1960s; Catalonia's reconciliation with Spain).*
5. *Potential ethnic conflicts that died out before they became serious (e.g., Catholic Bavarians and Protestant North Germans; Singapore; Tanzania; Paraguay; Switzerland).*

Together, conference participants would begin the long-term task of establishing scientific conclusions that could then be applied to predict, forestall, and ameliorate ethnic conflict in the future. An annotated list of potential conference participants is provided as Appendix 1. In addition to academics, a few key members of international governmental and non-governmental organizations, and some political figures, would be invited to attend the conference. All would contribute their experience and knowledge, and learn from the exchange of information and opinions. The conference would only be a first step toward establishing a continuing program of research and education in this field, but it would be a major advance toward our goal of identifying and solving one of the world's most pressing problems.

Institute for Psychological Study and Intervention Against Ethnopolitical Conflict

The major objective of the APA/CPA initiative is to organize a multi-center, multi-national Institute for Psychological Study and Intervention Against Ethnopolitical Conflict. Each Center will offer three kinds of training: academic instruction, research supervision, and field placement in an area in or close to ethnopolitical conflict. Academic instruction will bring trainees up to data on current research related to understanding, predicting, preventing, and intervening against ethnopolitical conflict. Intervention here includes not only what can be done to de-escalate ethnic conflict, but also what can be done to bring clinical psychology to serve the mental health needs of those caught up in conflict as both as victims and perpetrators of violence. Research supervision will involve each trainee being paired with one or more Institute professors in a continuing program of research related to ethnopolitical conflict. Academic instruction and research supervision should begin before a trainee embarks on a field placement.

The field placement program will be crucial for success of the Centers; the current weakness of psychology and psychologists in regard to problems of ethnopolitical conflict stems directly from lack of first-hand experience of the phenomenon. Each Center will develop at least one field site in which trainees can work with governmental or non-governmental agencies (e.g., U.N., Red Cross, International Rescue Organization, Catholic Relief Services) in assisting victims of ethnopolitical conflict.

Training will be offered initially to people holding a Ph.D. degree. We anticipate that most of these will have earned a Ph.D. in psychology. Some of the trainees may be fresh from their Ph.D. program, but others may come from and return to academic or practice careers. It is anticipated that graduates of the training program will contribute as consultants and staff members for non-governmental organizations working with victims of ethnopolitical conflict.

Institute Progress and Current Needs

An APA/CPA steering committee has been formed to direct the Institute and the development of Centers within the Institute (see Appendix 2).

The first Center is under way at the University of Pennsylvania, beginning with a planning grant (submitted to the Mellon Foundation) for development of an intensive course/curriculum and a postdoctoral program including field experience. Other Centers are being organized at the University of British Columbia, University of Ulster in Northern Ireland, and University of Capetown in South Africa. Centers will be sought in India and in Sri Lanka, where English-based academic institutions are in close proximity to significant ethnic conflict (Muslim vs. Hindu in India, Hindu vs. Buddhist in Sri Lanka).

- *Each Center will need financial support for planning and offering academic instruction relevant to ethnopolitical conflict, for initiating and developing research collaborations relevant to ameliorating ethnopolitical conflict, and for developing field placements with government and NGO agencies working with victims of conflict or participants in conflict.*
- *Communication between Centers also needs support; Centers will be mutually reinforced by sharing of faculty, instructional programs and materials, and field placement sites. Some of this kind of communication can be accomplished by email, but travel expenses are unavoidable at the start-up phase where personal contacts must be developed for collaboration in research and field placements. Centers will join in planning and conducting international conferences that will bring together researchers and practitioners interested in ethnopolitical conflict. These conferences will have the additional value of advertising the work of the Institutes for academic administrators, government officials, and the general public.*
- *Further interest in the problems of ethnopolitical conflict will be fostered by books written by the Institute faculty, proceedings of meetings, and books written by others who have important perspectives to consider. Support will be needed to bring these works to publication for an audience wider than that of typical academic monographs.*
- *The core of the training program is the postdoctoral fellows. Postdoctoral trainees will participate in programs that, depending on the Center, may be as brief as a summer or as long as two or three years. The limiting factor on the impact of the Institute may be the number of postdoctoral fellows who can be funded. A one-year "postdoc" typically costs about $50,000, including stipend of about $30,000, insurance and other benefits, and travel costs for field placement.*
- *Exchanges among Institute faculty, and between faculty and people directly involved in interventions, are critical to progress on both the basic research and intervention agendas, and to development of a curriculum that will prepare its students to deal with research and intervention at field sites.*
- *To this end, support will be needed for: faculty visit programs, particularly between field sites and centers, for periods ranging from a week to six months.*
- *A longer term intellectual exchange among some of the leaders in the field, perhaps in the form of a one-year working group at a major "think-tank," such as the Center for Advanced Study in the Behavioral Sciences, at Stanford.*

☐ Conclusion

Before we were born, cultural patterns of thought and action were already in place to guide our thinking, influence our behavior, and to help us make life decisions. We inherited these cultural patterns from our parents and teachers who taught us the "rules of the game." Only later, sometimes much later and sometimes never, did we learn that our culture was one of the many possible patterns of thinking and acting from which we could choose. By that time, most of us had already come to believe that "our" culture was the best of all possible worlds. Even if we recognized that traditional values were false or inadequate, when challenged by the stress of radical social changes, it was not always possible to replace the worn-out habits with new alternatives (Pedersen, 1991).

In science, experiences are categorized according to their qualities, dimensions, or variables. These variables are related to one another in systematic relationships and lawful ways. Theories depend on this network of relationships or laws to predict the future. When these predictions are confirmed, the theory is supported. This book has explored the possibility that we are moving toward a generic theory of multiculturalism as a "fourth force" or dimension, complementary to the other three forces of psychodynamic, behavioral, and humanistic explanations of human behavior. This perspective assumes that multiculturalism is relevant throughout psychology as a generic rather than an exotic perspective. Labels—such as "multiculturalism"—tend to oversimplify complicated relationships, and to that extent they are dangerous. This book has attempted to call attention to the ways in which a multicultural perspective is better able to address the complicated and dynamic cultural context in which psychology is practiced than the alternative monocultural models.

Gielen (1994) describes specific ways that the field of psychology can appropriately respond to the multicultural imperative for positive change: (1) Textbook authors should be asked to provide examples from a variety of societies in order to encourage reflection on the strengths and limitations of existing theories and research; (2) textbooks should introduce cross-cultural perspectives alongside other perspectives; (3) psychological theories should be routinely contextualized within a cross-cultural framework regarding research design and theory construction; (4) psychological theories must be consistently understood within historical frameworks as products of a specific cultural context; (5) journals in the United States and elsewhere should invite foreign authors, editors, referees, and authors to submit materials; (6) American journals should systematically encourage authors to cite relevant foreign literature; (7) textbooks can be jointly authored by authors from different cultural backgrounds; and (8) institutional support and funding should be available for collaborative research and scholarship across cultural boundaries. If psychology fails to respond appropriately then the field of psychology is likely to be divided up among other related fields as a sub-specialty.

Whether or not multiculturalism emerges as a fourth force in psychology and/or counseling psychology at a level of magnitude equivalent to that of psychodynamic, behavioral, and humanistic theories, culture will continue to provide a valuable metaphor for understanding ourselves and others. It is no longer possible for psychologists to ignore their own cultural contexts or the cultural contexts of their clients. Until the multicultural perspective is understood as having positive consequences toward making psychology more, rather than less, relevant and increasing, rather than decreasing, the quality of psychology, little real change is likely to occur.

☐ References

Bütz, M. R. (1997). *Chaos and complexity: Implications.* Washington, DC: Taylor & Francis.

D'Souza, D. (1991). *Illiberal education: The politics of race and sex on campus.* New York: Free Press.

Dana, R. H. (1998). *Understanding cultural identity in intervention and assessment.* Thousand Oaks, CA: Sage Publications.

Eysenck, H. J. (1995). Cross-cultural psychology and the unification of psychology. *World Psychology, 1*(4), 11–30.

Gielen, U. P. (1994). American mainstream psychology and its relationship to international and cross-cultural psychology. In A. L. Comunian and U. P. Gielen (Eds.), *Advancing psychology and its applications: International perspectives,* pp. 26–40. Milano, Italy: Franco Angeli.

Ho, D. Y. F. (1994). Introduction to cross-cultural psychology. In L. Adler and U. P. Gielen, *Cross-cultural topics in psychology,* pp. 3–13. Westport, CT: Praeger.

Huntington, S. P. (1993). The clash of civilizations. *Foreign Affairs, 72*(3), 22–49.

Inglis, C. (1995). *Multiculturalism: New policy responses to diversity.* New York: United Nations MOST Policy Paper #4.

Kagitcibasi, C. (1996). *Family and human development across cultures.* Mahwah, NJ: Lawrence Erlbaum.

Kuhn, T. S. (1970). *The structure of scientific revolutions* (2nd ed.). Chicago: University of Chicago Press.

Lonner, W. J., & Adamopoulos, J. (1997). Culture as antecedent to behavior. In J. W. Berry, Y. H. Poortinga, and J. Pandey (Eds), *Handbook of cross-cultural psychology: Volume 1,* pp. 43–83. Needham Heights, MA: Allyn & Bacon.

Mesarovic, M. D., McGinnis, D. L., & West, D. A. *Cybrenetics of global change: Human dimension and managing of complexity.* New York: United Nations MOST Policy Paper #3.

Pedersen, P. (1991). Multiculturalism as a generic approach to counseling. *Journal of Counseling & Development, 70*(1), 6–12.

Pedersen, P. (1997). Recent trends in cultural theories. *Applied and Preventive Psychology, 6,* 221–231.

Rosensweig, M. R. (1992). Psychological science around the world. *American Psychologist, 39*(8), 877–884.

Shore, B. (1996). *Culture in mind: Cognition, culture and the problem of meaning.* New York: Oxford University Press.

Sinha, D. (1997). Indigenizing psychology. In J. W. Berry, Y. H. Poortinga, and J. Pandey, *Handbook of cross-cultural psychology: Volume 1*, pp. 129–170. Needham Heights, MA: Allyn & Bacon.

Sue, D. W., Cartger R. T., Casas, J. M., Fouad, N. A., Ivey, A. E., Jensen, M., LaFromboise, T., Manese, J. E., Ponterotto, J. G., & Vasquez-Nutall, E. (1998). *Multicultural counseling competencies*. Thousand Oaks, CA: Sage Publications.

Tanaka-Matsumi, J., & Draguns, J. G. (1997). Culture and psychopathology in J. W. Berry, M. H. Segall, and C. Kagitcibasi, *Handbook of cross-cultural psychology: Volume 3*. Boston: Allyn & Bacon.

Thompson, M., Ellis, R., & Wildavsky, A. (1990). *Cultural theory*. San Francisco: Westview Press.

Triandis, H. C. (1997a). Forward. In J. W. Berry, P. R. Dasen, and T. S. Saraswathi, *Handbook of cross-cultural psychology: Volume 2*, pp. ix–x. Boston: Allyn & Bacon.

INDEX

distribution, individual epistemological
types, 44–46
diversity
cultural, 20, 21
elimination of, 30

E
ecological forces, factor in behavior, 4
economic changes, Turkish society and,
81–82
education
counseling for educational systems,
58–59
deaf community, 123–124, 140
developing countries and western,
149
H-type mindscape's influence on, 58
integration and, 30
ego identity, formation of, 37
emic process, 8–9, 76
emigration, 52
environment
impact on/from people, 196
individual/social psychological. *See* life
space; social space
epistemological types. *See also*
G-epistemological type;
H-epistemological type;
I-epistemological type;
S-epistemological type
individual distribution, 44–46
psychological test, 46–52
suppression of, 55
epistemologies
fallacious assumptions of 20th century,
40
types, 40–44
ethnicity
context of culture, 76–77
political construct in South Africa,
95–96
ethnocentrism, 64–65
ethnopolitical conflicts
American/Canadian initiative to solve,
201–202. *See also* APA/CPA Initiative
description of problem, 204–205
different levels of, 206
multiculturalism and, 200–201
psychology and, 205–206
etic process, 8–9, 76
European Common Market, 39, 63

exclusion, monocultural perspective and,
11
existentialism, 5

F
family
culture and, 115
impact on Asian youth, 157
individual and Turkish, 80–81
psychological distress and Japanese, 171
separation in South Africa, 93
structure, 80
Farkas, Andr s, 48
Food and Agriculture Organization
(FAO), 29
force-field analysis, application to social
movements, 61, 62
Fourth Force construct
integration and, 33
psychology development of, 4–10
review of, 192–194
separatism and, 33
single global culture, 32

G
Gay Power movement, 39
gender, impact on self-realization and
altruism, 156
G-epistemological type, 41, 42, 58. *See also*
epistemological types
Germany, multi-ethnic employee mix,
52–53
Gray Power movement, 39

H
Harvey, O. J., 46
healing, as a mental health resource in
South Africa, 103–107
health, Western concept of psychological,
169
health policy, South Africa, 102, 105
hearing impairment. *See also* deaf
community
statistics, 123
Heidegger, Martin, 42
H-epistemological type, 41–42, 44. *See also*
epistemological types
influence on education systems, 58
heterogeneity
cross cultures individual, 47
minority culture and, 37–38

pairing with different-culture client, 180–181. *See also* pair therapy
working with individuals from Confucian heritage societies, 158–159
Third World development, cultural encapsulation and, 12–13
TOB Test # 1, 48–50
TOB Test # 2, 50–52
training
of counselors to work with Asian youth, 149–150
of local psychologists, 204
of South African practitioners, 101–102
transpersonal psychology, 5
travel, 63
truth, scientific experimentation and, 69
Turkish culture
hierarchical/relatedness of individualism/collectivism, 80
psychotherapy in the context of, 77–78
Western culture *vs.*, 79–80
Tu Wei-Ming, 151

U
UNESCO, 29
uniqueness effect, false, 12
United Nations, 28, 29
universalism, in South Africa, 95–96

V
values
beliefs *vs.*, 68–69
multiculturalism and, 20

W
Western culture
Confucian heritage societies *vs.. See* Confucian heritage societies
education and developing countries, 149
individualism, 150–152, 154
vs. Turkish culture, 79–80
witchcraft, indigenous healing and, 104
within-society contacts, 23
Women Power movement, 39
women's movement, backlash phenomenon, 67
workforce, multi-ethnic, 52–53
working life, deaf/hearing workers' interaction, 134–139
World Bank, 29
World Health Organization (WHO), 28, 29

Y
Yellow Power movement, 38, 39

Z
Zulu identity, 98